EGYPT

HOW A LOST CIVILIZATION WAS REDISCOVERED

EGYPT

HOW A LOST CIVILIZATION WAS REDISCOVERED

Joyce Tyldesley

UNIVERSITY OF CALIFORNIA PRESS

Berkeley   Los Angeles

University of California Press, one of the most distinguished university presses in the United States, enriches lives around the world by advancing scholarship in the humanities, social sciences, and natural sciences. Its activities are supported by the UC Press Foundation and by philanthropic contributions from individuals and institutions. For more information, visit www.ucpress.edu.

University of California Press
Berkeley and Los Angeles, California

© 2005 by Joyce Tyldesley

Cataloging-in-Publication data is on file with the Library of Congress.

ISBN-13: 978-0-520-25020-8 — ISBN-10: 0-520-25020-6

First published in 2005 by BBC Books, an imprint of
BBC Worldwide Publishing, BBC Worldwide Limited,
Woodlands, 80 Wood Lane, London W12 0TT.

BBC Worldwide would like to thank the following individuals and organizations for providing photographs and for permission to reproduce copyright material. While every effort has been made to trace and acknowledge copyright holders, we would like to apologize should there be any errors or omissions.

Plate section one: 1t: By permission of the British Library (746.e.7); 1b: akg-images/ Laurent Lecat; 2t: akg-images; 2b: Topfoto.co.uk/Collection Roger Viollet; 3: By permission of the British Museum; 4t: Photo RMN/René-Gabriel Ojéda; 5t: The Art Archive/British Library; 5b: By permission of the British Library (1899.g.33); 6t: Werner Forman Archive/Sir John Soane's Museum, London; 6b: Archivio Geodia, Italy; 7: Photo RMN/Gérard Blot; 8: Werner Forman Archive.

Plate section two: 1t: Topfoto.co.uk/Collection Roger Viollet; 1b: Courtesy of the Egypt Exploration Society; 2-3t: J. Stevens/Ancient Art and Architecture Collection Ltd.; 2b: akg-images/François Guénet; 3b: Ancient Art and Architecture Collection Ltd.; 4t: Robert Partridge/The Ancient Egypt Picture Library; 4-5b: Petrie Museum of Egyptian Archaeology, University College, London; 5t: akg-images/Erich Lessing; 5br: akg-images/Erich Lessing; 6: Petrie Museum of Egyptian Archaeology, University College, London; 7t: akg-images/François Guénet; 7b: www.bridgeman.co.uk/Egypt National Museum, Cairo; 8t: The Art Archive/Egyptian Museum, Cairo/Dagli Orti (A); 8b: Corbis/Roger Wood.

Plate section three: 1t: Birmingham Library Services; 1b: M. Jelliffe/Ancient Art and Architecture Collection Ltd.; 2: Werner Forman Archive/Egyptian Museum, Cairo; 3: Borromeo/Art Resource, NY; 4t: Griffith Institute, Oxford; 4b-5: Ancient Art and Architecture Collection Ltd.; 6-8t: UNESCO; 8b: Courtesy of the Manchester Mummy Project.

Manufactured in the United States of America

15   14   13   12   11   10   09   08   07   06
10   9   8   7   6   5   4   3   2   1

This book is printed on New Leaf EcoBook 50, a 100% recycled fiber of which 50% is de-inked post-consumer waste, processed chlorine-free. EcoBook 50 is acid-free and meets the minimum requirements of ANSI/ASTM D5634-01 (*Permanence of Paper*).

CONTENTS

ACKNOWLEDGEMENTS

This book has been written to accompany the BBC series *Egypt*, which focuses on the lives and work of Jean-François Champollion, Giovanni Battista Belzoni and Howard Carter. I would like to thank all who have helped with its progress. Dr Patricia Spencer of the Egypt Exploration Society kindly gave permission to quote from EES published works. Lisette Flinders Petrie generously gave permission to quote from her grandfather's autobiography, and I'm grateful also to Dr Jaromir Malek of the Griffith Institute, Oxford, for kind permission to quote from the published works of Howard Carter. Phil Dolling at the BBC, and Sally Potter and Martin Redfern at BBC Books, deserve special mention. Finally, I would like to thank those Egyptologists, past and present, whose dedication and hard work has brought ancient Egypt to life for us all.

INTRODUCTION

>—<

FIVE THOUSAND YEARS AGO the land of the papyrus and the land of the lotus united to form one long, thin country ruled by one semi-divine king, or pharaoh. For the next 3000 years Egypt would maintain a culture so distinctive that even today, some 2000 years after the last pharaoh occupied the throne of the Two Lands, it has instant, universal recognition.

That this ancient culture holds a powerful fascination for Western observers is undeniable. Why this should be so is less obvious. Why are the Egyptian galleries of our museums packed with visitors, while neighbouring galleries remain empty? Why do television programmes about Egypt attract huge audiences, while programmes about other, equally ancient cultures do not? Why, at a time when the study of the classical languages is dwindling at an alarming rate, are more and more people choosing to study hieroglyphics? There is no simple answer to these questions, and many Egyptophiles cannot themselves explain the attraction that they feel so strongly. Are they approaching ancient Egypt in a quest for enlightenment, hoping to answer specific questions concerning life, death and religion? Is it the undeniable beauty of Egyptian art, architecture and literature that attracts them, or maybe the theological certainties and bizarre burial practices? Most, I suspect, find themselves drawn to Egypt as a land that is both pleasingly exotic, yet at the same time comfortingly recognizable and safe. The people of ancient Egypt, or so it often seems, have many of our own interests and preoccupations – we feel that we almost know them.

Our obsession with anything and everything Egyptian has inspired many to search for treasure in Egypt's sands. All of these can be loosely classified as 'Egyptologists' – specialists in the study of ancient Egypt – but their methods and motives vary widely. Some are archaeologists who travel to Egypt to excavate under the hot sun. Some are linguists who work in dark libraries, barely seeing the light of day. Increasingly, many are scientists who view ancient Egypt through a microscope lens. A few have worked openly and unashamedly for financial reward, cashing in on the Western willingness to pay for artifacts and information. Others have been inspired by scholastic curiosity and the quest for greater understanding. More than a handful, it has to be admitted, have been spurred on by a desire to find personal fame through what is now perceived as a glamorous, even romantic career. Indiana Jones has a lot to answer for!

Together, their work combines to become the story of the discovery of ancient Egypt – the story of this book. But first a word of warning. All of Egypt's explorers, through necessity, have worked within the understanding and limitations of their time. Slowly but surely increasing linguistic and scientific awareness, as well as a growing sensitivity to other cultures, has converted the crude treasure hunters of two centuries ago into the precise scientists of today. We must be very careful not to apply modern value judgements to the explorers of the past. The first collectors simply, and ruthlessly, exploited a source of unwanted antiquities in a land whose ancient history had vanished, seemingly never to be restored. It is hard not to wince when we read of Giovanni Belzoni carelessly crushing heaps of mummies underfoot, and certainly no reputable Egyptologist would behave this way today. But we must wince and read on. Belzoni was a man of his time and he knew no better – indeed, he was considerably more careful in his work than many of his contemporaries. He at least understood the importance of recording what he saw.

Egyptology is a relatively new science, barely two centuries old. Even so, it has been blessed with more than its fair share of intriguing characters, some of whom, by virtue of their larger-than-life personalities, their curious habits or spectacular finds, have come to dominate the subject at the expense of their less flamboyant colleagues. Many of these Egyptologists – Champollion, Belzoni, Edwards, Petrie and Carter included – have been the subjects of their own lengthy biographies, and some have also written autobiographies. It has been impossible to include here the work of every single Egyptologist – this book, already lengthy, would have swollen to the size of an encyclopedia. I have concentrated primarily on the work of European Egyptologists. Even so, I am fully aware that artists who did so much to preserve the now-vanished monuments, and the linguists who worked so hard to translate the newly deciphered texts, have been sadly neglected. I can only apologize to the readers who feel that their own particular hero has been slighted. It is probably no consolation that my own favourite, the Reverend James Baikie, a man who wrote entertainingly and with great authority on all matters Egyptian from the decidedly unexotic setting of his manse in Torphichen, Scotland, without ever actually visiting Egypt, is also left out. Although, as he was one of the first to write a history of Egyptology, I am allowing him a voice in this and all subsequent introductions. Baikie, never one to mince his words, sets the scene well:

> ... the early story of Egyptian exploration is not the story of pure research, conducted for love of truth and antiquity, but very often merely the story of how the representative of France strove with the representative of Britain or Italy for the possession of some ancient monument whose capture might bring glory to his nation, or profit to his own purse. There are few more melancholy chapters in the story of human frailty than those in which the early explorers of Egypt (if you can dignify them by such a name) describe how they wrangled and intrigued, lied and cheated, over relics whose mutilated antiquity might have taught them enough of the vanity of human wishes to make them ashamed of their pettiness.[1]

We cannot appreciate Egypt's archaeology properly without some understanding of her long history.

A BRIEF HISTORY OF EGYPT

Readers new to Egyptian history are often confused and irritated by the use of reign lengths and dynasties rather than conventional calendar dates. Why, they ask, is Egypt's history dated in this idiosyncratic and inconvenient way? The answer is simple. This is without question the most accurate dating method available. Ancient Egypt never developed a continuous calendar such as we have today, and years were not numbered in consecutive order from a chosen Year 1. Instead, scribes dated events by reference to the current king's reign: Year 5 of the reign of Ramesses II, Year 6, Year 7 and so on. With every change of monarch, dating had to start all over again from Year 1. With some obvious hiccups – co-regencies, or two or even three kings reigning in one year cause obvious problems – the system worked well for 3000 years, and it works well today, although modern archaeologists faced with the task of cataloguing a storehouses full of wine jars simply labelled 'Year 7, Year 8, Year 9, etc.' have good reason to curse the lazy scribes who neglected to add the all-important name of the king.

In order to keep track of their lengthy history, Egypt's scribes were forced to maintain 'king lists' – chronological catalogues of kings and their reign lengths preserved on papyrus or carved into temple walls. Fortunately, enough of these king lists have survived to allow Egyptologists to reconstruct the sequence of monarchs with a fair degree of accuracy. However, there are gaps, errors and deliberate omissions that make it impossible to fully align the king lists to our own calendar, providing precise dates BC for each reign. So, in order to ensure maximum dating accuracy, Egyptologists avoid the use of calendar dates, and use reign lengths instead. For convenience the reigns are grouped into dynasties of connected, but not necessarily related, kings, and the 31 dynasties are subdivided into periods with shared characteristics:

Archaic Period	Dynasties 1–2
Old Kingdom	Dynasties 3–6
First Intermediate Period	Dynasties 7–11 (early)
Middle Kingdom	Dynasties 11(late)–13
Second Intermediate Period	Dynasties 14–17
New Kingdom	Dynasties 18–20
Third Intermediate Period	Dynasties 21–25
Late Period	Dynasties 26–31
Graeco-Roman Period	

The Archaic Period is the time when Egypt is forced to adjust to her newly unified status as one land. The three Kingdoms are times of strong, centralized government. The three Intermediate Periods are times of weak or fragmented rule, and the Late Period is the confused time immediately preceding the conquest of Alexander the Great.

Late predynastic or prehistoric Egypt had seen the Nile Valley and Delta dominated by a series of independent city-states and their satellite town and villages. At the start of the Archaic Period the southern warrior king Narmer marched northwards to conquer and unite his land. In so doing, he became the first king of the 1st Dynasty. He, and his successors, ruled Egypt from the north, but built his mud-brick tomb at the southern cemetery site of Abydos. As the country united, her many local gods and goddesses also united to form one flexible pantheon. Different kings would favour different deities at different times, and gods and goddesses would rise and fall in popularity, but the basic pantheon would last beyond the end of the dynastic age.

The Old Kingdom monarchs ruled Egypt from the northern capital, Memphis (near modern Cairo). They worshipped the sun god, Re, at Heliopolis, and buried their dead in the nearby pyramid-cemeteries of Giza and Sakkara. This was an age of strict feudal rule when omnipotent kings were revered as semi-divine beings, the sole link between the people and their gods. The king's most important responsibility was the maintenance of *maat*, the state of rightness, justice or order that kept chaos (*isfet*) at bay. This need to maintain *maat*, to keep things in an unchanging state of correctness – 'if it ain't broke, don't fix it' – was to persist throughout the dynastic age, reinforcing the authority of the king and encouraging a natural conservatism that caused the Egyptians to shy away from experimentation for experimentation's sake. The king demonstrated his allegiance to *maat* in many ways: he destroyed the enemies who lurked at Egypt's borders, maintained law and order within his land, restored the damaged monuments of his predecessors, and made offerings to the gods.

Already it was understood that the dead could live beyond death as spirits if – but only if – the physical body survived in a form that the spirit could recognize. The Egyptians knew that, unlikely though it might seem, bodies could be preserved intact in the grave because the desert cemeteries occasionally yielded shrunken but otherwise perfect corpses. Originally buried without coffins in simple pits, these bodies had desiccated quickly and naturally through contact with the hot, sterile sand. So the theory was simple. A corpse could be preserved if it was buried in direct contact with the hot desert. But the upper classes did not want to be buried in humble peasant graves. They wanted splendid cemeteries, stone tombs, wooden coffins and plenty of space to store the grave goods that they expected to use in the next life, and all these things, of course, separated them from the preserving sand. Snugly sleeping in their coffins, surrounded by their earthly treasures, the upper classes started to decompose in their stone-lined tombs.

This launched the undertakers on a centuries-long quest to develop an artificial means of preserving the dead. Their earliest efforts, which involved wrapping corpses in bandages, coating them with plaster, then moulding the features, did nothing to halt the decay of the flesh beneath the hardened wrappings; it is not surprising that few of these early mummies have survived. But eventually the undertakers – perhaps drawing on their experience of preserving meats for cooking – refined a system of evisceration, drying with natron salt, then bandaging, that would preserve the corpse in a reasonable semblance of life.

Slowly but surely the highly centralized Old Kingdom failed, the inevitable end hastened by a series of low Nile levels that saw high inflation and food shortages within Egypt, and famine on her borders. The collapse of central government left no one in overall control, and the First Intermediate Period saw Egypt once again a land of independent city-states ruled by local governors. This was a temporary state of affairs. Gradually the city-states formed alliances until there were two power bases: a dynasty based at Thebes (modern Luxor) in the south and a dynasty based at Herakleopolis in the north. History was beginning to repeat herself.

The Theban kings marched north to reimpose central authority, establishing a new capital city at the now vanished city of Itj-Tawy, which we know was close to Memphis. *Maat* had been restored to Egypt, and she blossomed. The Theban kings brought a new style of kingship. Gone were the hard, invulnerable god-kings of the Old Kingdom. The Middle Kingdom pharaohs presented a more human face – they were the shepherds of their people, and their statues show them as compassionate men coping bravely with the responsibilities of office. Under their care, Egypt grew peaceful and prosperous again. Literature and the arts flourished, there was increased foreign trade and, lest anyone should mistake the new-style compassion for weakness, a series of successful military campaigns in Nubia. The Middle Kingdom pharaohs continued the pyramid building tradition, but their pyramids were built of mud-brick covered with stone.

The Nile Valley, isolated by its deserts and high cliffs, was secure against invasion. The Delta, however, was open and easily accessible. Throughout the Middle Kingdom there had been a peaceful inflow of easterners, or 'Asiatics', tempted from less fertile lands by Egypt's prosperity. At first the new arrivals were welcomed, their craft skills much appreciated. But as they started to form semi-independent communities, the Egyptians grew resentful. At the same time the local governors started to rebel against central government. A series of abnormally high Nile floods signalled the beginning of the end. The Middle Kingdom collapsed, and the Second Intermediate Period saw an Egyptian dynasty ruling from Thebes, while the Palestinian Hyksos ruled the north from their new eastern Delta capital, Avaris.

The Theban kings were not prepared to share their land with foreigners. War was declared, and once again a Theban warrior marched northwards to reunite Egypt. King Ahmose expelled the Hyksos, chasing them eastwards into Canaan. In so doing, he established the New Kingdom. If the Old Kingdom pharaohs were demigods, and the Middle Kingdom pharaohs were shepherds, the New Kingdom pharaohs were wise soldiers who knew only too well that they might be called upon to defend their realm. A succession of successful warrior kings ensured that Egypt, once so isolated, acquired an enormous empire stretching from Nubia in the south to Syria in the east. Suddenly Egypt was prosperous as she had never been before. This was the age of some of Egypt's best-known kings: the warrior pharaohs Tuthmosis I and Tuthmosis III, the female King Hatshepsut, the heretic Akhenaten and his beautiful wife Nefertiti, the boy-king Tutankhamen, and the long-lived Ramesses II.

Amen, 'The Hidden One', god of the Karnak temple, was now revealed to all as Egypt's principal deity, while Thebes, his home-town, became Egypt's religious capital. This change of allegiance was marked by a revolution in funerary traditions. Pyramids, strongly associated with the northern sun cult of Re, were not entirely suitable for the burial of Theban kings. Instead, the New Kingdom monarchs would be interred in secret in rock-cut tombs carved deep into the Theban mountain. The mountain itself would serve as a natural pyramid for those who required such solar-based comfort. Here it was hoped that the kings would rest for all time, their precious mummies protected from the thieves who had already emptied the pyramids. Mortuary or memorial temples, physically separate from the tombs but spiritually linked to them, offered a more public refuge for the cults of the dead kings. Today archaeologists use a numbering system devised by John Gardner Wilkinson to identify the tombs in the Valley of the Kings (KV) and the nearby Western Valley (WV): KV16, for example, is the tomb of Ramesses I, KV62 the tomb of Tutankhamen.

The late New Kingdom was a time of extensive population shift in the eastern Mediterranean, and fertile Egypt again found herself targeted by displaced nomadic groups who could not be kept out. By now Egypt's kings were facing multiple problems. Low Nile levels, inflation, civil disobedience, a corrupt bureaucracy and an increasingly powerful priesthood of Amen all combined to destabilize the country. First the eastern empire, then Nubia were lost. The end of the New Kingdom saw Egypt once again divided, with a local dynasty ruling the north from a new capital, Tanis, and the high priests of Amen ruling the south from Thebes.

At first the southern and northern courts cooperated, but it was perhaps inevitable that their good relationship would collapse. A confusing period followed, with various local chiefs simultaneously proclaiming themselves king. Kashta, King of Nubia, took full advantage of the chaos and, in 770 BC, marched on Thebes. He was proclaimed King of Upper and Lower Egypt, but it was his successor, Piye, who reached the Delta and so reunited the divided land. A century of stability followed. Egypt was at peace, but outside her borders the situation was deteriorating rapidly. In 671 BC an Assyrian invasion force captured the Delta, forcing King Tanutamen to flee to Nubia. In 663 BC the Assyrians reached Thebes.

The beginning of the Late Period saw the withdrawal of the Assyrians, and the country reunited under a dynasty of Egyptian-born kings ruling from the Delta city of Sais. There followed a century of

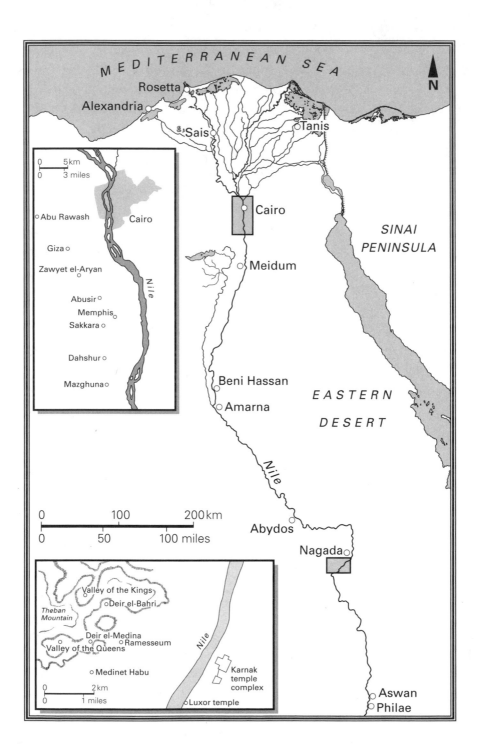

MEDITERRANEAN SEA

N

Rosetta

Alexandria

Sais

Tanis

0   5km
0   3 miles

Abu Rawash

Cairo

Cairo

Giza

Zawyet el-Aryan

SINAI
PENINSULA

Abusir

Memphis

Sakkara

Meidum

Dahshur

Mazghuna

Nile

Beni Hassan

Amarna

EASTERN

DESERT

0   100   200km

0   50   100 miles

Nile

Abydos

Valley of the Kings

Deir el-Bahri

Theban
Mountain

Nagada

Deir el-Medina
Valley of the Queens

Ramesseum

Nile

Medinet Habu

Karnak
temple
complex

0   2km
0   1 miles

Luxor temple

Aswan

Philae

cultural renaissance as the Saites took their inspiration from the glorious days of the Old and Middle Kingdoms. But Egypt's hard won independence could not last. In 525 BC the Persian army conquered Egypt, installing its own dynasties. Finally, in 332 BC, Alexander the Great arrived. The age of the Egyptian pharaohs was over.

GEOGRAPHY

In addition to understanding her history, we also need an appreciation of the geography that has had a huge effect on the preservation of Egypt's remains.

The ancients lived in a land of two very distinct parts, joined by a shared dependence on the river Nile. Lower, or northern, Egypt was the papyrus land of the Delta, the region where the Nile split into seven branches before emptying into the Mediterranean Sea. It was a wide, flat, moist expanse of fields, canals and papyrus marshes, whose extensive coastline and Sinai land bridge allowed links to the wider Mediterranean world. Here, amidst the green meadows, the Egyptians raised splendid cities, building extensive mud-brick palaces that they coated with plaster, then tiled and painted so that they sparkled in the bright sunlight. Unfortunately, damp conditions are not conducive to the preservation of mud-brick, the building material of choice for all urban architecture in Egypt. Mud-brick was cheap, easy to obtain, cool in the hot daytime, and warm in the colder nights, but it was relatively fragile. This did not matter to the Egyptians. They did not expect their palaces to last for more than a few generations, and they were more than happy to rebuild as necessary. But it causes great problems for archaeologists. Today the once-magnificent mud-brick cities of the Delta have almost entirely vanished beneath the cultivated fields, while the Delta cemeteries have dissolved into the soil. Until relatively recently few archaeologists chose to excavate in the Delta as the rewards were thought to be negligible.

By contrast, Upper Egypt, the land of the Nile Valley, was a long, narrow, hot, self-contained region focused on the river Nile. Along both banks of the river ran the narrow strip of Black Land, the dark, rich, fertile soil. Beyond the Black Land stretched the inhospitable Red Land, the desert, and beyond this again towered the cliffs that provided Egypt's builders with stone. The Egyptians built their mud-brick houses on the edge of the Black Land. The first urban temples, too, stood here, built of mud-brick, reeds, wattle and daub. But fashions changed, stone was readily available, and Egypt's gods soon found themselves housed in impressive stone temples that dominated the mud-brick housing. While almost all the domestic architecture has now disappeared – dissolved, corroded, flattened under later constructions or spread on the fields as fertilizer – the stone temples remain to bear silent witness to the lost cities.

Meanwhile, the Red Land, the barren desert, was one vast cemetery. Here, in the land of ghosts where none but the dead could live, the Egyptians built the pyramids, mortuary temples and tombs that housed and celebrated the deceased. This architecture, the architecture of death, has survived in the hot, dry sand more or less intact. It is not surprising that the first Egyptologists targeted the elite burial sites in the sure and certain knowledge that they would yield rich pickings. And it is little wonder, as Western museums quickly filled with mummies, mummy cases, sarcophagi, canopic jars and grave goods, that the Egyptians gained an undeserved reputation as a deeply morbid people obsessed with thoughts of death. Today this imbalance is being redressed, as current excavators reject the cemeteries and turn instead to the Delta, and to the few surviving domestic and military sites.

The building of the Aswan High Dam in the late 1960s brought a welcome regularity to the Egyptian water and electricity supplies, but completely transformed the natural rhythm of the agricultural cycle. For thousands of years the Nile had swollen and burst her banks in the late summer months, spreading water and fertile silt over the fields that lined the river. This time of inundation, the time when the fields were inaccessible, left a vast workforce available to labour for the state. The retreat of the waters left the fields moist and ready for planting, with no need for any form of artificial irrigation. A fertile harvest could then be gathered in the spring, before the hot sun baked the land and killed its pests.

With the building of the dam, this annual inundation came to an abrupt stop. Now Egypt has a permanently high water table. The effect on her monuments has been intensely damaging. Ancient mud-brick buildings – and this includes all of Egypt's royal palaces – are more prone than ever to dissolve and disappear. Stone buildings, designed to be wet for three months of the year and then bone dry for nine, now find themselves sitting in damp soil for the full 12 months. More than ever, there is a need to excavate, investigate and conserve Egypt's treasures before it is too late.

THE EXPLORERS

≻—≺

THE STORY OF THE BEGINNINGS
OF RESEARCH INTO THE WONDERS
OF ANTIQUITY IN EGYPT IS UNIQUE
IN AT LEAST ONE POINT. IN NO
OTHER LAND DOES A CONQUERING
ARMY MARCH AT THE HEAD OF THE
PIONEERS OF EXPLORATION ...

J. Baikie, *A Century of Excavation in
the Land of the Pharaohs* (1923)

CHAPTER ONE

>—<

THE FIRST
EGYPTOLOGISTS

IN 1400 BC the three Giza pyramids, the tombs of the 4th Dynasty kings, were already 1000 years old. Long abandoned by their priests, they lay open and stripped of their contents, their precious mummies vanished. At their feet crouched the once-mighty Sphinx, now buried up to his noble neck in windblown sand. Pyramids were out of fashion. Kings were being buried in secret rock-cut tombs in southern Egypt, and the northern royal cemeteries were curiosities – tangible reminders of a vanished, almost mythical age.

It was a hot day and Prince Tuthmosis, younger son of the 18th Dynasty King Amenhotep II, was hunting gazelles in the Giza desert. At noon the exhausted Tuthmosis sought shelter from the fierce sun. Taking advantage of the shade offered by the ancient ruins, he leapt from his chariot and flung himself on the ground. He drank deep from his water flask and, with his back resting against the Sphinx's limestone head, started to doze. Soon he was fast asleep and dreaming a curious dream. The god Hor-em-akhet (Horus on the horizon), the falcon-headed spirit of the Sphinx, stood before him. The god was unhappy. He implored Tuthmosis to restore his neglected statue. In exchange, he would ensure that Tuthmosis became king of Egypt. The ambitious Tuthmosis swore to carry out the god's wishes. He cleared away the sand to reveal the Sphinx's long, leonine body, repaired a broken paw, and plugged a hole in the battered chest. Then he repainted the Sphinx, using the brightest blues, reds and yellows so that the god sparkled in the sunlight. The god was delighted with his colourful statue, and Tuthmosis did indeed become king of Egypt. The newly crowned Tuthmosis IV had the story of his extraordinary dream carved on a stone tablet – the Dream Stela – and set between the paws of the Sphinx, where it still stands today.

A hundred and fifty years later, Ramesses II was on the throne. The ancient pyramid cemeteries of Sakkara and Giza were now attracting tourists, and a steady stream of day-trippers made their way into the desert to marvel at the monuments and carve graffiti into their stone:

> Year 47, 2nd month of winter, day 25 [January 1232 BC], the Treasury-Scribe Hednakht, son of Tjenro and Tewosret, came to take a stroll and enjoy himself in the west of Memphis, along with his brother Panakht ... He said: 'O all you gods of the West of Memphis ... and glorified dead ... grant a full lifetime in serving your good pleasure, a goodly burial after a happy old age, like yourself' ...[1]

But the cemeteries were ill maintained, the royal tombs were in disrepair and everything was once again covered in sand. Prince Khaemwaset, the fourth son of Ramesses II, was a respected scholar and antiquary who would be revered as a magician after his death. Now the prince undertook the restoration of the monuments. Of course, Khaemwaset did not get his own princely hands dirty, but he supervised closely as his workmen tidied, swept, repaired, and carved conspicuous labels – officially sanctioned graffiti – into the pyramids, tombs and temples. Each label bore the name of the original monument owner, the name of Ramesses II and, of course, the name of Khaemwaset himself.

Both Tuthmosis IV and Prince Khaemwaset have been burdened with the title 'world's first Egyptologist'. But they were by no means the first Egyptians to show an interest in preserving and restoring their country's past. Already, in 2680 BC, the 3rd Dynasty King Djoser had included approximately 40,000 old stone vessels, plates and cups, some inscribed with the names of 1st and 2nd Dynasty pharaohs, in the storage galleries beneath his Sakkara Step Pyramid. It seems unlikely that these second-hand vessels represent Djoser's own collection of antiques – perhaps some had come from the old tombs and storerooms that must have been demolished to build Djoser's own pyramid? Whatever their provenance, it is interesting that Djoser was reluctant to throw them away.

In fact, Djoser was acting with utmost propriety in caring for his ancestors' property. All of Egypt's monarchs were burdened with the duty of maintaining and renewing the monuments of past kings. This was an important aspect of their duty to preserve *maat*, or order, and banish chaos. Restoring the sacred sites – the temples and tombs – was a very obvious means of proving that chaos was indeed being kept at bay. So when the 18th Dynasty female king Hatshepsut boasted that she had restored the monuments of her fathers, damaged during the turbulent Second Intermediate Period, she had her own agenda. In an inscription carved on the Speos Artemidos, a temple dedicated to the lion-headed goddess Pakhet in Middle Egypt, she showed that, although female, she was an eminently suitable king:

> I have done these things by the device of my heart. I have never
> slumbered as one forgetful, but have made strong what was
> decayed. I have raised up what was dismembered, even from the
> first time when the Asiatics were in Avaris of the North Land, with
> roving hordes in the midst of them overthrowing what had been
> made ... [2]

In theory the royal commitment to the maintenance of *maat* should have ensured that Egypt's many ancient monuments remained in an excellent state of preservation. But not all kings had the financial resources to renovate their land, and those who did tended to concentrate on renewing the monuments of their immediate predecessors. Tuthmosis and Khaemwaset were unusual in venturing so far back into the past. Renewal, in all too many cases, meant 'restoration': complete demolition followed by rebuilding on a far grander scale. This was particularly the case during the New Kingdom, when the Karnak temple of Amen at Thebes suffered wave after wave of restoration. Some of the most beautiful parts of the temple complex, including the 12th Dynasty White Chapel of Senwosret I and the 18th Dynasty Red Chapel of Hatshepsut, were dismantled at this time. Fortunately, the frugal labourers salvaged their disjointed blocks for reuse as filling in gateways and walls, and modern archaeologists have been able to retrieve the blocks and fit them back together as gigantic 3-D jigsaw puzzles. These two lost buildings have been recreated, and modern *maat* has defeated ancient chaos!

As the New Kingdom drew to a close, Egypt was plunged into economic crisis. At Thebes, the mayor found himself unable to pay the workmen employed in the royal cemeteries. The consequences were inevitable: the workmen turned to robbery, and the Valley of the Kings became unsafe. Hastily, Ramesses XI abandoned his partially completed tomb, and made plans to be buried in the north. Soon the royal tombs were in a disgraceful condition. Alarmed by what they saw, the priests of Amen embarked upon an archaeological rescue mission. Egypt's kings were to be excavated and reburied.

The priests opened the tombs, and transferred their sorry remains to temporary workshops. Fortunately, they had lost track of Tutankhamen, and he was left to lie in peace. The priests repaired the mummies using contemporary bandages, mending broken limbs and patching and darning as required. At the same time they stripped the bodies of their surviving jewels and amulets, a brutal desecration that they perhaps justified on the grounds of protecting the bodies from future thefts. The rewrapped mummies were replaced in their original wooden coffins, now denuded of all gold leaf. Mummies and coffins were labelled, then groups of mummies were stored in chambers dotted in and around the Valley. From time to time these groups were amalgamated, until eventually there was a large cache of royal mummies housed in the family tomb of Pinodjem II at Deir el-Bahari, and a second, smaller cache in the Valley tomb of Amenhotep II. With the Valley now stripped of its treasures, the robbers lost their interest in the royal tombs and the priests lost their interest in archaeology.

The 26th Dynasty Saite kings showed an interest in exploring and restoring Egypt's ancient monuments that went far beyond their duty to maintain *maat*. Newly independent, flushed with the triumph of breaking free from Assyrian control, and with the Kushite kings humbled and confined to Nubia, Late Period Egypt could once again be proud of her heritage. A wave of patriotism swept the country. Drawing inspiration from the art and sculptures of the Old and Middle Kingdoms, Egypt's artists set to work to prove cultural continuity with their glorious past. The Saite kings built their own tombs safe within their Delta temple precincts, where the ever-vigilant priests could guard them. But they felt a strong reverence for the pyramid builders, and many Saite nobles aspired to be buried in the ancient pyramid cemeteries. At Sakkara a new entrance was built to allow access to a network of Saite passageways cut under the Step Pyramid. And at Giza the pyramid of Menkaure, a particular hero of the Saites, was provided with an inscribed wooden coffin dedicated to the dead king:

> Osiris, the King of Upper and Lower Egypt, Menkaure, living forever. Born of the sky, conceived by Nut, heir of Geb, his beloved. Thy mother Nut spreads herself over you in her name of 'Mistress of Heaven'. She caused you to be a god, in your name of 'God'. O King of Upper and Lower Egypt Menkaure, living forever.[3]

We must assume that the Saite coffin came fully equipped with a Saite mummy, a substitute for the missing body of Menkaure that would help his dead spirit to live again. When rediscovered in the nineteenth century the coffin did indeed hold body parts: a motley collection of human remains, including a pair of legs, a lower torso, and some ribs and vertebrae. These, however, have been dated by radiocarbon analysis to the Roman Period, while the coffin, firmly dated to the Saite Dynasty, is 600 years older. It seems that the mummy thoughtfully interred by the Saites must at some time have been replaced by a Roman corpse.

The Saite kings were defeated by the Persians. Now the Emperor Cambyses was pharaoh of Egypt, and, as the admittedly biased Greek historians record, he was not remotely interested in respecting or restoring the ancient traditions. In response to an attempted uprising he completely obliterated the 2000-year-old temple of Re at Heliopolis. He even ordered that the sacred Apis bull of Memphis be slaughtered. He did, however, have a certain curiosity about the local burial practices, and is rumoured to have opened up the ancient tombs so that he might examine their contents.

For centuries Egypt had maintained close political and economic ties with Greece. Both countries were part of a circular Mediterranean trade network, which saw ships sailing anti-clockwise from Memphis, through the Delta, along the Levantine coast, and westwards past Turkey and Greece before crossing to the African coast and returning eastwards to Memphis. We do not know when this trade link was first established, but it was already functioning efficiently during the New Kingdom, and probably existed well before. Egyptian goods (not antiquities, but everyday products such as linen and grain) made their way to Greece on a regular basis, while Greek delicacies, including wine and oil, travelled in the opposite direction. People travelled, too. By Saite times there were significant numbers of Greek mercenaries in the Egyptian army, and in 610 BC a Greek settlement had been established at Naukratis, in the western Delta, close by Sais. Inevitably, Egypt started to attract Greek tourists who, in time-honoured tradition, carved their graffiti into her temples and tombs. Homer, writing his *Odyssey* in the eighth century BC, tells us that King Menalaeus was among these early visitors, lingering in Egypt on his way home from the Trojan war.

The historian Herodotus of Halicarnassus (*c.* 484–420 BC) travelled to Egypt soon after the end of the Saite Period, roaming extensively in the Delta and perhaps venturing as far south as Aswan, although from his writings it seems that he never visited Thebes. Details of his adventures were included in his nine-volume *Histories*, with the entire second book, *Euterpé*, being devoted to his own personal experience of the land of the pharaohs. His account is an engaging mixture of history, geography, economics and anthropology linked by accounts of his visits to some of Egypt's most ancient sites and flavoured by his own personal prejudices. It is as enjoyable today as it was over 2000 years ago – an impressive achievement for any author.

Herodotus, accustomed to patriarchal Greek culture, where the men participated in public life while their womenfolk remained modestly at home weaving wool, was intrigued and slightly shocked by the sheer difference of the people he met:

> Not only is the climate different from the rest of the world, and the rivers unlike any other rivers, but the people also, in most of their manners and customs, exactly reverse the common practice of mankind. For example, women attend the markets and trade, while the men sit at home at the loom; and here, while the rest of the world works the weft up the warp, the Egyptians work it down. The women carry burdens upon their shoulders, while men carry them upon their heads. Women urinate standing up, men sitting down. To ease themselves they go indoors, yet they eat their food outside in the streets ... A woman cannot serve as a priest, either for god or goddess, but men may be priests to both. Sons need not support their parents unless they choose, but daughters must, whether they wish to or not ... Dough they knead with their feet, but they mix mud, and even take up dirt, with

their hands. They are the only people in the world – they at least, and those who have learned the practice from them – who use circumcision. The men wear two garments apiece, their women but one.[4]

Like all good tourists, Herodotus paid a visit to the Giza pyramids, which he correctly identified as the tombs of Egypt's long-dead kings. Here he listened to the tour guides, and remembered their stories:

> Cheops [Khufu] succeeded to the throne and plunged into all kinds of wickedness. He closed the temples and forbad the Egyptians to sacrifice, compelling them instead to labour, one and all, in his service. Some were required to drag blocks of stone down to the Nile from the quarries in the Arabian hills; others received the blocks after they had been conveyed in boats across the river ... A hundred thousand men laboured constantly, and were relieved every three months by a fresh lot. It took ten years' oppression of the people just to build the causeway for the transportation of the stone ...
>
> The wickedness of Cheops reached such a pitch that, when he had spent all his treasure and wanted more, he sent his daughter to the brothels, with orders to procure for him a certain sum – how much I cannot say, for I was never told. She procured it, and at the same time, determined to leave a monument to her own memory, she required each man to make her a present of a stone. With these stones she built a pyramid ...[5]

To some Herodotus will always be the venerable 'Father of History', the affectionate term first used by the Roman statesman Cicero. His works will always be respected as they preserve a wealth of small detail and oral tradition that would otherwise be completely lost. To take just one example, Herodotus's account of mummification, where he describes in suitably gory detail the entire process from death to bandaging, has proved particularly helpful and, as scientific analysis has recently confirmed, almost entirely correct:

> The method of embalming, according to the most perfect process, is as follows. First they take a crooked piece of iron and use it to draw out the brain through the nostrils. Rinsing with drugs clears out anything remaining in the skull. Next they cut along the flank with a sharp Ethiopian blade, and take out the whole contents of the abdomen, which they then cleanse ... After this they fill the cavity with the purest crushed myrrh, with cassia and every other sort of spice except frankincense, and sew up the opening. Then the body is placed in natron for seventy days, and entirely covered over. After that time has passed, and it must not be exceeded, the body is washed and wrapped round, from head to foot, with fine linen bandages coated with resin ... Finally they hand back the body to the relatives, who place it in a wooden coffin in the shape of a man before shutting it up in a tomb, propped upright against the wall.[6]

Others, less charitably, have classified him as the 'Father of Lies', casting doubt on many of his stories, and even suggesting that he might have been an armchair travel writer, fantasizing about exotic Egypt without ever leaving home. This seems unduly harsh. While Diodorus loftily announces, 'We shall omit from our history the tales invented by Herodotus and certain other writers in Egyptian affairs, who deliberately prefer fables to fact,' Herodotus himself is critical of lazy historians who place their trust in dubious sources: 'The Greeks tell many tales without due investigation.' He does indeed tell a number of unlikely stories, and in some instances he is quite clearly wrong. Almost every one of his stories crumbles slightly under scrutiny. There is no evidence to support his claim that Khufu was a cruel king. The Great Pyramid was not built by 100,000 men toiling in conditions of abject oppression, but was built by gangs of 20,000 well-fed free workers, who were treated with a degree of respect by their supervisors. And so on. But Herodotus was not omniscient – he was a foreigner writing about a very strange land. Honest errors are surely forgivable. Herodotus had no reference books to consult. He obtained his information from the priests and scribes whom he met on his travels, and quite often these self-styled 'experts' were themselves wrong. In some cases, indeed, it seems that his sources may have succumbed to the temptation, well known to modern tour guides, of misleading the gullible foreigner.

Contemporary readers had no problem accepting Herodotus's stories, and many used him as the primary source for their own works. Chief among these were the historian Diodorus Siculus (first century BC) and the geographer Strabo (*c.* 63 BC – AD 21). Diodorus includes a detailed description of Egypt in his *Bibliotheca Historica* (Library of History*)*, an ambitious history of the world covering all known events up to Caesar's conquest of Gaul. Although he draws heavily on Herodotus, Diodorus has some original passages and includes facts that Herodotus omits. His description of the mummification process, for example, is subtly different from that given by Herodotus:

> ... One of them inserts his hand through the wound in the body
> into the breast and takes out everything except the kidneys and
> the heart. Another man cleans each of the entrails, washing them
> with palm wine and with incense. Finally, having washed the whole
> corpse, they first diligently treat it with cedar oil and other things
> for thirty days, and then with myrrh, cinnamon and spices ...
> Having treated it, they return it to the relatives with every
> member of the body preserved so perfectly that even the eyelashes
> and the eyebrows remain, the whole appearance of the body being
> unchanged and the cast of the features recognisable.[7]

Diodorus tells us the cost of this elaborate ritual – one talent of silver – and adds that most undertakers, not unreasonably, required this payment in advance.

Strabo lived for a time at Alexandria and so knew Egypt and her people well. He travelled the length of the Nile Valley with his friend Aelius Gallus, the Roman-appointed governor of Egypt, and together they visited all the main cities. His multi-volume *Geography* includes an extensive coverage of the Delta region, plus descriptions of the better-known Theban tourist attractions, including the Colossi of Memnon and the west bank tombs of the New Kingdom kings:

> Above the Memnonium [the Ramesseum], in caves, are the tombs
> of kings, which are hewn from stone, are about forty in number,
> are marvellously constructed and a sight worth seeing.[8]

The arrival of Alexander the Great saw a new capital city established at Alexandria and, after the untimely death of Alexander, a new royal family on the throne. Now Egypt was ruled by the Greek-born Ptolemies. The Greeks were very interested in the intellectual achievements of the Egyptians. Alexandria, home to a splendid museum and the world's greatest library housing an estimated million books, attracted scholars of international renown, eager to learn from the Egyptian masters. Soon Egyptian philosophy, religion, architecture and mathematics were being exported to a wider Mediterranean world. Meanwhile, the Greeks who lived in Egypt in ever-increasing numbers became to a certain extent Egyptianized. They accepted Egyptian traditions, including mummification and the custom of brother-sister marriage in the ruling family, and they built temples to the old gods, including the temple of Isis at Philae, in a slightly distorted but still recognizably Egyptian style.

When Julius Caesar visited the last queen of Egypt, Cleopatra VII, they took a break from their busy schedules to enjoy a pleasure cruise down the Nile accompanied, somewhat unromantically, by a fleet of troop-carrying ships. The days they spent marvelling at the antiquities, the nights they spent together on Cleopatra's state barge. The Romans, interested primarily in Egypt's grain, took a robust, materialistic approach to Egypt's treasures. They adopted Egypt's gods – Isis was to have particularly successful career in the Roman world – and seized her more portable monuments. Having annexed Egypt in 30 BC, they were free to take what they liked. So while in Egypt the traditional way of life was being slowly stifled beneath a thick blanket of Roman culture, in Rome and her provinces Egyptian sphinxes and obelisks were standing (or in the case of the sphinxes, lying), slightly self-consciously, alongside the statues of noble Romans that adorned the public squares. In Rome's Field of Mars an Egyptian obelisk now served as the gnomon (rod) for a gigantic sundial. The historian Pliny the Elder (AD 23–79) was very impressed by this novel way of telling the time:

> Augustus used the obelisk in the Campus Martius in a remarkable way: to cast a shadow and so mark out the length of the days and nights. An area was paved in proportion to the height of the monolith in such a way that the shadow at noon on the shortest day would reach to the edge of the pavement. As the shadow shrank and expanded, it was measured by bronze rods fixed in the pavement.[9]

The Romans were expert engineers, but the lowering, transportation and re-erection of at least 13 obelisks, plus sundry large-scale statues, posed an unprecedented challenge. Obelisks are long, thin shafts cut from hard granite. Dedicated by the king to the sun god Re, they were raised in pairs before Egypt's temple gates, where their tips, coated with gold foil, sparkled in the sunlight. Some of the larger obelisks were over 100 feet in length and weighed upwards of 450 tons; they could only be transported on huge barges, and there was a constant worry that they might crack while being loaded on or off the ship. Pliny devoted an entire chapter in book 36, *Stone*, of his 37-volume encyclopedia *Natural History* to obelisks and their transportation:

A canal was dug from the river Nile to the spot where the obelisk lay, and two broad vessels, loaded with blocks of similar stone a foot square – the cargo of each amounting to double the size and consequently double the weight of the obelisks – was put beneath it. The extremities of the obelisk remaining supported by the opposite sides of the canal. The blocks of stone were removed and the vessels, being thus gradually lightened, received their burden.[10]

Genuine Egyptian artifacts spread throughout the Roman world, leaving trails guaranteed to confuse the archaeologists of the future. Meanwhile, the imported Egyptian antiquities were being copied and adapted by local craftsmen, so Egyptian-style Roman artifacts became commonplace. Now small-scale pyramids enhanced the cemeteries of Rome, and meaningless fake hieroglyphics decorated purely Roman objects. At least one genuine obelisk was enhanced with a pseudo-Egyptian text to increase its appeal. When Antinous, the cherished favourite of the Egyptophile Emperor Hadrian, drowned in the Nile in AD 129, his grieving master had him deified as a form of Osiris; his statue, recovered from the Villa Adriana, Tivoli, shows him in the typical pose of a pharaoh, complete with *nemes* headcloth and kilt. Only the beard is missing – presumably it was felt that this would have marred Antinous's flawless, and entirely classical, face.

Back in Egypt, there had been a cultural disaster. In 47 BC, as Julius Caesar attempted to take Alexandria, the great library had burned to the ground. With it went many of the books detailing Egypt's glorious past, including the irreplaceable *History of Egypt*, a complete account of all of Egypt's kings painstakingly compiled by the priest Manetho for Ptolemy I. Fortunately, fragments of Manetho's great work had been preserved in the writings of other authors.

Worse was to come. Christianity had already arrived in Egypt, where it slowly but steadily persuaded converts from the old religion. In AD 391 the Christian Emperor Theodosius hastened matters by prohibiting all pagan cults, and closing all the pagan temples in his empire. This forced conversion saw the abrupt end of over 3000 years of religious continuity in Egypt. With it came the inevitable end of the art of mummification. The Greeks and Egyptians who had died in Egypt had been happy to accept the local funerary rites, adapted to fit with their own beliefs. But Egypt's Christians, the Copts, were a stricter, more ascetic cult. They believed that they would cast off their earthly bodies at death, and had no interest in paying to preserve an empty corporal shell, favouring instead a simple burial, unembalmed and without grave goods. Mummification was, in any case, too tainted with the cult of Osiris to be acceptable to the Christians.

Now the temples fell into disrepair, their precious libraries abandoned, their metal idols melted and their stone statues smashed. Fundamentalists attacked the Serapeum, the underground catacombs designed by Prince Khaemwaset to house the burials of the sacred Apis bulls, and its precious library was burned. Meanwhile curious tourists continued to visit the dynastic cemeteries, leaving behind the inevitable graffiti. The lonely Valley of the Kings became home to a community of Christian hermits who braved the harsh conditions to build churches and houses in the disused tombs. Here Christian slogans were painted on the walls to coexist, somewhat unhappily, alongside the images of Egypt's ancient gods:

> I beseech thee, Jesus Christ, my Lord, suffer me not to follow after my desire; let not my thoughts have dominion over me; let me not die in my sins, but accept thy servant for good.[10]

With the temples closed and their priests scattered, the hieroglyphic script became redundant. Hieroglyphs had always been reserved for official pronouncements – religious, funerary, historical and royal texts – usually carved in stone. The intricate hieroglyphic characters were beautiful to look at but time-consuming to reproduce, and they had never been considered suitable for routine office work.

Egypt's busy scribes, working with papyrus and paintbrush rather than carving in stone, preferred the quicker, cursive hieratic script – a form of hieroglyphic shorthand. This, by the end of the dynastic age, had evolved into the equally speedy demotic writing. Demotic, used from 700 BC to AD 500, was in turn replaced by the new-style Coptic script. The Copts retained the old Egyptian language, but they wrote using a combination of Greek letters and demotic signs. Now, as the old priests died, there was no one left who could read the lengthy texts preserved in Egypt's temples and, of course, on the obelisks that still graced the squares of Rome. Egypt's long history simply disappeared, and the curious inscriptions started to take on the status of magical, mystical runes.

For 250 years, as the Roman Empire gave way to Byzantine rule, Egypt remained a Christian country. Then, in 640, came the Arab conquest. Alexandria fell to the forces led by General Amr Ibn-al-As, and almost instantly Egypt became isolated from the Western world. Within Egypt the Christian Church quickly dwindled as the masses converted to Islam and increasingly strict penalties were applied to those who would not conform. Coptic became an essentially dead language confined to the few remaining churches, and Arabic was now the official language and script of Egypt. When, in 1517, the Turkish Ottoman Empire took control, Egypt was ruled from Constantinople, but little else changed. Two hundred and fifty years later the Turks remained in nominal control, but real power lay in the hands of the Mamluk Beys, the descendants of slaves imported from Central Asia and the Caucasus, who had developed into a ruling military caste.

It would be a grave mistake to imagine Arabic Egypt as a benighted cultural backwater. Cairo, at least, flourished under Arabic rule, becoming a sophisticated centre of Muslim culture. But to all intents and purposes, Egypt was now hidden from Western eyes and Christians were unwelcome.

CHAPTER TWO

>—<

A REDISCOVERED LAND

EGYPT HAD BECOME a veiled land, her glories glimpsed through the Bible and the works of the classical authors. Arabic merchants had little trouble moving around the country, but were indifferent to the curious relics of a long-vanished people. The few European traders who did manage to reach Cairo marvelled at the pyramids, but were advised that it was both difficult and dangerous to journey further south. The German friar Felix Fabri was one of the few who recorded his adventures in northern Egypt. His *Evagatorium in Terrae Sanctae* (published in English as *The Wanderings of Felix Fabri*), tells of his 1482 visit to Egypt, when he travelled across the Sinai to St Catherine's Monastery (supposedly the site of Moses' burning bush) and visited the Cairo crypt where the Holy Family is reported to have hidden from King Herod.

The Egyptians themselves had no interest in archaeology for archaeology's sake but, like the Romans, the Greeks, the Persians and the ancient Egyptians before them, they recognized that their ancient temples and tombs made excellent quarries. No one of any sense would go to the trouble of cutting, shaping and transporting a stone block when the deserts were full of gently decaying tombs whose stone walls were just begging to be reused. Recycling was common, and a conveniently shaped stone might have a long and useful life as an integral part of several disparate buildings before finally coming to rest in a museum.

Even Tuthmosis IV, the 'first Egyptologist' and restorer of the sand-encrusted Sphinx, had seen nothing wrong in carving his Dream Stela on a door lintel liberated from King Khaefre's redundant mortuary temple. Tuthmosis would not, however, have been amused by the malicious actions of the Sufi sheikh Sayim al-Dahr – the Perpetual Faster – who in 1378 attacked the face and ears of the Sphinx. Once again Hor-em-akhet took action to protect his statue, this time covering a neighbouring village with sand. The sand-coated villagers, highly irritated by this turn of events, retaliated by lynching the meddlesome sheikh. Later French soldiers serving under Napoleon would be blamed for his act of vandalism.

The three Giza pyramids had originally been covered in a fine limestone cladding that caused them to shine like mirrors in the bright desert sunlight. Already part of this cladding had been removed and ground up to make Roman mortar. Now the remainder was stripped and re-employed in the building of medieval Cairo. Today only the pyramid of Khaefre retains, at its very tip, a trace of its original casing. Once dazzling white, the Tura limestone has been yellowed by centuries of Cairo smog. This story of destruction was repeated along the Nile, as everywhere builders helped themselves from the ancient remains. Meanwhile, treasure seekers, convinced that the monuments held untold riches, were conducting their own excavations. The explicitly titled *Book of Buried Pearls and of the Precious Mystery: Giving the Hiding Places of Finds and Treasures* offered an invaluable guide to the antiquities, for not only did it promise to pinpoint fabulous treasures, it also listed potent spells guaranteed to defeat the guardian spirits of the pyramids and tombs. No one stopped to query why the authors of the guide would prefer to publish this valuable information rather than excavate the treasures themselves, and many were inspired to dig. Even though the guide was a blatant fraud, it seems unlikely that all the treasure seekers came away empty-handed.

The physician Abd el-Latif of Baghdad, who visited Cairo at the end of the twelfth century, kept a detailed record of his travels. He tells the revolting tale of one excavation that certainly did not go to plan:

> A credible person told me that, joining once in a search for treasures near the pyramid, his party found a tightly sealed jar, on opening which and finding honey, they ate it. One of them noticed a hair that had stuck to his finger: he pulled it towards him and a small infant appeared, the whole of the limbs of which appeared to have preserved their original freshness ...[1]

The best known of the early excavators – and one of the few who has left any record of his work – is the eighth-century Caliph el-Mamun, son of Caliph Harun el-Rashid. The enterprising caliph is reported to have doused the north face of the Great Pyramid with hot vinegar in a vain attempt to crack its blocks and access its treasure, for he, like everyone else, was absolutely convinced that the pyramid was stuffed full of gold and jewels. Eventually he resorted to brute force and used a battering ram to force his way in – his hole forms the entrance that tourists use today. He was able to tunnel upwards, burrowing around the stone plugs that blocked the internal passageways, until he found himself in a room (now known as the Queen's Chamber) filled with grotesquely large bats and intrusive Late Period mummies. Moving ever upwards, he eventually discovered the burial chamber (the King's Chamber) where, it is rumoured, he discovered the gold-encrusted mummy of King Khufu lying in his coffin, a sword in his hand and a ruby the size of an egg on his forehead. However, given that the pyramid is known to have been opened and emptied by the Middle Kingdom, and, indeed, that rubies were unknown in Old Kingdom Egypt, it seems unlikely that this could have been the original Khufu. If the caliph found anything at all – and false rumours of spectacular finds of gold are associated with all of Egypt's excavations – it must have been a substitute Khufu, thoughtfully interred by the Saite kings.

In Europe the Renaissance, or cultural rebirth, of the fifteenth and sixteenth centuries deflected the introspection of the Middle

Ages and encouraged a greater curiosity about the wider world. The Near East, Egypt included, had at last attained a stability that made her attractive to merchants. This was an age of intrepid explorers, of the opening of trade routes and of varied and widespread reading. The Bible was slowly becoming accessible to all, and there were many mentions of Egypt in the Bible. There was a fresh interest in the civilizations of Greece and Rome, and the infant science of archaeology developed as the tales of the classical authors – Homer and Herodotus among them – tantalized scholars with hints of vanished cities and long-lost knowledge.

This renewed awareness of the classical world went hand in hand with a keen desire to decipher the hieroglyphics that adorned so many classical monuments. Many believed, as the Imperial Romans had believed, that the ancient Egyptians had been the possessors of true esoteric wisdom. Maybe they even knew the true story of the origins of the world and its people? It was felt that the Coptic language, which was still being used by Egypt's Christians, might hold the key to unlocking that wisdom for the benefit of mankind. Unfortunately, the would-be translators were confused by the pseudo-hieroglyphs and error-filled copies of genuine texts that adorned the faux Egyptian pieces, and their efforts were doomed to fail.

One major conceptual problem was handicapping the development of archaeology. Everyone in Christian Europe accepted that the Bible told the literal truth; it was the word of God revealed to man, and no one dared to think otherwise. It therefore followed that ancient history – and prehistory, geology, biology and all the sciences – had to be made to fit with the Bible stories. The first book of the Bible recorded, in beautiful and very clear language, the details of the creation of the world:

In the beginning God created the heaven and the earth. And the earth was without form, and void; and darkness was upon the face of the deep. And the Spirit of God moved upon the face of the waters. And God said, Let there be light: and there was light.

And God saw the light, that it was good: and God divided the
light from the darkness.

And God called the light Day, and the darkness he called
Night. And the evening and the morning were the first day ...
And God said, Let us make man in our image, after our likeness:
and let them have dominion over the fish of the sea, and over the
fowl of the air, and over the cattle, and over all the earth, and over
every creeping thing that creepeth on the earth.

So God created man in his own image, in the image of God
created he him; male and female created he them ...

And the evening and the morning were the sixth day.[2]

In 1650 James Ussher, Archbishop of Armagh, calculated a date for
this momentous event: the world had been created at noon on 23
October 4004 BC. However did he reach such a precise date? As he
knew that 'one day is with the Lord as a thousand years', and that
the world had been created in six days, he deduced that world was
to last for a mere 6000 years. He apportioned his 6000 years to
4000 years before the birth of Jesus, and 2000 years after. Then he
made a slight adjustment. He knew that Herod had died in 4 BC;
this meant that Jesus must have been born in 4 BC. The date of 4004
BC was fixed. As for the month, he chose noon on the first Sunday
after the autumnal equinox (the time when day and night are of
equal duration) because he knew that in the beginning, God created
light.

The official date for the beginning of life was printed boldly in
the Bible for all to read. Nothing could have existed earlier than this
date. So although the Greeks and Romans had known that the world
was far older, all of human history and prehistory now had to be
crammed into a very short time frame. British archaeologists were
forced to accept that flint handaxes found beside fossilized mam-
moths must be curious relics of the Roman invasion (perhaps the
Romans had brought elephants with them?), while Egyptologists
had to dismiss the early kings of Egypt, preserved in the writings of

Manetho, as fiction. This was clearly unsatisfactory, and it grew increasingly difficult to accept as more and more archaeological discoveries came to light. For many years archaeologists, Egyptologists among them, dared to think the unthinkable. But it was not until 1859, the year that Charles Darwin published his *On the Origin of Species*, that the true age of the world won general acceptance.

In 1580 English merchants were subject to a formal trade agreement with the Sublime Porte, the Turkish court and government. Most trade bypassed Egypt, but there was one very active, and specifically Egyptian, trade link with the West. In 1564 the King of Navarre had sent his personal physician, Guy de la Fontaine, to Alexandria in search of human mummies. In 1586 the British merchant John Sanderson exported five hundredweight of assorted mummy pieces to the apothecaries of London. These bodies and body parts were destined to be ground to a powder and mixed with herbs and spices, then swallowed or applied as a poultice. They were the cure-all wonder drug, the Viagra of their age. The apothecaries had confused '*mumia*', a rare and extremely expensive bitumen or tar believed to seep from the Persian mountains, with 'mummies' – long-dead, bandaged and resin-coated Egyptians. The Greek physician Dioscorides (AD 40–90) and the Persian physician Avicenna (AD 980–1037) were just two who made this crucial mistake: both maintained that powdered mummy could cure a wide variety of diseases, ranging from abscesses to paralysis and – somewhat surprisingly, given that many who took the black powder immediately vomited it back up again – nausea. In 1657 *The Physical Directory* included '*mumia*, a thing like pitch', and warned those of delicate susceptibilities that this useful substance was indeed extracted from ancient tombs.

This hint of the macabre did nothing to halt its appeal. Celebrity endorsements came from Catherine de Medici, Francis I of France and from Francis Bacon, who avowed that 'mummy hath great force in staunching blood', and hundreds of bodies were shipped from Alexandria. Some of these were undoubtedly genuine dynastic mummies. But supplies were running short, genuine mummies were expensive, and there was a cheap alternative to hand. Many of the mummies that found their way into the medicine cabinets of Europe were crude fakes: the recently dead (often criminals, the unclaimed or the severely diseased) who had been bandaged, then either buried for a couple of years or sun-dried before being ground up for export to the sick and gullible. The unsavoury trade came to an end in the eighteenth century, when the Ottoman (Turkish) rulers of Egypt, wary of any kind of trafficking in dead bodies, slapped a heavy tax on the mummies The first mummy to have entered Britain intact rather than in powdered form was probably the mummy that Charles II is rumoured to have given to his mistress, Nell Gwyn. This mummy is now stored in the British Museum, London.

Explorers and missionaries started to leave increasingly detailed accounts of their travels in Egypt. The 'Anonymous Venetian', an unknown merchant, left a record of his adventures in *A Journey I Made in the Year 1589 from Cairo to Ebrin Sailing up the Nile*: 'truth to say, many a time my life was in danger and I suffered from the torrid heat, and I often had a shortage of onions as well as other food ...' George Sandys, the youngest son of the Archbishop of York, visited Egypt in 1610 and found unimagined strangenesses: pyramids and crocodiles. He published *A Relation of a Journey* in 1615. Thirty-one years later the astronomer John Greaves published *Pyramidographia*, the first scientific account of the pyramids. A series of determined European travellers reached the small and rather scruffy town of Luxor, where all failed to recognize the many collapsed and partially buried stones as the remains of the once great city 'Hundred-Gated Thebes', so eloquently described by Homer. It was not until 1707 that a Jesuit missionary, Father Claude Sicard, made the connection and recognized the true nature of the Valley of the Kings:

These sepulchres of Thebes are tunnelled into the rock and are of astonishing depth. Halls, rooms, all are painted from top to

bottom. The variety of colours, which are almost as fresh as
the day they were painted, gives an admirable effect. There are as
many hieroglyphs as there are animals and objects represented,
which makes us suppose that we have there the story of the
lives, virtues, acts, combats and victories of the princes who are
buried there, but it is impossible for us to decipher them for
the present.[3]

Sicard travelled further south, becoming the first European to reach
Aswan for many centuries. He was able to visit an impressive 20 pyramids and 24 temples before succumbing to the Cairo plague in
1726. In the 1730s the Reverend Richard Pococke became the first
British traveller to pass beyond Cairo; his two-volume publication
Description of the East and Some Other Countries (1743) included
details of the Aswan monuments and plans showing the location of
the Theban tombs which, being somewhat inaccurate, have puzzled
archaeologists for centuries. His Danish contemporary Friderik
Norden travelled even further south, reaching Derr in Nubia and
publishing, posthumously, the heavily illustrated *Travels in Egypt*.
Soon after, in 1768, the British explorer James Bruce made his way
to the Valley of the Kings, where he discovered the decorated tomb
of the 20th Dynasty pharaoh Ramesses III (KV11), although he, of
course, had no idea what he had discovered:

It [the Valley] is a solitary place: and my guides, either from a
natural impatience, and distaste that these people have at such
employments, or that their fears of the banditti that live in the
caverns of the mountains were real, importuned me to return to
the boat, even before I had begun my search, or got into the
mountains where there are many large apartments of which I was
in quest.
  Within one of these sepulchres, on a panel, were several musical
instruments strewed upon the ground, chiefly of the hautboy
[oboe] kind, with a mouthpiece of reed ... In the three following

panels were painted, in fresco, three harps, which merited the utmost attention ...[4]

Bruce started to sketch one of the harpists, but was forced to abandon his artwork when his guides, growing nervous of the local bandits, encouraged him to withdraw for his own safety:

> With great clamour and marks of discontent ... dashed their
> torches against the largest harp, and made the best of their way
> out of the cave, leaving me and my people in the dark: and all the
> way as they went, they made dreadful denunciations of tragical
> events that were immediately to follow upon their departure from
> the cave. There was no possibility of doing more.[5]

The publication of the sketch caused great public interest: henceforth, the tomb was known as the 'Tomb of the Harpists' or 'Bruce's Tomb'.

Slowly but surely Egypt was casting off her veil. Then, in 1798, Egyptology took a huge, unintentional leap forward.

The 29-year-old French general Napoleon Bonaparte had developed a breathtakingly audacious plan. The French ports seethed with activity as the fleet prepared to sail. The intended target – a closely guarded secret – was Egypt. Napoleon had determined to follow in the footsteps of his hero Alexander the Great. By liberating and civilizing the downtrodden Egyptians he hoped to strike an oblique blow at France's arch-enemy, Britain. He also had more practical plans to cut a canal through Suez, allowing French ships unhindered access to the rich markets of East Africa and Asia. After replacing Egyptian Ottoman rule with French, he would move on to India where, with some local help, the British would be overthrown and lucrative trade routes opened up. His strategy met with the full agreement of his superiors in Paris; it seems that they were only too pleased to have the over-ambitious young general out of the way. It certainly worried the British who, gazing across the Channel, had to watch their traditional enemy make ready for war. On Easter Sunday *Bell's Weekly Messenger* spoke for many in London:

> Terrible, indeed, would be the necessity of a war. To fight to restrain French ambition ... England, already bending under the weight of a too extended Colonial dominion, can have little ambition for an inheritance of perpetual slaughter and invincible rebellion ...

From a military viewpoint Napoleon's campaign was to prove an over-ambitious disaster, but it started well enough. First Malta was seized from the Knights of St John, who had held the island for over 250 years. Next Alexandria fell, and the French naively set off across the desert, with the aim of capturing Cairo. It was to be a horrific march. The Bedouin, happy in their own climate, would not leave the French troops alone. Handicapped by their unsuitable thick clothing and heavy equipment, and driven to the point of madness by constant thirst, hunger, sunstroke and flies, several hundred French died on the journey, including many who shot themselves. Morale plummeted, only to be revived by the first victorious skirmish with the Egyptian forces. By 21 July 1798 the French had rallied enough to defeat the Mamluks in the Battle of the Pyramids (which actually took place in a field ten miles to the north of the Giza Pyramids). Here Napoleon gave his famous address to the troops: 'Soldiers! From the top of these Pyramids, forty centuries gaze upon you.' No one then knew the true age of the pyramids, and Napoleon was impressively accurate in his guess, being only three centuries adrift.

Cairo formally surrendered on 24 July, and a triumphant Napoleon set up his headquarters in the city. But on 2 August the Royal Navy, under the command of Admiral Horatio Nelson, attacked the French fleet. The 13 large warships and 4 frigates had been anchored in a defensive line over 1.5 miles offshore across the curve of Abuqir Bay, to the east of Alexandria. The British ships, being smaller and lighter than the French ones, were able to slip between the vessels and the shoreline and, with the French ships seriously undermanned and the French cannons all pointing in the wrong direction, they wreaked havoc with little fear of reprisal. Napoleon's flagship, *L'Orient*, blew up in spectacular fashion, taking with it the 13-year-old son of its captain, Louis Casabianca. The boy's heroic decision to stand by his wounded father would inspire the poet Felicia Dorothea Hemans to write 'The boy stood on the burning deck'. All but four of the French ships were lost, as were the irreplaceable treasures of the Knights of St John, and approximately 1700 French sailors died. So many French prisoners were taken that the British, who had lost a mere two ships and 218 men, couldn't cope with the numbers. Admiral Nelson found himself a national hero. Newly ennobled as Viscount Nelson of the Nile and Burnham Thorpe (the latter being his birthplace), the grateful nation awarded him a generous yearly pension of £2000.

The Battle of the Nile left the French forces stranded, depleted, demotivated and extremely short of cash. They were to hold Cairo for three years, eventually extending their control as far south as Aswan, but they were permanently vulnerable to the Turks, to the British, to the Mamluks, to local uprisings and to local illnesses that now included the plague. Pointless campaigns against the Turks in Palestine further depleted their numbers. On 18 March 1801 the British landed, and Alexandria was taken three days later. Three weeks after that the Turkish army arrived to support the British. The French were forced to retreat, and the British took plague-stricken Cairo. Ottoman rule was restored, and the French were free to make a peaceful, if ignominious, withdrawal. By this stage, an estimated one man out of every three had died. Napoleon himself was surprisingly unconcerned about this unfortunate turn of events. Commandeering a swift ship, he had escaped the British blockade on 22 August 1799 and, after a successful military coup, had proclaimed himself Emperor of France. No one back home realized the full humiliation of the Egyptian debacle. Officially, the campaign had been a great success – a coin had even been struck to celebrate Napoleon as 'Liberator of Egypt'.

From an archaeological viewpoint, the campaign was indeed a great success. Included on Napoleon's civilian staff was the Commission des Sciences et Arts d'Égypte, an illustrious band of 167 scholars, or savants, made up of: 52 engineers; 11 surveyors; 8 surgeons; 7 chemists; 6 interpreters; 5 architects, 5 designers and 5 printers; 4 mineralogists, 4 astronomers and 4 economists; 3 botanists, 3 zoologists, 3 pharmacists, 3 painters and 3 archaeologists; 2 writers and 2 musicians; 1 engraver and 1 sculptor, as well as sundry assorted students. Together they were charged with the task of investigating, recording and publishing the natural and ancient history of Egypt.

Most notable among these august men was Baron Dominique Vivant Denon, a man of great personal charm. An artist, writer and diplomat of international renown, he had been a close friend to the notorious Madame de Pompadour and, it was rumoured, lover to more than one European queen. Having served under Louis XV and Louis XVI, he was closely linked to the monarchy. Luckily, Denon had been visiting Venice when the Revolution started, so although he lost all his property and was forced to earn a rather ignominious living selling his own drawings, he managed to retain his head. Josephine introduced Denon to Napoleon and, after a period of mutual distrust, the two eventually became firm friends. Napoleon had extended a personal invitation to Denon to head his mission to Egypt. Now Denon set to work, travelling with the army as it marched south. He was to record, plan and draw Egypt's monuments under the most trying of conditions – it was not unknown for him to stray into the line of fire as his great friend General Desaix chased the remaining Mamluks beyond the Aswan border. Life was dangerous, but satisfying:

There are some unlucky moments, when everything one does is followed by danger or accident. As I returned ... to Benesuef, the general charged me with carrying an order to the head of the column; I gallop on to execute it; when a soldier who was marching out of his rank turning suddenly to the left as I was passing to the right, presents his bayonet against me, and before I could avoid it, I was unhorsed by the blow, whilst he at the same time was thrown down. 'There is one savant less,' said he while falling (for with them, every one who was not a soldier was a savant); but some piastres which I had in my pocket received the point of the bayonet, and I escaped with only a torn coat.[6]

Denon became the first European to find a papyrus scroll intact and *in situ*; he tells us how, although he was theoretically opposed to the desecration of mummies, his delight at being offered the scroll quickly overcame his scruples:

... I was conscious that I grew pale; I was just going to scold those who, in spite of my urgent requests, had violated the integrity of this mummy, when I perceived in its right hand and under his left arm a roll of papyrus which perhaps I should never have seen without this violation. My voice failed me. I then blessed the avarice of the Arabs, and the good fortune which had put me in possession of such a treasure, the most ancient book known, which I hardly dared to touch for fear of injuring it. I neither dared to entrust it to anyone, nor to lay it down anywhere; all the cotton of my bed quilt seemed to me to be insufficient to make a soft enough wrapping for it.[7]

Back in Cairo, the Commission had converted a confiscated Mamluk palace into a fully equipped research centre complete with meeting rooms, laboratories and an impressive library of reference books brought from France. There was even a printing press – the only press in the whole of Cairo. The prestigious Egyptian Institute of Arts and Sciences had been born. Denon escaped from Egypt with Napoleon in 1799, and in 1802 published his influential and highly popular *Voyage dans la Basse et la Haute Egypte (Journey in Lower and Upper Egypt)*. In 1804 he became Director General of the Museums of France. His position entitled him to travel on all of Napoleon's campaigns, and he drew architecture and collected antiquities in Austria, Spain and Poland. In so doing he laid the foundations of the Louvre collections. Denon died in 1825, leaving the world a precious legacy. Today his beautiful, precise drawings offer our only view of some of Egypt's vanished monuments, including the Elephantine temple of Amenhotep III, which was demolished in 1822.

After a series of thwarted escape attempts, the remaining Commission members eventually made their way back to Paris. Twenty-seven years later, and with their sometime emperor now exiled to St Helena, they completed the publication of the lavish and impressively titled *Description de l'Égypte, ou, Recueil des Observations et des Recherches qui ont été faites en Égypte pendant l'expédition de l'armée française, publié par les ordres de Sa Majesté l'empereur Napoléon le Grand (Description of Egypt, or, an anthology of observations and researches conducted in Egypt during the expedition of the French army, published by order of His Majesty the Emperor Napoleon the Great)*. The *Description*, heavily illustrated and including scores of detailed maps and accurate plans, was first published (1809–29) as 9 volumes of text and 11 volumes of plates; the subsequent reissue (1820–30) had 24 volumes, including 5 volumes devoted to Egypt's antiquities. It is hard to imagine any modern publisher being courageous enough even to consider such an ambitious undertaking, but the *Description* was far more than a guide to Egypt. It was a justification of Napoleon's entire Egyptian campaign, designed to make the superiority of French scholarship obvious to all.

Instantly, it was a huge success. It was not the first book to take Egypt as its theme. Denon's own book was already enjoying considerable popularity; it had been reprinted, and had been translated into English and German, the English version being both smaller and cheaper than the French. But it was the *Description* that opened European eyes to Egypt's archaeological potential, and sparked a Europe-wide fashion for anything and everything with 'Nile-style'. Suddenly the biblical stories, and the stories of the classical authors, had become real, and genuine Egyptian antiquities were in demand. Included in Napoleon's own collection was a piece we have already met: the Emperor Hadrian's Egyptian-style figure of Antinous, which had been seized from the Capitoline Museum in 1798 (and which would be returned to Rome in 1815).

Meanwhile, back in Egypt, there had been a significant discovery. A month before Napoleon fled Egypt, the French were expecting a Turkish assault on the western Delta. French troops, led by engineer and Commission member Pierre François Xavier Bouchard, were ordered to strengthen the defences at Fort Julien. Also known as Borg Rashid, Fort Julien was the medieval fortress of Rosetta which, slightly set back from the coast, lay about 50 miles beyond Alexandria. As the soldiers demolished a ramshackle old wall, they discovered a curious stone: a large, dark grey, damaged granite slab, at first sight not an obviously valuable or attractive piece. But the slab was polished on one face and it had been inscribed in three different styles of script. Peering at his find, Bouchard recognized, and could read, a Greek text written in Greek characters. Above this were carved two texts, the lower one written in unreadable scrawl (demotic) that looked something like modern Arabic, and the upper one written in recognizable but equally unreadable hieroglyphs. In 1828 the *Description* would include a brief description, and plentiful illustrations, of this curious stone and its texts:

> The stone is black granite: its average thickness is 0.27 metres, the width of its lower part 0.735 metres and its height, in its present state, 0.963 metres, for unfortunately the upper part has been greatly truncated, and one cannot even conjecture how much is missing from the stone ... About one fourth of the sole remaining part of the hieroglyphic text is missing, because of the truncation

of the right and left sides, without mentioning all that is lacking above the first line ...[8]

The Greek text confirmed that the decree had been issued by the priesthood at Memphis on 27 March 196 BC, in honour of the anniversary of the accession of King Ptolemy V Epiphanes. It had been issued in three scripts so that it could be read by both the native Egyptians and the Greeks. Archaeologists have since speculated that the stone, or stela, must first have been raised in nearby Sais and then, during the medieval period, have been relegated to the status of building-site fill.

Bouchard reported his find to his commanding officer, General Menou. Menou toyed with the idea of classifying the stone as his own personal property – many of the French took a 'finders, keepers' approach to Egypt's antiquities, building up fine private collections – but he quickly relented. Perhaps the stone was simply too big for him to handle. It was transported by boat to Cairo, where, on 29 July 1799 (or, as the Commission were now using the new revolutionary calendar, on 11th Thermidore Year VII), news of the discovery was announced to the Institute. The potential of the stone was immediately obvious. Linguists could read the Greek version of the decree, and that Greek version confirmed that the Egyptian texts were copies of the same text, both written in the ancient Egyptian language but using different writing styles:

> This decree shall be inscribed on a stela of hard stone, in sacred writings [hieroglyphs], the script of documents [demotic] and the script of the Greeks, and it shall be erected in each of the temples of the first, second and third rank, near to the divine image of the king, may he live for ever.[9]

Although neither the language nor the scripts of the Egyptian texts could be understood, the bilingual stone offered a real possibility that the mystery of hieroglyphics could at last be solved. Copies of the texts were made and sent to Paris, but the stone itself was to go to London. Under the 1801 Treaty of Alexandria, the scholars of the Commission were entitled to retain all their field notes, plans and natural history collections, but the British laid claim to their large-scale archaeological finds. These included, as well as the Rosetta Stone, two obelisks, three complete sarcophagi, and many statues and statue parts. The Rosetta Stone went first to the library of the Society of Antiquaries in London, then in 1802 it was officially presented to the British Museum as a gift of King George III. Today the Rosetta Stone (safely protected by a state-of-the-art display case) stands at the heart of the Egyptian Gallery, attracting visitors from all over the world.

CHAPTER THREE

>—<

DECODING THE
STONES

T HE MEMBERS OF Napoleon's Commission made their way back
from Egypt laden with drawings, diagrams and plans that they
circulated among fellow academics and eventually published in
admirable detail in the *Description*. For the first time European
scholars had access to accurate copies of hieroglyphic texts which,
most frustratingly, no one could either read or understand. Locked
in the hieroglyphs was the whole of Egypt's vanished history.
Linguists were determined to crack the code, but where to start?
The Rosetta Stone, with its three different scripts, offered a promising beginning.

The classical writers, who had lived alongside the hieroglyph-
writing Egyptians, had shown surprisingly little interest in the native
language, and had left disappointingly few clues for the would-be
translators:

> In the education of their sons the Priests teach them two sorts of
> writing; that which is called sacred writing [hieroglyphs] and that
> which is used in the more day-to-day instruction [demotic].[1]

> The language of the first Egyptians did not have, like modern
> languages, a set number of characters corresponding to all
> the needs of thought. The value of a noun or verb was attached

to each letter, and sometimes a letter constituted a complete meaning.[2]

Some of their clues were downright misleading, and more than a little bizarre:

When they wish to show a man dead from sunstroke they draw a blind beetle, for this dies when blinded by the sun.[3]

Already, however, there had been some progress. In 1636 the Jesuit scholar and mathematician Athanasius Kircher, inspired by the inscribed obelisks of Rome, had realized that the Coptic still being used in Egypt's churches was a distorted form of the ancient Egyptian language. Kircher's interpretations of the hieroglyphic script were less reliable. Famously, he translated the name of King Apries as, 'the Benefits of the divine Osiris are to be procured by means of sacred ceremonies and of the chain of the Genii, in order that the benefits of the Nile be obtained'.

Then, in 1761 the Abbé Barthélemy, fresh from his triumph in deciphering the Phoenician and Palmyrian alphabets, experienced a flash of inspiration. Cartouches – the loops or ovals that enclosed some of the hieroglyphs – might be being used to indicate the names of gods, or perhaps the names of kings and queens. This deduction proved to be entirely correct.

Finally, in 1797, the Danish scholar Jörgen Zöega suggested that there might be a phonetic element to the hieroglyphic script.

Unfortunately, these three truths were hidden in a thicket of mis-understandings – hieroglyphs were a secret language accessible only to the initiated; hieroglyphs were used to write a religious code; hieroglyphics were purely symbolic; there were no early alphabets; Chinese had evolved from hieroglyphics (a logical deduction for those who believed that China had been an early Egyptian colony); Coptic was a version of ancient Greek.

The starting point for the decoding of both hieroglyphs and

demotic on the Rosetta Stone had to be the Greek text. But the stone was now in London, and there was an unexpected difficulty with the copies available for study. In Cairo the Institute, conscious of the need for total accuracy, had rejected simple hand-copying as both time-consuming and prone to human error. Instead they had commissioned three separate scientific copies of the inscriptions from three separate experts. Jean-Joseph Marcel of the Cairo Press had used a system of 'autography'. The stone was cleaned, its carved characters were filled with water, then ink was applied to the entire surface. The water in the carvings repelled the ink, and so when damp paper was pressed against the stone, it received a negative impression of its text – a black background with the characters preserved in white – which could be read only with the use of a mirror. Nicholas Conté, famous today as the inventor of the graphite pencil, had used a method similar to copperplate engraving. The carvings, filled with grease, retained ink while the surface of the stone, coated in a thin layer of rubber and nitric acid, did not. Finally, Adrien Raffeneau-Delile took a cast of the stone, using the sulphur process.

Scientific these methods may have been, but they can have done little to preserve the original colour and texture of the stone. Worse was to come. The British Museum staff, in an effort to make the carved text stand out from its grey background, would later whiten the carvings with chalk and coat the stone with protective wax – some archaeologists have suspected that this might actually have been boot polish – which subsequently darkened with age and dust. Today the stone has been restored to its natural dark grey appearance, although a small dark square has been retained deliberately in the lower left-hand corner, and the delicate pink vein running through the upper left-hand portion of the stone has been revealed. But older photographs show it as black and basalt-like. And, although we are accustomed to seeing the Rosetta Stone with white writings, scientific analysis has shown that the carvings were originally filled with red pigment.

The Society of Antiquaries, too, had copied the stone. Their printed copies had been widely distributed in Europe and North America, with the universities of Oxford, Cambridge, Dublin and Edinburgh each being honoured with full plaster casts. These gifts were not made out of pure altruism. The Society needed help in developing the definitive translation of the Greek inscription, but the only response came, in Latin and with an accompanying commentary in French, from the polyglot Professor Heyne of Göttingen University. Now it was becoming obvious that there were discrepancies between the French and British versions of the text, although the three French versions seemed to be in perfect agreement. There were suspicions – voiced in Paris, not London – that the British engraver might have succumbed to making 'improvements' as he copied. In 1803 a French linguist known as Citizen Amelihon published a transcription of the Greek text accompanied by a precise Latin translation and a more speculative French translation. His was to remain the standard translation for many years, although alternative published versions were also available in English (1802), Latin (1816), German (1822), and Italian (1833).

The Greek text included the names of several kings and places which, of course, must also have been included in the two Egyptian versions of the text and which, being Greek rather than Egyptian in origin, must have been given in precise transliteration – one hieroglyphic or demotic 'letter' representing one Greek letter. Simple mathematics allowed linguists to calculate, rather crudely, where these names might be found. If a name was a third of the way in from the end of the Greek text, it was likely to be found approximately a third of the way in from the end of the demotic or hieroglyphic text. Already, in Cairo, Jean-Joseph Marcel, working in collaboration with Louis Rémi Rage, had isolated the name Ptolemy, which appeared 11 times in the Greek, and had tentatively identified the letters P and T in demotic. But they could get no further. Baron Antoine Isaac Silvestre de Saçy, working in Paris, developed a different method. He looked for words in the Greek that could be translated into Coptic, and then sought them in the demotic text. He succeeded with Ptolemy and Alexander, realizing in the process that the two Egyptian texts could not be exact, word-for-word translations of the Greek, but then he drew a blank. The Swedish linguist Johan David Åkerblad was able to take Silvestre de Saçy's work further, identifying all the Greek proper names in the demotic script, and reading the words 'temples' and 'Greeks'. Then he too ground to a halt, foiled by his mistaken belief that demotic was an entirely alphabetic script.

JEAN-FRANÇOIS CHAMPOLLION was an exceptionally talented and fiercely determined young Frenchman born in difficult but stimulating times. The Revolution and its uncomfortable aftermath would form an unsettling and occasionally dangerous background to his life's work, yet it was the Revolution and, more specifically, Napoleon Bonaparte's Egyptian ambitions that made his life's work possible. Jean-François was the youngest child, born on 23 December 1790, of the travelling bookseller Jacques Champollion and his wife Jeanne-Françoise in the small town of Figeac, Lot, southwest France. As the Revolution had forced the closure of the schools run by the religious orders, and his father was often away working and his illiterate mother invariably ill, the young Jean-François was educated at home by his self-educated brother Jacques-Joseph and his three doting sisters, Thérèse, Pétronille and Marie-Jeanne. By the time he was able to attend primary school he was recognized as something of a prodigy, but his isolated upbringing had also made him something of an oddity; an ill-disciplined and determined individual prone to sudden bursts of rage, intensely focused on subjects that interested him, and supremely indifferent to subjects, such as mathematics and spelling, that did not. If this makes him seem unlikeable, he was not – or at least he was not to his brother, his sisters, and later to his wife and daughter, all of whom were happy to support the young Jean-François in his unconventional career without, as far as we can tell, any word of complaint about their own hardships. Now, as he struggled to cope with the school system, his parents bowed to the inevitable, and a private tutor was hired.

At the age of ten Jean-François was sent to live with his older brother in Grenoble. Peaceful Grenoble, it was felt, offered good opportunities for a gifted boy, and Jacques-Joseph, who had always regretted his own lack of formal education, had generously offered to supervise and pay for his brother's schooling. Jacques-Joseph Champollion had by now changed his name to Jacques-Joseph Champollion-Figeac. Jean-François would remain plain Champollion, but was occasionally referred to as Champollion le Jeune (Champollion the Younger) to distinguish him from his brother.

Jean-François started to attend private school. Happy in his work, he mastered Latin and Greek, and quickly progressed to Arabic, Hebrew, Syriac and Chaldean. He was even lucky enough to meet Jean-Baptiste Joseph Fourier, a member of Napoleon's Commission, who had a passionate interest in everything Egyptian. Fourier had retired to Grenoble to work on the *Description*. Now he employed Jacques-Joseph to research part of the preface, and it seems likely that it was he who gave the 11-year-old Jean-François his first glimpse of hieroglyphics.

When the new government lycée, or secondary school, was established in Grenoble, Jean-François passed the examination to become one of its first boarding pupils, receiving a state bursary that covered two-thirds of his fees. The ever-generous Jacques-Joseph would pay the remaining third. Jean-François hated his new life with a deep and barely concealed passion. He loathed the pointless military discipline, the compulsory mathematics, and the fact that he was compelled to adhere to a strict national curriculum which, unsurprisingly, did not allow for the study of Arabic, Hebrew, Syriac and Chaldean. But, realizing that there was no better education on offer, he managed to stick it out for several years, cheered, perhaps, by his own private study of Coptic, Italian, English and German. Only when, in 1807, there was a riot against harsh conditions at the lycée, did Jacques-Joseph finally relent, allowing his brother to live at home and attend only the occasional class at the school. The school term came to an end that August, and the younger Champollion prepared to move to Paris where he could continue his study of ancient languages.

Already Jean-François had dedicated himself to Egypt and the decoding of hieroglyphics. He was not the only one. Closeted in their libraries, hunched over their books, the intellectuals of Europe were engaged in a discreet but determined battle to be the first to solve the riddle. There was no prize on offer, save perhaps the chance to be the first to read the lost wisdom of the Egyptians, but for many, hieroglyphics had become an obsession. The highly focused academics had no wish to share their evolving work with others. They each wanted to be the first to spring the solution on the world in its entirety, and they were all haunted by the thought that someone else, an unknown rival in Britain or Germany perhaps, might get there first. In consequence they worked in secret, and no one had any idea how well, or how fast, their rivals were progressing. Indeed, no one really knew who was working on the puzzle. The sense that time was running out intensified the pressure on Jean François. It was perhaps fortunate that the linguistically gifted Jacques-Joseph understood his compulsion – he already had one failed attempt to decode the Rosetta script behind him. He was prepared to keep supporting his younger brother, both financially and mentally, even though he now had a wife and a growing family to maintain:

> Do not be discouraged about the Egyptian text – this is the time
> to apply Horace's precept; a letter will lead you to a word, a word
> to a sentence, and a sentence to all the rest, and so everything is
> more or less contained in a single letter. Keep working until I can
> check your work myself ...[4]

Like Athanasius Kircher before him, the younger Champollion believed that the key to understanding the Egyptian language lay in a thorough understanding of Coptic, something that all previous would-be translators had lacked. He now made Coptic his first focus of study. Through Coptic he hoped to understand the demotic inscription and then, with the Egyptian language revealed, decipher the hieroglyphic writing. Studying variously at the College of France, the School of Oriental Languages and the National Library in Paris, and learning liturgical Coptic from an Egyptian priest, he was able to devise a timetable that suited his own, very specific needs. The renowned hieroglyphic expert Silvestre de Saçy was one of his new tutors. The only problem – and it was a pressing one – was his lack of paid employment and the constant, hovering threat that he might be drafted into the army, which was now desperately short of able-bodied young men. Jean-François grew thin, his clothes were little more than rags, and his health deteriorated as he sank into depression. Again, he was not the only one. France as a whole was suffering, with high inflation, food shortages and the demoralizing effects of Napoleon's constant campaigning.

In 1809 his fortunes turned as the 18-year-old Jean-François published his geography of Egypt, the first section of an intended much longer work, and was rewarded with a position as professor of ancient history in the newly formed University of Grenoble. At the same time Jacques-Joseph was offered a post as professor of Greek literature in the same institution, and both brothers were awarded doctorates. There were some drawbacks – Jean-François's salary was disappointingly low, it was embarrassing having to teach former fellow students from the lycée, and hieroglyphic copies were harder to come by in Grenoble than they had been in Paris – but it seemed that at long last the talents of the Champollion brothers were being recognized. Neither brother was blessed with the kind of diplomatic charm that would ensure an uneventful university life; both were outspoken and had a knack of annoying those in authority, and both had an unhealthy interest in politics. But for the time being at least, both were settled. By 1813 Jean-François felt that he was in a position to propose marriage to Rosine Blanc. Unfortunately, her family did not agree; a poor professor was no catch for the beautiful young daughter of a wealthy glove-maker.

Across the Channel in London, another genius was at work: Dr Thomas Young was a polymath – an accomplished scientist, astronomer and musician, a respected physician and a professor of natural philosophy at the Royal Institute. Young had been another infant prodigy, reading fluently by the age of two. Thirty-nine years later, in 1814, he was also fluent in Latin, Greek, Italian, French, Hebrew, Arabic and Persian, but he showed little interest in the ancient Egyptian language until Sir William Broughton gave him a collection of papyrus fragments. Sir William had personally 'rescued' a papyrus scroll from a genuine Egyptian tomb, thrillingly complete with bandaged mummy, but somehow the papyrus had been soaked in sea water and shredded on the way to England. It was certainly not the easiest text to start with, but it inspired Young to start studying hieroglyphs. Soon he was working on the Rosetta inscription and, after one published but not particularly successful attempt to decode the demotic, he was also studying Coptic. A dedicatory hieroglyphic text and accompanying Greek inscription, found on a fallen Gracco-Roman obelisk in the temple of Isis at Philae, proved particularly useful to him, as the cartouches in the hieroglyphic text could be compared to the Greek text. The English explorer William Bankes had laid claim to the obelisk, and had already identified the name Cleopatra in its text. Now Young found that he was also able to read the name of Queen Berenice.

If Champollion was short of money – and he always was – Young was desperately short of time. His interests were many and varied, he had his professional duties to perform, and he simply could not devote the hours to linguistics that Champollion could. But he did succeeded in correctly identifying at least 40 hieroglyphic signs. His published analyses were helpful to Champollion – he was able to work through Young's list, correcting it – and the two became long-term, if rather sporadic, correspondents, casual friends and occasional bitter enemies. Young was the first to fully realize that demotic, or enchorial as he called it, was not an entirely alphabetic script like English or Greek, but that it did use alphabetic characters to spell out foreign words, such as Ptolemy. He was clear-sighted enough to be able to summarize his own contribution to the subject. Although some of the discoveries that he classes as original were actually known or guessed at before, his summary is worth quoting in full:

> ... First that many simple objects were represented, as might naturally be supposed, by their actual delineations; secondly, that many other objects, represented graphically, were used in a figurative sense only, while a great number of the symbols, in frequent use, could be considered as the pictures of no existing objects whatever; thirdly, that, in order to express a plurality of objects, a dual was denoted by a repetition of the character, but that three characters of the same kind, following each other, implied an infinite plurality, which was likewise more compendiously by means of three lines or bars attached to a single character; fourthly, that definite numbers were expressed by dashes for units, and arches, either round or square, for tens; fifthly, that all hiegraphical inscriptions were read from front to rear, as the objects naturally follow each other; sixthly, that proper names were included by the oval ring, or border, or cartouche, of the sacred characters, and often between two fragments of a similar border in the running hand; and, seventhly, that the name of Ptolemy alone existed on this pillar, having only been completely identified by the assistance of the analysis of the enchorial [demotic] inscription.[5]

In 1814 Napoleon abdicated and left France for Elba, and Louis XVIII took the throne of France. Grenoble breathed a collective sigh of relief – Napoleon's abrupt departure had averted a threatened attack by the Austrian army, which had declared war on France the previous year. Not everyone was happy, though. The Champollion brothers may have been mildly critical of the Napoleonic regime, but they were Revolutionaries at heart, and they did not know when to keep quiet. They now took to openly criticizing the monarchy.

In March 1815 Napoleon returned from Elba, and marched to spend a day in Grenoble en route to Paris. Both Jacques-Joseph and Jean-François met their hero, and Jacques Joseph was inspired to abandon his family to follow him north. Back in Grenoble, Jean-François published an article that made his loyalties obvious to all: 'Napoleon is our legitimate prince'. His timing could not have been worse. Napoleon met his Waterloo and found himself back in exile, this time on far-away St Helena. Meanwhile, Grenoble, still loyal to Napoleon, was shelled by a combined Austrian and Sardinian army. The outspoken brothers were in deep trouble, and they knew it. Jean-François wrote to his brother, still in Paris, urging him to 'save yourself first of all ... I have neither a wife nor child'. In 1816 they were dismissed from their posts at the university and condemned to internal exile. They found themselves living once again in Figeac, sharing the family house with their aged, alcoholic father and the unmarried Thérèse and Marie-Jeanne. It was not until 1817 that Jean-François, his sentence lifted, returned to Grenoble. In December 1818 he finally married his Rosine.

By late 1821 Champollion had made definite progress with his hieroglyphic studies. He had proved to his own satisfaction that hieratic was a simplified or shorthand form of hieroglyphic writing, and that demotic was a later, even more simplified version of hieratic. All three scripts had been used by the ancients to write the same Egyptian language. He was now able to draw up a table comparing more than 300 hieroglyphic, hieratic and demotic signs and could effectively transcribe between the three. Even though he could not understand their meaning, his knowledge of Coptic was allowing him some feeling for the sense of the ancient language. And he had had a moment of inspiration. He had counted the number of Greek letters and the number of hieroglyphic signs in the corresponding section of the Rosetta Stone, and had realized that there were three times as many hieroglyphs as there were Greek letters. So each hieroglyph could not, as some experts maintained, represent a single word: Egyptian hieroglyphs were not the direct equivalent of Chinese characters. There must, as he had always suspected, also be a phonetic element to the language. Furthermore, he had realized that Egyptian employed determinatives – hieroglyphs that convey an impression of the sense of other hieroglyphs – an idea that had first been mooted by Young.

His personal life was not going so well. He was now ill, depressed, unemployed and living in Paris. The two brothers shared a house on the rue Mazarine, close by the Institute of France, where Jacques-Joseph had found employment.

Jean-François was able to read the Greek royal name Ptolemy on the Rosetta Stone – this meant that he could recognize the hieroglyphic characters P, T, W, L, M, Y and S wherever he found them. But the Rosetta Stone was broken – its hieroglyphic text cut short. Moving on to other hieroglyphic sources, he examined the Bankes obelisk and found that he could recognize both Ptolemy and Cleopatra. There was, however, one curious discrepancy. In the name Ptolemy, T was written with a 'segment of a sphere'. In the name Cleopatra it was written as a hand. The two were, as Champollion realized, homophones: letters that sounded the same but that could be written in different ways. Clearly, hieroglyphics were far more complicated than anyone had previously supposed. From these two names he was able to look at inscriptions from the Karnak temple at Thebes and reconstruct the name Alexander. He was soon able to reconstruct a phonetic alphabet that could be applied to all Graeco-Roman names written in Egyptian. He was now ready to look backwards, at actual Egyptian royal names.

On 14 September 1822 Jean-François was working, as usual, at home. He had recently received accurate copies of the texts decorating the magnificent Ramesside temples of Abu Simbel, Nubia. These texts were genuine Egyptian writings, 1500 years older than the text on the Rosetta Stone. Now, as he glanced over the copies, he automatically looked for the cartouches that would denote a

ABOVE: The Great
Temple of Abu Simbel,
Nubia, illustrated by
David Roberts. The
temple façade displays
four seated colossi of
Ramesses II 'the Great',
and, above the doorway,
a much smaller image
of the solar god,
Re-Herakhty.

RIGHT: Napoleon's
Egyptian campaign
sparked an interest in
anything and every-
thing Egyptian. Here
Napoleon's image
decorates a nineteenth-
century tobacco tin.

LEFT: Vivant Denon, member of the French Commission, records the curiously steep Egyptian pyramids.

BELOW: Not all the early illustrations of Egypt's archaeological wonders were true to life. Here the Great Sphinx of Giza has a youthful, rounded face and an expression of total surprise.

The Rosetta Stone is carved with the same text written in two languages and three types of script: Egyptian written in hieroglyphic script (top), Egyptian written in demotic script (middle) and Greek written in Greek script (bottom).

LEFT: Léon Cogniet's 1831 portrait of Jean-François Champollion, linguistic genius and decoder of the hieroglyphic script.

RIGHT: Cartouches, the ovals drawn around the names of Egypt's kings and queens, allowed Champollion to recognize the royal names within hieroglyphic texts. This page from Champollion's *Précis du système hiéroglyphique* illustrates the names of Egypt's Ptolemaic rulers.

LEFT: Giovanni Battista Belzoni, the Patagonian Sampson, carrying his human pyramid at the Sadler's Wells Theatre, Easter Monday 1803.

ABOVE: Belzoni's workmen drag the 'Younger Memnon', a colossal head of Ramesses II, from the Ramesseum to the Nile. This sculpture is today displayed in the British Museum, London.

ABOVE: The translucent sarcophagus of Seti I, retrieved by Belzoni from the Valley of the Kings, was deemed too expensive for the British Museum to purchase. Today it is displayed in Sir John Soane's Museum, London.

LEFT: The memorial engraving commissioned by Sarah Belzoni to celebrate her husband's life. We can recognize the Younger Memnon, the sarcophagus of Seti I, a pyramid and the Philae (Bankes) obelisk.

RIGHT: François Auguste Ferdinand Mariette – discoverer of the Serapeum, the Sakkara cemetery of the Apis Bulls.

Neat columns of hieroglyphic texts – a collection of spells known today as the 'Pyramid texts' – decorate the interior of the Sakkara pyramid of the 5th Dynasty King Unas.

royal name. To his great astonishment, he found that the previously unreadable cartouches held recognizable names – names that he had already met in the works of classical authors. Here were the truly Egyptian names of Ramesses and Thothmes, or Tuthmosis. It was a moment of uncontrollable emotion. Rushing from his home to his brother's office in the nearby Institute, he burst through the door, shouted '*Je tiens l'affaire!*' ('I've got it!'), and collapsed, unconscious, on the floor. For one terrible moment, Jacques-Joseph thought that his younger brother had died.

On 27 September 1822 Jean-François Champollion's discovery was presented to the Academy of Inscriptions, Paris, in the form of a formal *Letter to M. Dacier relating to the phonetic hieroglyphic alphabet used by the Egyptians* (Bon-Joseph Dacier being the Secretary of the Academy). The *Letter* would subsequently be translated and published in many languages. Champollion's system of decoding did not meet with universal acclaim; there were some, Thomas Young included, who would accuse him of stealing his ideas from others, and some who simply refused to believe his translations. But Jean-François persevered; visits to Turin Museum in Italy, home to many hieroglyphic texts, helped him to refine his work. In 1824 he felt ready to publish *Précis du Système hiéroglyphique des anciens Égyptiens* (*A Summary of the Hieroglyphic System of the Ancient Egyptians*). Here he explained the complex nature of hieroglyphics:

> Hieroglyphic writing is a complex system, a script simultaneously figurative, symbolic and phonetic, in one and the same text, in one and the same sentence, and, I should say, almost in one and the same word.

In 1826, in recognition of his work, Jean-François was appointed curator of the Egyptian collection of the Louvre Museum. His new job involved collecting exhibits, organizing displays and battling with colleagues who were reluctant to treat his ideas with the respect that he felt they deserved. He won the fight to have his artifacts displayed in a sensible, chronological order, but lost the war to have the Egyptian rooms decorated in true Egyptian style.

Two years later Champollion paid his first and only visit to Egypt as part of a joint Franco-Tuscan mission that included the Italian Egyptologist Ippolito Rosselini, as well as 12 artists, draughtsmen and architects. This was the ideal opportunity for Jean-François to collect more bilingual inscriptions from Egyptian temples, and, of course, to correct inscriptions that had been copied carelessly in the days when reading the hieroglyphs seemed an impossible dream. Landing at Alexandria on 18 August 1828, the mission sailed first to Cairo, where they caught their first glimpse of the pyramids. They travelled southwards, reaching Aswan on 4 December, then passed into Nubia to visit the Ramesside rock-cut temples of Abu Simbel. Jean-François, an indefatigable correspondent and enthusiastic sightseer, described his first impressions to his brother:

> The great temple of Abu Simbel is alone worth the journey to Nubia: it is a marvel which would be a rather beautiful thing even at Thebes. The labour that this excavation cost terrifies the imagination. The façade is decorated with four seated colossal statues, no less than sixty-one feet in height. All four, of superb workmanship, represent Ramesses the Great: their faces are portraits and perfectly resemble the figures of this king which are at Memphis, at Thebes and everywhere else. Such is the entrance; the interior is completely worthy of it, but it is a rough job to visit it. On our arrival the sand, and the Nubians who take care to shift it, had closed the entrance. We had it cleared so as to ensure as well as possible a small passage that they had opened, and we took all precautions possible against the internal flow of the sand which, in Egypt as in Nubia, threatened to engulf everything. I almost completely undressed, only keeping my Arab shirt and underpants of cotton, and went forward flat on my stomach to the little opening of a door, which, if cleared, would be at least twenty-five

feet in height. I thought I was going forward into the mouth of an oven, and sliding entirely into the temple, I found myself in an atmosphere heated to fifty-two degrees ... After two and a half hours of admiration and having seen all the reliefs, the need to breathe a little pure air made itself felt, and it was necessary to get back to the entrance to the furnace.[6]

At last Jean-François was living the life of a true archaeologist; heat, sand, flies, upset stomach and all. He was enjoying himself hugely, but his health was starting to suffer. After 16 months in the field, exhausted yet elated, he returned to France to complete his *magnum opus*, his *Grammaire égyptienne* (*Egyptian Grammar*). Jean-François Champollion was created professor of archaeology at the College of France in March 1831. His portrait, painted in 1823, shows him as a robust-looking, thoughtful man with a fine head of curly dark hair. But appearances can be deceptive. On 4 March 1832 Jean-François, aged 41 and suffering from consumption, diabetes, gout, paralysis, kidney and liver disease, died from a stroke. It was left to the devastated Jacques-Joseph to complete and posthumously publish his *Grammar* in 1836.

The foundations had been laid, but there was still much more work to be done, and not everyone was convinced by Champollion's arguments. Armed with the Champollion system, the brilliant German scholar and mathematician Karl Richard Lepsius was able to take the Egyptian language further, proving beyond a shadow of a doubt that Champollion had been right. In 1842 Lepsius headed the Prussian expedition to Egypt and Nubia, a survey mission sponsored by Friedrich Wilhelm IV, which was to spend three years surveying, copying, excavating and collecting antiquities – including, unfortunately, a column removed with the aid of dynamite from the tomb of Seti I. Their results were to be published in the *Denkmäler aus Aegypten und Aetheopien*, Germany's 12-volume answer to the *Description*, which is still used by Egyptologists today.

THE
COLLECTORS

>—<

IN THE EARLY YEARS OF THE NINETEENTH CENTURY ...
THERE WAS A PERFECT ORGY OF SPOLIATION CARRIED
ON, NOT IN THE INTERESTS OF SCIENCE, BUT PARTLY
OUT OF VANITY, AND PARTLY OUT OF GREED. EVERY
IMPORTANT OR NOBLE CHARACTER HAD TO
ADD A FEW CURIOS FROM EGYPT TO HIS
MISCELLANEOUS COLLECTION GATHERED FROM
HALF A DOZEN OTHER LANDS, AND SCULPTURES,
INSCRIPTIONS, AND PAPYRI OF THE GREATEST VALUE
WERE THUS USELESSLY DISPERSED IN PALTRY PRIVATE
COLLECTIONS, WHERE, WHEN THEY HAD GRATIFIED A
PASSING CURIOSITY OR MINISTERED TO A MOMENTARY
SPIRIT OF EMULATION, THEY WERE ALLOWED TO
GATHER DUST THROUGH YEARS OF NEGLECT, TILL AT
LAST THE FUTILE CABINET OF CURIOS WAS DISPERSED,
AND ITS ITEMS WERE LOST SIGHT OF ALTOGETHER.

J. Baikie, *A Century of Excavation in
the Land of the Pharaohs* (1923)

CHAPTER FOUR

⊱—⊰

THE GREAT
BELZONI

GIOVANNI BATTISTA BELZONI, born in Padua on 5 November 1778, was another poor boy whose adolescence was shaped by the upheavals and uncertainties of the Napoleonic wars. Both Champollion and Belzoni were the sons of tradesmen – Champollion a bookseller, Belzoni a barber. Both were exceptionally determined, driven individuals with a supreme disregard for their own (and their loved ones') comfort. Both were blessed with supportive brothers and sympathetic wives. Curiously, neither could spell when writing in their native tongue. But there the similarities between Belzoni and Champollion end. Belzoni came late and by accident to Egyptology. Adopted by the fashionable upper classes, he became a legend in his own lifetime: an amusing, entertaining legend admired far more for his handsome features and impressive physique than for his academic prowess.

Today, while Champollion is revered for his work in decoding hieroglyphs, Belzoni is generally relegated to the rank of adventurer, his impressive achievements – and, even if we disagree with his aims and methods, we cannot deny that his achievements were impressive – classified as little more than cunning tricks of engineering. A few experts, Howard Carter among them, have dared to challenge this rather lazy approach. To Carter at least, Belzoni was a hero, 'one of the most remarkable men in the whole history of Egyptology', while his published account of his exploits was quite simply 'one of the most fascinating books in the whole of Egyptian literature'.[1] This is Belzoni's story. The reader must make up his or her own mind.

The first thing that struck everyone about Belzoni was his size: he stood at least 7 ft tall according to his overawed contemporaries although it seems likely that they, craning their necks upwards, were exaggerating somewhat. Certainly he was several inches taller than his brother, Francesco, who was reportedly a 'mere' 6 ft 1in. The brothers must have appeared startling in an age when the average English male was likely to have been less than 5 ft in height. This extraordinary size was matched by an almost super-human strength. Giovanni was blessed with broad, powerful shoulders and long, muscular arms, and, as he proved time after time in his stage act, was capable of carrying up to 12 full-grown men in – most appropriately, given his future career – a human pyramid. Georges Depping, who knew Belzoni well, described him as being 'of colossal stature, shaped like Hercules. He had broad shoulders, his head was covered with long hair, and his features were gentle'.[2] His portraits and playbills, some of which show him as a stereotyped circus strongman, others as an oriental potentate dressed in flowing robes and turban, confirm his dark good looks – his thick hair, deep blue eyes, commanding stare and, from time to time, full beard and moustache.

> My native place is the city of Padua: I am of a Roman family, which had resided there for many years. The state and troubles of Italy in 1800, which are too well known to require any comment from me, compelled me to leave it, and from that time I have visited many different parts of Europe, and suffered many vicissitudes ...[3]

The 16-year-old Giovanni abandoned the Padua barber's shop to seek his fortune in Rome. We are not sure how he supported himself – there are various reports of him studying hydraulics and preparing to enter a Capuchin monastery – but we do know that he was still there, and still poor, in 1797, when Rome fell to the French.

Giovanni, who had little wish to be drafted into the French army, took to his heels. First he travelled alone to Paris. Then, with his brother Francesco, he made his way to Holland to learn the science of hydraulics from the Dutch. Eventually the brothers arrived in England, where they soon found employment at the Sadlers Wells summer theatre, working alongside such stars as Joe Grimaldi the clown, Jack Bologna the harlequin, and 'Mr Bradbury', who performed a curious act with a live pig. The 'Patagonian Sampson' – a strongman of unparalleled powers – had been born.

By September 1803 Belzoni was performing in a booth at Bartholomew Fair, Smithfield, where the human pyramid again proved a great crowd-pleaser. Years of provincial touring followed, with Belzoni appearing in theatres throughout Britain, not only lifting weights, but acting, conjuring, presenting optical illusions and even playing the glass harmonica. In later life he preferred to forget this less than dignified chapter of his life, and it is excluded from his autobiography, but we can track his career through old playbills and contemporary diaries. He pops up in a circus in London, in a theatre in Perth where despite his strong Italian accent he plays Macbeth, in Plymouth where he once again supports a human pyramid, and in Edinburgh where he bravely, some might say foolishly, acts alongside a live bear. Some theatres are even treated to that most fashionable of entertainments: Belzoni's 'curious exhibition of Hydraulicks'. By this time he had married Sarah Banne, an Irish or English woman of unknown origins. Happy to support her husband in all his schemes (being small in stature, she was occasionally to be found standing on top of the human pyramid, gamely waving a flag), happy to live an itinerant, childless way of life, happy to live alone when necessary, and fully capable of setting off alone on her own adventures, Sarah made the perfect wife for the Patagonian strongman.

The small Belzoni family – Giovanni, Sarah and their teenage Irish servant James Curtin – had grown restless. Nine years in Britain had been long enough and Europe, peaceful once again, beckoned. Crossing the Channel, they journeyed through Portugal, Spain and Sicily, ending their travels with a six-month sojourn in Malta, now firmly in British hands. Here fate intervened, and the course of Egyptology was irreversibly altered, as Belzoni was introduced to Captain Ishmael Gibraltar.

The Captain was the agent of Pasha Mohammed Ali, the former mercenary of Albanian origins whom the Turks had confirmed as Governor General of Egypt. After years of civil unrest, the utterly ruthless Mohammed Ali had successfully eliminated the remaining Mamluks, his campaign culminating in 1811 with a massacre that saw 500 Mamluk leaders trapped and slaughtered in the Cairo Citadel. Egypt was at peace again, and she was eager to re-establish contact with the West. Tourists were officially welcome; those with the skills to transform medieval Egypt into a modern industrialized nation even more so. The Captain had been specifically instructed to look out for European engineers who might be tempted to work in Egypt, and it seems that the Pasha, as ruler of a dry country, was particularly interested in acquiring new water-lifting devices that could be used alongside the traditional *sakkiya* (water-wheel) to extend the fertile strip of land that ran alongside the Nile. Belzoni, already interested in hydraulics, sensed a business opportunity too good to be missed. He was hooked.

On 19 May 1815 the Belzonis left Malta for plague-ravaged Egypt. Soon, after a period of quarantine in Alexandria, they found themselves living in a dilapidated house in Cairo. From here they undertook the usual sightseeing trips. There was an enjoyable visit to Giza, to climb over and crawl into the Great Pyramid, and a trip to Sakkara to view the Step Pyramid and inspect the animal catacombs, but as yet there was no overwhelming interest in Egypt's antiquities, as Belzoni's own account of these early days confirms:

> Though my principal object was not antiquities at that time, I
> could not restrain myself from going to see the wonder of the
> world, the pyramids ... We went there to sleep, that we might

ascend the first pyramid early enough in the morning, to see the rising of the sun; and accordingly we were on top of it long before the dawn of the day. The scene here is majestic and grand, far beyond description; a mist over the plains of Egypt formed a veil, which ascended and descended gradually as the sun rose and unveiled to view that beautiful land, once the site of Memphis. The distant view of the smaller pyramids on the south marked the extension of that vast capital; while the solemn, endless spectacle of the desert inspired us with reverence for the all-powerful creator. The fertile lands on the north, with the serpentine course of the Nile, descending towards the sea; the rich appearance of Cairo, and its numerous minarets, at the foot of the Mokatam mountain on the east; the beautiful plain which extends from the pyramids to the city; the Nile, which flows magnificently through the centre of the sacred valley, and the thick groves of palm trees under our eyes; all together formed a scene, of which very imperfect ideas can be given by the most elaborate description. We descended to admire at some distance the astonishing pile that stood before us, composed of such an accumulation of enormous blocks of stone, that I was at a loss to conjecture how they could be brought thither; and presently we entered the pyramid: but I must reserve for some other time the more minute account of this wonderful work.[4]

If Belzoni felt little interest in the monuments around him, there were many who did. Napoleon's soldiers had, quite literally, put Egypt on the map. Now everyone knew what delights lay to the south of Cairo, and, as the Nile was more or less safe, many were eager to experience the sights for themselves. Egypt had become annexed to the 'grand tour', and a small but persistent trickle of Europeans in search of a frisson of adventure made their way south-wards, sailing in native boats, sleeping in tents, donning native dress, and returning home to publish lengthy, inaccurate, and very popular, guidebooks. More often than not, they retuned home with souvenirs.

Mohammed Ali had no interest in the huge carved stones that littered his land. Keen to modernize, to look forward and not back, he was happy to continue the centuries-old tradition of tearing down and reusing the monuments. He was also happy to give them away, or sell them, to anyone who could arrange their export. Antiquities were becoming big business, and a select group of European entrepreneurs was supplying a booming market. Many of these suppliers were diplomats, charged with obtaining the antiquities that would boost their national museums. Less official, but still perfectly legal, were the private collectors who were competing for the better pieces.

One diplomat who was already heavily involved in collecting was the Piedmont-born Bernardino Drovetti, a former French army officer who was to enjoy two spells as French Consul-General (1810–15 and 1820–9), and who, having the confidence of the Pasha, was to play an important role in modernizing Mohammed Ali's army. Drovetti employed permanent teams of men to seek out and salvage antiquities, and he was not averse to directing the occasional excavation himself. The fruits of his labours now form the basis of the Egyptian collections in Turin, Paris and Berlin. At first a good friend to the Belzonis, it was perhaps inevitable that Drovetti, intensely loyal to France, should soon became a rival. The Belzoni party – husband, wife and servant – all travelled under a British passport, and clearly felt that their loyalties lay with Britain.

Belzoni immediately arranged an interview with the Pasha, or as he called him, the 'Bashaw' so that he might explain his design for a new, highly efficient water-wheel. He knew that there was no time to lose. The British government had already presented the Pasha with a mechanical water-lifting device, a machine that was rumoured to have cost an astonishing £10,000. Fortunately, they had neglected to send an engineer along with their gift, and no one in Egypt could get it to work properly. Or perhaps, as Belzoni himself suspected, the Egyptian engineers were pretending to find the machine less efficient than promised because they were worried about job losses. On 15 July 1815 Belzoni set off for the palace, riding through the crowded streets of Cairo on a donkey. But the meeting was not to be. On the way he encountered a Turkish officer who, entirely unprovoked, lashed out at the large 'Frank' (the general word used to describe Europeans), cutting his calf to the bone. As the victim tells it, it was a dramatic incident:

> The staves of the Turks, which are like shovels, cut very sharp; and one of the corners, catching the calf of my leg, tore off a piece of flesh in a triangular form, two inches broad and pretty deep. After this he swore two or three oaths at me, and went on as if nothing had happened. The blood ran out copiously ... I was taken home to my house in Boolak, where I remained under cure for thirty days, before I could stand on my legs.[5]

When the delayed appointment finally took place the Pasha, after making polite enquiries about Belzoni's still obvious limp, agreed to inspect the wonderful water-lifting machine that would apparently raise as much water with one ox as a conventional *sakkiya* could raise with four. Now all the self-styled hydraulics expert had to do was to build it.

Fortunately, Mohammed Ali was prepared to pay his new engineer a salary of £25 per month (paid in Spanish dollars), and that was just about enough for the small household to live on. For a year Belzoni laboured in secret over his machine until, in December 1816, it was finished. Designed on the principle of a crane to be powered by a single ox in a revolving drum, the prototype wheel was to be demonstrated in the garden of a house owned by the Pasha at Shubra, just outside Cairo. Six traditional *sakkiyas* were set up next to the new wheel so that their output might be compared. All went splendidly. The new machine functioned superbly well, and everyone agreed that it did indeed match the output of at least four *sakkiyas*. But this did not please everyone. Greater efficiency would naturally lead to greater unemployment, and there were many who felt that the Pasha's interest in modernity had gone far enough. This unvoiced current of discontent may help explain what happened next. Mohammed Ali, a great practical joker, decided to see what would happen if the one ox was replaced by 15 men. A group rushed into the drum, the young James Curtin included. The men ran, the wheel turned, the water poured, and everyone cheered. Then, at a prearranged signal, the men leapt out of the drum, leaving James alone. He did not have the weight to keep the machine turning and he was flung out, his thighbone broken. Only Belzoni's immense strength stopped his servant being crushed beneath the wheel. This was seen as a very ill omen indeed. The new machine was clearly very dangerous – it could never be used. Giovanni had lost his great business opportunity and the Belzonis found themselves penniless and unemployed in a foreign land.

There was just one possible employment opportunity. Belzoni had already met, and greatly enjoyed the company of, the Swiss explorer Johann Ludwig Burckhardt, who was also known in the Anglicized form of his name as John Lewis Burckhardt. Burckhardt had been one of the first Europeans to travel the length of Egypt, passing beyond the first Nile cataract at Aswan to journey deep into Nubia, where he had discovered the two lost Ramesside temples of Abu Simbel. His most recent, and most impressive, exploit had been a daring extended pilgrimage to Mecca and Medina. Disguised as the Muslim Sheikh Ibrahim, Burckhardt was probably the first European to visit the sacred shrines and live to tell the tale. He was already planning his next adventure – a journey by caravan across the Sahara to Timbuktu. Now, as he recovered from a bad bout of fever in Cairo, he talked to Giovanni and Sarah, entrancing them with long tales of adventure and sand-buried ruins. In particular, he told them about the beautiful, huge, carved stone head that lay abandoned in a remote, ruined temple on the west bank of the Nile at Gurna, opposite modern Luxor (ancient Thebes).

In 1275 BC the 19th Dynasty King Ramesses II built himself a splendid mortuary temple, a 'Mansion of Millions of Years'. This temple, which the Greeks called the 'Memnonium' or the 'Tomb of Ozymandias' (Ozymandias being a corruption of Ramesses's official name Usermaatre Setepenre Ramessu Meryamen), is today better known as the Ramesseum. Here the divine, dead Ramesses, forever linked with the state god Amen, could be worshipped for all eternity. Unfortunately, the temple had not lasted as long as Ramesses hoped, and by the time Burckhardt visited it was an earthquake-damaged ruin. Behind an impressive gateway or pylon lay two open-air colonnaded courts. The first was dominated by the colossal 'Re of the Rulers', a seated statue (now fallen), which had greatly impressed Diodorus Siculus:

> Beside the entrance [to the temple] are three statues, each carved from a single block of black stone from Syene. One of these, which is seated, is the largest of any in Egypt, its foot alone measuring over seven cubits ... it is not merely for its size that this work merits approbation. It is also marvellous because of its artistic quality and excellent because of the nature of its stone, since in a block of so great a size there is not one single crack or blemish to be seen. The inscription on it runs: 'King of Kings I am, Ozymandias. If anyone would know how great I am and where I lie, let him surpass my works'.[6]

Beyond the enormous fallen statue a ramp led upwards to the second court, where the eastern and western porticoes were lined with colossal statues of Ramesses in the form of the mummified god of the dead Osiris. Here lay the shattered statue, which explorers had named the 'Younger Memnon' after the hero son of Eos and Tithonus who, as Homer told, had been killed by Achilles. The Younger Memnon was one of a pair of broken statues of Ramesses, smaller than the huge Re of the Rulers, but still well above life-size. Its beautifully sculpted head and upper torso had already attracted attention as 'certainly the most beautiful and perfect piece of Egyptian sculpture that can be seen throughout the whole country'.[7] The other statue, once equally beautiful, now had a badly disfigured face and was essentially worthless.

Burckhardt had already asked Mohammed Ali to give the Younger Memnon to the Prince Regent. The Pasha, seeing no value in the carved stone, had been puzzled by the request but had readily agreed. Now the time had come to transport the head to London, but it was enormous, and Burckhardt was uncertain how to proceed. Napoleon's troops had already tried to take the Younger Memnon but they had been defeated by its sheer size, and by the locals, who were unwilling to cooperate in such a pointless exercise. At 9 ft tall, and carved from granite, the statue weighed between 7 and 8 tons. French engineers had calculated that it might be possible to separate the head from its unwanted torso by blowing the two apart with powder, but after drilling a hole into the right shoulder they had – fortunately – abandoned the plan, realizing, perhaps, that the powder was likely to damage the face, making the statue worthless. Now Belzoni offered to go and get the head for Burckhardt. Eagerly, Burckhardt agreed and, as he couldn't afford to pay for the transportation himself, the two paid a visit to the British Consul-General, Henry Salt.

Just as Drovetti had a brief to collect antiquities for France, so Salt was authorized to collect on behalf of the British Museum. In particular, it was hoped that he might be able to trace the missing pieces of the Rosetta Stone, which – God forbid – might otherwise fall into French hands! Salt was a former portrait painter with a genuine interest in Egyptology; he conducted his own excavations, and would later publish a monograph on hieroglyphics. But he was relatively poor, and couldn't afford to employ a permanent team of excavators as his French counterpart Drovetti did. The Younger Memnon, however, was far too tempting a piece to miss. Belzoni talked his way into the job, and soon found himself engaged to transport the head of Ramesses from Luxor to Alexandria. Belzoni's exact status troubled Salt little, if he thought about it at all. His own records suggest that he viewed Belzoni as a simple employee:

> Mr Belzoni will have the goodness to keep a separate account of
> the expenses incurred in this undertaking, which, as well as his
> other expenses, will gladly be reimbursed: as, from the knowledge
> of Mr Belzoni's character, it is confidently believed they will be as
> reasonable as circumstances will allow.[8]

Salt, not unreasonably, assumed that the objects collected by his new agent were his to dispose of as he liked. Belzoni, a proud and sensitive man who had avoided conventional employment all his life, saw things very differently. Conscious of his own expertise, he regarded himself as an independent consultant rather than an employee. While he was happy enough to work for the British Museum, he had no wish to be seen to be working for Salt in a personal capacity, as that would make him little more than a servant. Furthermore, he wanted the credit for his own discoveries. It may have been a throwback to the insecurity of his days on the stage, but it worried him that Salt might receive the publicity which he thought was his due. Maybe, one day, he might need to rely on the publicity generated by his work in Egypt. Finally, he reserved the right to make his own collection while working for, or with, others. Belzoni considered this a matter of such great importance that he dedicated a substantial part of his autobiography to explaining his position:

> It has been erroneously stated, that I was regularly employed by
> Mr Salt, the consul-general of his Britannic majesty in Egypt, for
> the purpose of bringing the colossal bust from Thebes to
> Alexandria. I positively deny that I was ever engaged by him in any
> shape whatsoever, either by words or writing; as I have proofs of
> the case being on the contrary. When I ascended the Nile, for the
> first and second time, I had no other idea in my mind, but that I
> was making researches for antiquities, which were to be placed in

the British Museum; and it is naturally to be supposed that I
would not have made these excursions, had I been previously
aware, that all I found was for the benefit of a gentleman, whom
I never had the pleasure to see before in my life.[9]

Giovanni hired a cheap boat, invested in some rope and timber,
and, on 30 June 1817, set sail with the patient Sarah, the limping
James, and an interpreter with an unfortunate fondness for
drink. The trip was a pleasurable one, and there was plenty of time
to stop and enjoy the sights on the way. Three weeks later they
reached Luxor and set up camp in the ruined Ramesseum.
Fortunately, as Belzoni tells us, 'Mrs Belzoni had by this time accustomed herself to travel, and was equally indifferent with myself
about accommodations.'

Belzoni realized that he had to act fast if he wanted to move the
head before the annual inundation caused the Nile to burst its banks
and flood the roads. Under normal circumstances, transporting
heavy stone by water was a good thing; the ancient Egyptians had
cut canals which took their statuary directly from the quarry, via the
Nile, to their temples. But Belzoni did not have the resources to cut
a canal linking the Ramesseum to the Nile, and he judged that the
floodwater, while preventing the use of the roads, would not be
deep enough to support any boat capable of carrying the head. The
last thing he wanted was to get the boat, and head, grounded at
Gurna for three months. So he determined to drag the head to the
river. With considerable difficulty, a team of workmen was recruited.
While the local chief was determined to save the head for Drovetti's
men and did everything in his power to hinder the British party, the
workmen themselves, having observed the antics of the French and
the British, decided that the seemingly worthless stone must be
filled with gold – naturally, they were reluctant to see such a precious
prize leave Gurna. In the end a mixture of tact, diplomacy, bribery
and threats proved effective, and work started.

The head was raised up by means of wooden levers, and a

wooden sledge, or 'car', was slid under it. The car was then pulled
forward on four wooden rollers by a team of 80 men – no easy task.
The Ramesseum was a complete ruin, and the car had to negotiate
sand, stone walls and the fallen Ozymandias, who lay tumbled from
his throne, blocking the entrance to the second courtyard. The
workmen, working through the heat of an August Ramadan, were
hungry and thirsty, tired and argumentative. James Curtin could not
cope with the climate, and had to be sent back to Cairo. Belzoni
himself, unaccustomed to the fierce sun, and dressed in unsuitable
European clothing, was suffering badly:

> On the 28th [July] ... in the evening I was very poorly: I went to
> rest but my stomach refused any aliment. I began to be persuaded,
> that there is a great difference between travelling in a boat, with
> all that is wanted in it, and at leisure, and the undertaking of an
> operation, which required great exertions in directing a body of
> men, who in point of skill are no better than beasts, and to be
> exposed to the burning sun of that country from morning to
> night.
> On the next day, the 29th, I found it impossible to stand on
> my legs ... I remained very ill the whole day, my stomach refusing
> to take almost any thing ...
> On the 9th [August] I was seized with such giddiness in my
> head, that I could not stand. The blood ran so copiously from
> my nose and mouth, that I was unable to continue the operation:
> I therefore postponed it to the next day.[10]

On future expeditions he would dress as the locals did, in cool, flowing robes. Only Sarah was well; she too was most inappropriately
dressed but, spending her days with the local women, she was able
to shelter from the heat in the cool of the ancient tombs cut into the
mountainside.

Sixteen days later, the Younger Memnon had travelled two
exhausting miles and had reached the bank of the Nile. Here it

rested, protected by a strong mud-brick wall, as it waited for a boat large enough to carry it north. His work accomplished and his health restored, Belzoni had time to relax and explore his surroundings. In the Valley of the Kings he went to inspect the pink granite sarcophagus of Ramesses III. The tomb of Ramesses III, Bruce's 'Tomb of the Harpists', had been discovered half a century earlier and was open to all who cared to visit. But the local guides led Belzoni not to the tomb entrance, but through a hot, dark 'hole' into a warren of confusing, winding pathways, where he sweated profusely as he crunched over heaps of human bones:

> Previous to our entering the cave, we took off the greater part of our clothes, and, each having a candle, advanced through a cavity in the rock ... In some passages we were obliged to creep on the ground, like crocodiles. I perceived that we were at a great distance from the entrance, and that the way was so intricate, that I depended entirely on the two Arabs, to conduct us out again ... The Arabs had intended to show me the sarcophagus, without letting me see the way by which it might be taken out, and then to stipulate a price for the secret.[11]

Belzoni was not fooled for long. Indeed, as one of the would-be con men fell into a pit in the dark and broke his hip, he ended up conducting a rescue operation. The sarcophagus actually lay close by the tomb entrance, and its separated lid, decorated with the image of the dead king supported by the goddesses Isis and Nephthys, lay hidden under layers of mud and rubble not far away. Drovetti had tried to remove the sarcophagus, but failed. Now Henry Salt had laid claim to it, while Belzoni himself claimed ownership of the lid. Ultimately, and most unsatisfactorily, the lid would be displayed in the Fitzwilliam Museum, Cambridge, while its base would be sold to the Louvre Museum, Paris.

The Younger Memnon still sat on the riverbank, waiting for its boat. The Belzonis, however, were sailing southwards. Inspired by

Burckhardt's tale of the lost temples of Abu Simbel, they had determined to visit the second cataract.

The river took the Belzonis past the sites of Esna, Edfu, Kom Ombo and Aswan, where Sarah, the first European woman to travel this way in many centuries, paid courtesy visits on the two wives of the local ruler. In her own memoir, 'Mrs Belzoni's Trifling Account of the Women' (which is a fascinating read, and by no means trifling), published as an appendix to her husband's longer work, she tells us how she drank coffee and smoked a water pipe, two luxuries denied to the wives, and how the two ladies marvelled at her strange European clothing:

> The first thing was my hat and hair; my neckerchief of black silk, which they coveted much; next the buttons of my coat: nothing could persuade them but money was hid in them. I opened one, to convince them of the contrary; this seemingly did not satisfy them, for, judging by their own tricks, they thought that it was one put there purposely to deceive. I verily believe, if the man [the local ruler, husband of the two women] had not now come in, they would have been very troublesome. However I learned sufficient in this my first visit to guide me in future, and to put on a greater degree of consequence with other women I might have to deal with; for by showing myself free with them, on account of my ignorance of their character, they would take advantage of it.[12]

At Philae they stopped for a picnic, examining with interest the fallen red granite obelisk that had once stood in front of the Graeco-Roman temple dedicated to the Egyptian goddess Isis. Belzoni believed that the obelisk could be moved, but now was not the time. He sailed on to Abu Simbel.

Early in his reign, Ramesses the Great had built two impressive temples on the west bank of the Nile at Abu Simbel, Nubia, some 40 miles to the north of the second cataract. Abu Simbel was a remote spot, lacking any form of sizeable settlement or cemetery, and we may guess that Ramesses was inspired by the local geography, which would allow him to cut into sandstone cliffs set at an angle to each other so that just twice each year, on 20 February and 20 October, the rising sun would penetrate the gloom of his Great Temple to highlight the gods sitting in his sanctuary.

The Lesser Temple of Abu Simbel was officially dedicated to a local form of Hathor, goddess of motherhood, beauty and drunkenness, who was strongly identified with Ramesses's consort, Nefertari. The façade shows six colossal standing figures: two of Nefertari wearing the insignia of Hathor, and four of Ramesses. The niche at the back of the sanctuary contains the carved image of Hathor in the form of a cow, protecting Ramesses who stands beneath her head.

The Great Temple belongs to Ramesses himself. Four colossal statues of Ramesses wearing the double crown of Upper and Lower Egypt sit two on either side of the central doorway. Harder to spot is the figure of the god carved high above the entrance. Here stands Re-Herakhty, holding the goddess Maat beside his left leg and the hieroglyphic sign for User beside his right so that the image of the god becomes a rebus (a symbolic representation) which may be read as the throne name of Ramesses, User-Maat-Re. Beyond the façade the temple cuts into the cliff. The great hall, bisected by two rows of pillars in the form of Ramesses as the mummified god Osiris, is decorated with scenes of the victorious king displaying his earthly triumphs before the gods. The inner pillared hall shows Ramesses as a divine king. In the gloom of the sanctuary, beyond the second hall, sit four gods: Ptah of Memphis, Amen-Re of Thebes, Re-Harakhty of Heliopolis and, seated between Amen and Re, Ramesses himself. Unfortunately, during Ramesses's regnal Year 30, the Great Temple suffered earthquake damage. The north doorjamb collapsed, the colossus to the north of the entrance lost an arm, and the colossus to the south of the doorway lost its upper body.

The Abu Simbel cult survived the reign of Ramesses but eventually the priests left and the temples were abandoned. Slowly but surely the temple façades were hidden beneath a blanket of wind-blown sand. When Greek soldiers visited the Great Temple in the sixth century BC they scrawled their graffiti at the new ground level, just under the knee of the southern colossus beside the entrance. By the time Burckhardt rediscovered the site in 1813 the temples were hidden by a massive sand mountain. Inevitably, the locals believed that the Great Temple was full of treasure – why else would so many Europeans come to visit it? Many Europeans, by contrast, believed that there was no temple behind the impressively carved façade. Belzoni begged to differ. He knew that there was a temple hidden under the sand.

Bernardino Drovetti had already paid a visit to assess the Abu Simbel temples, but his attempt to clear the façade of sand had proved unsuccessful. Encouraged by the thought of his rival's failure, Belzoni set to work. Employing 40 local men, and erecting a wooden fence to hold back the sand, he made a good start. But, still some way off a complete clearance, he had to stop work. He was running out of money, the job was taking longer than he had anticipated, and he needed to get the Younger Memnon back to Salt.

The return journey saw another stop at Philae, where Belzoni identified and paid for the pieces he wanted – the fallen obelisk, and a series of decorated blocks that were to be cut into thin slabs for ease of transport:

> When the Aga [local chief] and the Reis [head workman] came, I made an agreement with them to have the obelisk taken down to the cataract; but, for want of a boat, it could not be effected that season. The obelisk is twenty-two feet long, by two wide at the base, so that it required a pretty large boat to convey it. It was agreed, and perfectly understood, that I took possession of this obelisk in the name of his Britannic Majesty's consul-general in Cairo; and I gave four dollars to the Aga, to pay for a guard for it till my return ...
>
> The blocks of stone, which formed the compartment of

fourteen feet long and twelve wide, were twelve in number. When they were put together on the ground, they were a beautiful group, consisting of the great god Osiris seated on his chair, with an altar before him, receiving offerings from priests and female figures, the whole surrounded by flowers and hieroglyphics. The blocks were three feet six inches long, and three feet wide; but as they were two feet three inches thick, they were too bulky to be embarked whole. As they could be easily cut, being a calcareous gritstone, I made an agreement for one hundred piastres, to have them cut to six inches.[13]

Back in Luxor, and still waiting for a boat to transport the head to Cairo, Belzoni found the time to excavate in the ruins of the Karnak temple. In the precinct dedicated to the goddess Mut, wife of the state god Amen, he found a cache of five statues depicting the lion-headed goddess Sekhmet, plus a white quartzite statue of Seti II. Over on the west bank, in an offshoot of the Valley of the Kings, he discovered the plundered tomb of Ay, successor to Tutankhamen (WV23). Lest there be any doubt over his discovery, he carved his own inscription over the entrance: 'discovered by Belzoni 1816'. Then it was time to load the head onto a boat and sail north.

Six months after his departure from Cairo, Giovanni Belzoni deposited the Younger Memnon in a warehouse in Alexandria. He was to be paid £100 for his troubles. The head travelled on to the British Museum, which at the time was housed in the sadly over-crowded Montague House. There was some discussion as to whether it would have to be placed in the courtyard, but there were worries about the effect of the British weather on the polished stone, and it eventually went on public display in the Egyptian Room. The arrival of the statue caused some public excitement, and the gallery was crowded with the great and the good. Included among these was the poet Percy Bysshe Shelley, who, in 1817, published his poetic impression of the once-mighty Ramesses. Shelley, an accomplished classical scholar, was surely influenced by Diodorus Siculus:

OZYMANDIAS

I met a traveller from an antique land
Who said: Two vast and trunkless legs of stone
Stand in the desert. Near them, on the sand,
Half sunk, a shattered visage lies, whose frown,
And wrinkled lip, and sneer of cold command
Tell that its sculptor well those passions read
Which yet survive, stamped on these lifeless things,
The hand that mocked them, and the heart that fed:
And on the pedestal these words appear:
'My name is Ozymandias, king of kings:
Look on my works, ye Mighty, and despair!'
Nothing besides remains. Round the decay
Of that colossal wreck, boundless and bare
The lone and level sands stretch far away.

CHAPTER FIVE

>—<

THE TREASURE SEEKERS

Henry salt was eager that his new 'employee' should assist the Italian adventurer Captain Caviglia in his exploration of the mysteries of the Great Pyramid of Giza. But Belzoni had other ideas. The sand-covered Great Temple of Abu Simbel beckoned, and he had determined to head south again. His second Nile journey started on 20 February 1817. This time Sarah chose to stay with friends in Cairo, and the heat-sensitive James Curtin stayed with her. They were replaced by Salt's secretary, the talented artist Henry Beechey, and Salt's agent and interpreter, the Greek collector Giovanni d'Athanasi (also known in his own language as Yanni Athanasiou). An Egyptian cook and a Turkish soldier completed the party.

Belzoni had intended to start his season by conducting further excavations in the Karnak temple precinct of Mut, where he had high hopes of finding more statues. But on arrival in Luxor, he found Drovetti's agents busily digging up 'his' site and gathering 'his' precious finds. Thwarted, he left a small group of men excavating, and living, in the temple, and turned his attention to the non-royal tombs that riddled the mountainous west bank:

> I can truly say, it is impossible to give any description sufficient to convey the smallest idea of those subterranean abodes and their inhabitants. There are no sepulchres in any part of the world like

them; there are no excavations, or mines, that can be compared to these truly astonishing places; and no exact description can be given of their interior, owing to the difficulty of visiting these recesses. The inconveniency of entering into them is such, that it is not everyone who can support the exertion.[1]

Here, in the spacious rock-cut tombs of the nobles, and in the dark and crowded 'mummy pits', the catacombs that stored the poorer burials, he specifically sought out mummies and the papyri that were buried with them. The mummies fascinated the tourists, but were basically worthless. But their papyri – illustrated copies of the Book of the Dead provided to help the deceased negotiate the trials of the Afterlife – were extremely valuable. Tourists and collectors would pay good money for a decorated scroll, or for part of a decorated scroll (dealers would routinely cut up their finds in order to sell them several times over), even though they had no hope of reading it. As far as we are aware, none of the tombs that Belzoni ransacked was in any way intact – all had been discovered, and thoroughly plundered, by the residents of Gurna many years before. Nevertheless, we might wish that he had kept better records of his work. His account, although providing a fascinating insight into the ethics of the time, certainly lacks scientific precision:

Of some of these tombs many persons could not withstand the suffocating air, which often causes fainting. A vast quantity of dust rises, so fine that it enters into the throat and nostrils, and chokes the nose and mouth to such a degree, that it requires great power of lungs to resist it and the strong effluvia of the mummies. That is not all; the entry or passage where the bodies are is roughly cut into the rocks, and the falling of the sand from the upper part or ceiling of the passage causes it to be nearly filled up. In some places there is not more than a vacancy of a foot left, which you must contrive to pass through in a creeping posture like a snail, on pointed and keen stones, that cut like glass. After getting through these passages, some of them two or three hundred yards long, you generally find a more commodious place, perhaps high enough to sit. But what a place of rest! Surrounded by bodies, by heaps of mummies in all directions; which, previous to my being accustomed to the sight, impressed me with horror. The blackness of the wall, the faint light given by the candles or torches for want of air, the different objects that surround me, seeming to converse with each other, and the Arabs with the candles or torches in their hands, naked and covered with dust, themselves resembling living mummies ... After the exertion of entering into such a place ... I sought a resting place, found one, and contrived to sit; but when my weight bore on the body of an Egyptian, it crushed it like a band-box. I naturally had to recourse to my hands to sustain my weight, but they found no better support; so that I sunk altogether among the broken mummies, with a crash of bones, rags and wooden cases, which raised such a dust as kept me motionless for quarter of an hour, waiting till it subsided again I could not remove from the place, however, without increasing it, and every step I took crushed a mummy in some part or other ...[2]

Over the river, back in the more hygienic environment of the Karnak temple, his men were assembling a respectable, and very heavy, collection of antiquities. They had a colossal head of Tuthmosis III, a matching arm, sundry Sekhmet statues, the 'altar' from the Karnak precinct of Montu, and the beautifully carved sarcophagus lid of Ramesses III, all ready for transport to Cairo. But the local governor, the son-in-law of Mohammed Ali, was anti-British and pro-French, and it was proving difficult to ship the cargo. Once again, the precious finds were left protected by a mud-brick wall as Belzoni sailed southwards.

At Philae, Belzoni flew into a rage. The series of decorated blocks that he had left to be cut into thin slabs for ease of transport had been attacked with a hammer, and someone had scribbled '*operation manquée*' (spoiled job) in charcoal across the defaced stone. The handwriting could not be identified, but it was not hard to work out who had committed this petty act of vandalism. Franco-British collecting rivalries were as fierce as ever, and three of Drovetti's agents had passed this way a few months previously.

By now the party had expanded. Sarah and James had arrived from Cairo, there was the 'Albanian' (actually a native-born Italian named Giovanni Finati, who also went by the name of Muhammad) sent by Salt to protect the party, and two Royal Navy captains, James Mangles and Charles Irby, who had been persuaded to abandon their sightseeing and go in search of archaeological adventure. The party had, in fact, grown too large, and too expensive, for the journey to Abu Simbel. As the boat pulled away from Philae, the ever-patient Sarah and James were left, together with the excess baggage, living on the roof of the temple of Isis and protected, inevitably, by a thick mud-brick wall.

After an eventful period of intensive sand-shifting, coloured by strikes, riots, thefts and the mutiny of the boat crew, the doorway to the Great Temple of Abu Simbel was partially revealed. By 1 August 1817 it was possible to slip between the sand and the doorframe, and slide inside the temple. The interior was both hot and humid. The party passed through the two decorated halls and entered the sanctuary set deep in the cliff face, where, by flickering torchlight, they were confronted by the four seated gods, including the great Ramesses himself. They could not read the hieroglyphs carved into the walls, and so could not fully understand what they had found, but they realized that they had made an extraordinary discovery and marvelled at the battle scenes that decorated the first hall. Yet, to Belzoni at least, the day was a slightly disappointing one. There were relatively few portable antiquities within the temple, and portable antiquities had been, as always, his main goal. Measurements were taken, a hasty plan was prepared, and a few scenes were copied; the extreme heat within the temple made this difficult, as the paper was soon drenched in sweat. The names of the explorers were carved on the sanctuary wall. Then, on 4 August, with food supplies running worryingly low, the party set sail for Philae. The Great Temple would not be properly recorded until 18 months later, when Salt, Beechey, Finati and Bankes arrived with a small team of draughtsmen. They would clear more of the façade, but the temple would always be vulnerable to wind-borne sand. The enterprising locals would allow it to silt up, and then take payments from tourists to clear the entrance again.

Back in Luxor, Belzoni discovered that Drovetti's agents had taken advantage of his absence, and started to plunder the non-royal tombs of the west bank. Irritated, and unwilling to work close by his enemies, he focused his attention on the more remote Valley of the Kings. The Valley – known locally as the Biban el-Moluk – was understood to be the last resting place of the New Kingdom pharaohs, who had abandoned pyramids in favour of hidden rock-cut tombs. Estimates as to the number of tombs in the Valley varied. Diodorus Siculus had suggested that there might be as many as 47, a mixture of royal and non-royal tombs. Napoleon's commission had recorded 11 in the Valley, as well as one (WV22, the tomb of Amenhotep III) in an offshoot known as the Western Valley. Belzoni himself had discovered the tomb of Ay (WV23) on his previous visit to the Western Valley. It seemed that this would be the best place to start his work.

Close by the tomb of Ay, Belzoni discovered another entrance (WV25). Having forced his way through its stone-blocked doorway with a palm-tree battering ram, he gained access to the unfinished tomb. A flight of steps led downwards to a burial chamber. Here were eight painted coffins, complete with 22nd Dynasty mummies but lacking inscriptions.

Eager to find a royal burial, Belzoni abandoned the Western Valley and returned to the Valley proper. Here his engineer's eye gave him an almost uncanny ability to detect hidden tombs. His rate of discovery was astonishing. On 9 October 1817 he discovered the unfinished, painted tomb of Prince Mentuherkhepshef, son of Ramesses IX (KV19). On the same day he found an uninscribed and undecorated tomb (KV21) holding two naked female mummies, 'their hair pretty long, and well preserved, though it was easily separated from the head by pulling it a little'. The next day, he found KV16, the tomb of Ramesses I, founder of the 19th Dynasty, and grandfather to Ramesses the Great.

Ramesses I had been adopted into the royal family as an elderly man. He had planned to build himself a magnificent tomb but had died too soon, when only two steep stairways, a corridor and a single room had been cut. The unfinished room became his burial chamber. Its walls were given a quick coating of plaster, and then painted to show the king and his gods. The red granite sarcophagus, too, had to be made ready in a hurry, and its inscriptions were painted rather than carved.

> I found the tomb just opened, and entered to see how far it was practicable to examine it. Having proceeded through a passage thirty-two feet long and eight feet wide, I descended a staircase of twenty-eight feet, and reached a tolerably large and well-painted room ... The ceiling was in good preservation, but not in the best style.
>
> We found a sarcophagus of granite, with two mummies in it, and in a corner a statue standing erect, six feet six inches high, and beautifully cut out of sycamore wood ... The sarcophagus was covered with hieroglyphics merely painted, or outlined: it faces south-east by east.[3]

The bodies that Belzoni found lying in the sarcophagus were intrusive Late Period burials. Ramesses's sarcophagus still lies in his tomb, surrounded by the veritable forest of wooden beams that are now needed to support the collapsing ceiling.

On 16 October, 'a fortunate day, one of the best perhaps of my life', Belzoni discovered the tomb which he first identified as the 'Tomb of Apis', then as the 'Tomb of Psammethis', but which we now know to be the tomb of Seti I, son of Ramesses I and father of

Ramesses the Great (KV17). This is one of the longest, deepest and most beautifully decorated tombs in the Valley of the Kings. An impressive sequence of stairways, corridors and pillared rooms led downwards to a high vaulted burial chamber decorated with an astonishing astronomical ceiling. All the walls glowed with vibrant colour – it was as if they were freshly painted. Although the tomb had been robbed in antiquity, Belzoni found hundreds of wooden *shabti* figures (models of servants provided to do the work of the dead king in the Afterlife), as well as the remains of an embalmed bull. The real treasure of the tomb was the king's anthropoid [human-shaped] alabaster sarcophagus, which was carved with scenes and verses from the Book of Gates:

> [the coffin] merits the most particular attention, not having its equal in the world, and being such as we had no idea could exist. It is a sarcophagus of the finest alabaster nine feet five inches long, and three feet seven inches wide. Its thickness is only two inches; and it is transparent, when a light is placed in the inside of it. It is minutely sculptured within and without with seven hundred figures, which do not exceed seven inches in height and represent, as I suppose, the whole of the funeral procession and ceremonies relating to the deceased, united with several emblems, etc.[4]

There were those who mocked Belzoni's description of the sarcophagus as 'transparent', but he was quite correct: if not strictly speaking transparent, it is translucent. Unfortunately, the lid of the sarcophagus had been broken by the ancient thieves who dragged the king from his coffin in the frenzied search for gold and jewellery.

The discovery of the tomb created great interest; visitors flocked to the Valley of the Kings, and Bernardino Drovetti came to inspect the tomb and offer his rather grudging congratulations. One of the first to arrive was Henry Salt, keen to congratulate 'his' team on their discovery. He brought bad news: Burckhardt, the discoverer of the Abu Simbel temples, and Belzoni's first patron, had died of dysentery in Cairo. As the Belzonis mourned their lost friend, Salt made plans to export the valuable sarcophagus to Britain.

Belzoni took an amazingly quick ten days to empty a tomb that would, to modern Egyptologists, represent a lifetime's work. Then he started to record the wall scenes, making a series of rather hasty and inaccurate watercolours, and taking wax impressions (having added resin and dust to the wax so that it did not melt in the heat), which, unfortunately, and unknown to him, dulled the brightly coloured paintwork. Twelve years later Jean-François Champollion, on his one and only visit to Egypt, would take a more robust approach: he wanted to cut the more beautiful scenes from the tomb walls and take them to France. Joseph Bonomi, a Roman-born British draughtsman and sculptor-turned-Egyptologist, attempted to stop this vandalism. In a state of panic, he wrote to Champollion:

> If it be true that such is your intention I feel it my duty as an Englishman and a lover of antiquity to use every argument to dissuade you from so Gothic a purpose at least until you have permission from the present Consul General or Mohammed Ali.[5]

Champollion, a proud and patriotic Frenchman, was not impressed by this approach:

> I am also performing a duty as a Frenchman in telling you that, as I do not recognise any authority in Egypt but the Pasha's I have to ask no other permission, much less that of the British Consul, who certainly does not make the ridiculous claims that you put forward for him ... rest assured, Sir, that one day you will have the pleasure of seeing some of the beautiful bas-reliefs of the tomb of Osirei [Seti I] in the French Museum. That will be the only way of saving them from imminent destruction ...

His argument was that the desecration was conservation rather than destruction: the scenes had to be removed before they were ruined by flood damage. It is true that the Valley is prone to flash-floods, which occur roughly once a century, carrying vast quantities of water, mud and rubble into the open tombs. Floods had already invaded Seti's tomb, and some of the walls had been irreparably damaged. Nevertheless, dismantling the tomb was a drastic solution. Bonomi, however, was convinced by Champollion's argument. Soon he was recommending that the British, too, take saws to the tomb walls, while Lepsius saw nothing wrong in dynamiting out a column for 'conservation' purposes.

Now, as his team set to work recording the tomb walls, Giovanni and Sarah returned to Cairo. The death of Burckhardt was clearly preying on their minds, and may well account for Sarah's next, surprising, move. She had determined on her own adventure; she would travel to the Holy Land. This is Giovanni's story, not Sarah's, but her exploits deserve some recognition. Disguised as Mamluks, Sarah and James Curtin set off. They had an exciting time: they bathed in the river Jordan and visited Nazareth and Jerusalem, where, with Sarah dressed as an Arab merchant, they entered the forbidden Mosque of Omar (as Burckhardt had before them). Their travels over, they returned to Cairo, where Sarah hired a boat and sailed to meet her husband at Luxor.

After a quick spell working at Giza, 'a little private business' as Belzoni rather coyly described it to Salt, he was ready to venture south again. On the west bank at Luxor he continued to record the tomb of Seti and, denied access to the best archaeological sites, started to excavate the area behind the Colossi of Memnon. These two immense seated statues of Amenhotep III had once stood in front of the king's mortuary temple but now, thanks to the collapse of the temple and the theft of its stone, stood alone beside the road. Almost at once Belzoni struck lucky, recovering a black granite statue of the king and some more Sekhmet statues. Then, his last excavation over, he set off across the desert towards the Red Sea, in search of the lost Graeco-Roman city of Berenice.

Belzoni had been inspired both by Burckhardt's tales and by the adventures of the French mineralogist Frédéric Cailliaud, whom he strongly suspected of being the vandal who had attacked his Philae slabs (perhaps using his mineralogist's hammer?). Cailliaud had been present as Drovetti tried, unsuccessfully, to clear the sand from the façade of the Abu Simbel Great Temple. Next he had entered the service of Mohammed Ali, and had been sent to look for Egypt's lost sulphur mines, which, it was rumoured, lay in the eastern desert. Two months later Cailliaud returned, having discovered not only the exhausted sulphur mines, but emerald mines too. In addition, he had found a small temple established by Seti I at the miner's encampment of Wadi Miah, and the ruins of a 'little Greek town' which the locals called Sakait. This little town grew in the popular imagination, until everyone accepted, even though it was many miles from the sea, that Cailliaud had discovered the port of Berenice, built by Ptolemy II Philadelphus to control Egypt's trade with India.

Belzoni set off from Edfu with a caravan of 16 camels and 12 men, including Beechey and two boys, retracing Cailliaud's route. It soon became apparent that the ruins were the remains of an insignificant mining village. Belzoni, now determined to find the real Berenice, pressed on. And eventually, on the Ras Banas peninsula, he did indeed discover the remains of the lost port. There was, however, no time to excavate. Food and, more worryingly, water supplies were running low, 'it was now three days since we had eaten anything but dry biscuit and water', and the party turned round almost immediately. Forty days after their departure, they were back in Luxor, where Sarah and Giovanni were reunited.

William Bankes and Henry Salt were passing through Luxor on their way to record the Abu Simbel temple. Bankes is the Dorset landowner and traveller who keeps hovering on the edge of our story. A friend to Lord Byron, Bankes had been one of the first Englishmen to visit Philae, where he had recognized the significance of the fallen obelisk, inscribed in both hieroglyphics and Greek. He had visited Abu Simbel, still covered in sand, and had gone on to enjoy a series of thrilling escapades in the Holy Land. On his return to Egypt, he had conducted his own excavations at Abydos, where he discovered, in the temple of Ramesses II, a list of the kings of Egypt. This was to prove an invaluable guide to the understanding of Egyptian history, as the cartouches on the wall could be matched with the names preserved in the writings of the classical authors. Bankes copied the list and left it where he found it, but it was later hacked off the wall and sold by the French to the British Museum.

Now Bankes had determined to claim the fallen Philae obelisk, not for the British Museum, but for his own country estate at Kingston Lacy, Dorset. He asked Giovanni Belzoni to get it for him. On 16 November a large and noisy party sailed southwards:

> The party was numerous – Mr Bankes, Mr Salt, Baron Sack, a
> Prussian traveller and a celebrated naturalist, Mr Beechey, Mr
> Linton, a draftsman, Doctor Ricci, and myself: a large boat was
> taken for the consul, a cangiar for Mr Bankes, a small boat for the
> baron, and a canoe for the sheep, goats, fowls, geese, ducks,
> pigeons, turkeys and donkeys, which occasionally joined the
> chorus with the rest of the tribes, and accompanied the fleet with
> a perpetual concert.[6]

But Drovetti had also claimed the obelisk for France, and his agents, too, were on their way to collect it. Belzoni had to work quickly. There were some technical hitches – at one point the obelisk ended up lying on the riverbed – but he successfully loaded the obelisk onto a boat and navigated it, undamaged, through the first cataract. By Christmas the obelisk was safely berthed at Luxor, where it acted as a prominent irritation to the French and their supporters. Giovanni thought this funny; he was less amused when his servant was attacked, and absolutely furious when he himself was nearly killed by a pistol shot fired by one of Drovetti's agents. Suddenly Luxor was too dangerous for comfort. Reunited, the Belzonis sailed northwards with the Philae obelisk, the records of the tomb of

Seti I, its alabaster sarcophagus, and the sarcophagus cover of Ramesses III.

With Luxor unsafe, Belzoni decided on a mission to explore Egypt's western desert, where he hoped to find the lost oasis of Jupiter-Amen. Leaving Sarah in Rosetta, he set off for the Faiyum, the largest oasis in the desert. Here he explored the ruins of the Hawara labyrinth, which had been eloquently described by Herodotus 2000 years before:

> I visited this place and found it to surpass description; for if all the walls and other great works of the Greeks could be put together in one, they would not equal either in labour or expense, this Labyrinth ... It has twelve courts, all of them roofed, with gates exactly opposite one another, six of them to the north and six to the south. A single wall surrounds the entire building. There are two different types of chambers throughout – half underground, half above ground, the latter being built upon the former; the whole number of these chambers is three thousand, fifteen hundred of each kind ... At the corner of the Labyrinth stands a pyramid, forty fathoms [235 feet] high, with large figures engraved on it; which is entered by a subterranean passage.[7]

The 'labyrinth', the inspiration behind the story of the labyrinth of Knossos and its Minotaur, was actually the remains of the mortuary temple attached to the mud-brick pyramid of the 12th Dynasty king Amenemhat III. Belzoni was less than impressed with what he saw:

> ... Whatever remains of beauty might be seen in this town, it does not appear that this was the place of the famous labyrinth, nor anything like it; for, according to Herodotus, Pliny &c. there is not the smallest appearance that can warrant the supposition that any such edifice was there. The Labyrinth was a building of 3,000 chambers, one half above and one half below. The construction of such an immense edifice, and the enormous quantity of materials

which must have been accumulated, would have yet left specimens enough to have seen where it had been erected, but not the smallest trace of any such thing is any where to be seen.[8]

On 16 May 1819 Belzoni set off with a small camel train to seek out the lost oasis. It took him six days to arrive at the Bahariya oasis, which he assumed was the oasis of Jupiter-Amen, home to the oracle who had first recognized Alexander's greatness. In fact he was wrong – the oasis of Jupiter-Amen is Siwa oasis, even further to the west.

In September 1819 Giovanni and Sarah left Egypt for Europe – 'thank God!' The first stop was Italy, where Giovanni paid his first visit to his home-town in 19 years. There was a civic reception – a thank you for his gift of a pair of Sekhmet statues – and a reunion with his family, who received a pair of gazelles as a present. Then the Belzonis moved on to London, where their arrival was reported in *The Times* on 31 March 1820:

> The celebrated traveller Mr Belzoni has arrived in this metropolis after an absence of ten years, five of which he has employed in arduous researches after the curious remains of antiquities in Egypt and Nubia ... Mr Belzoni's Journal of his discoveries in Egypt and Nubia and the Oasis will be published as soon as possible. The model of the beautiful tomb discovered by Mr Belzoni in Thebes will be erected as soon as a convenient place shall be found for its reception.

The first priority was the publication of Belzoni's book, the British response to the French *Description*. The lengthily titled *Narrative of the Operations and Recent discoveries within the pyramids, temples, tombs and excavations in Egypt and Nubia; and of a journey to the coasts of the Red Sea, in search of the Ancient Berenice; and another in the oasis of Jupiter Ammon* was published in London in 1820 and became an instant success. It was subsequently published in French (some of the anti-French sentiments had to be toned down), German and Italian. It is a wonderful book packed with tales of adventure, yet it has all the flaws of a hastily written autobiography. Its many omissions (there is no mention of the Patagonian Samson, for example), its errors, curious language and strong biases tend to enhance rather than detract from its appeal. The one person who did not enjoy the book was Henry Salt; consumed with jealousy, he resumed his own excavations, employing Giovanni d'Athanasi as his archaeologist.

Then came the exhibition. The Egyptian Hall had been designed by the architect Peter Robinson, who, heavily inspired by Denon's illustrations of the Graeco-Roman temple of Hathor at Dendera, had produced an elaborate and highly imaginitive Egyptian temple façade standing in the middle of a row of conventional terraced houses and shops in Piccadilly, London. Happily, the Hall was untenanted, and it made a splendid and highly conspicuous setting for Belzoni's display. At the centre of the exhibition was a re-creation of two of the finest chambers in the tomb of Seti I. There was also a model of the entire tomb, drawings and casts from other sites, and a rather random display of artifacts, statues and mummies. After a grand unrolling of a mummy, and a good preview in *The Times*, the doors were opened to the public in May 1821. Almost 2000 visitors came that first day. Belzoni, always in touch with the people, had a success on his hands. He was the toast of London, and Egyptology was the new British craze.

Belzoni loved his newfound fame, and the money that went with it, but, true to form, he soon developed itchy feet. In 1822 he travelled alone to Russia, where he met Tsar Alexander I (who gave him an amethyst ring), then returned to London via Finland, Sweden and Denmark. On his return he auctioned off the unwanted contents of his exhibition – Lot 15 was the now naked mummy – and moved to Paris, where he opened the exhibition once again. Here, despite Champollion's timely announcement of the decoding of hieroglyphics, the display was not such a great success.

It was time for another adventure – maybe one that would raise some much-needed funds. With Egypt effectively out of bounds, Belzoni had resolved to complete Burckhardt's unfinished voyage; he would trace the origins of the river Niger, and discover the lost city of Timbuktu. James Curtin, who had been taking a leaf out of his employer's book by enjoying his own Ethiopian adventures, returned to take charge of the Paris exhibition. Sarah travelled as far as Fez, Morocco, before returning home, taking her husband's last will and testament with her. Belzoni eventually reached Benin, but there he caught dysentery. He died on 3 December 1823, aged 45, and was buried that night under a large tree. His grave has since disappeared.

What happened to everyone else?

SARAH, ACCUSTOMED to long periods of separation followed by happy reunion, refused to believe that her beloved Mr B. would not be returning. Only when she received his Masonic signet ring, 18 months after his death, did she accept the truth. Devastated, she commissioned a memorial engraving that showed Belzoni the gentleman explorer surrounded by some of his more important discoveries: the Younger Memnon, the head and arm of Tuthmosis III, the Philae obelisk and the sarcophagus of Seti I. She was left almost destitute, and it was not until 1851, when she was nearly 70 years old and living in Brussels, that she was granted a British state pension of £100 per year. Filled with wanderlust to the last, she made a final move to the warmer climate of the Channel Islands, where she died on 12 January 1870, aged 87.

HENRY SALT offered his first collection of antiquities, including the alabaster sarcophagus of Seti I, to the British Museum. Still recovering from the public outcry caused by the purchase of the Elgin Marbles for an astonishing £35,000, the Trustees were reluctant to meet his asking price of £8000. Eventually, after some hard bargaining, they bought most of the collection for a knockdown

£2000 – less than the amount Salt had spent excavating and transporting it – while the sarcophagus was sold separately to the architect Sir John Soane for a further £2000. Today it is displayed in Sir John Soane's Museum, London. Undaunted, Salt continued to collect antiquities: by now he and Drovetti had reached a gentlemen's agreement to split Egypt's sites between them. His second collection (made between 1819 and 1824) was sold to Charles X of France for a more realistic £10,000, subsequently becoming an important part of the Louvre collection. A third collection (1824–7) was sold posthumously at Sotheby's and raised over £7000. Henry Salt died in Alexandria in 1827.

BERNARDINO DROVETTI continued to excavate alongside Salt. A year after Belzoni's death he discovered, in the northern cemetery site of Sakkara, the tomb of the great 18th Dynasty General Djehuty, the inspired tactician, who, as legend tells us, caused his men to hide in baskets and be carried into the siege town of Joppa. His tomb included a fine assortment of canopic jars, scribal palettes, jewellery, tools and presumably much more. Unfortunately, the grave goods were quickly sold to collectors and dispersed, and, as there was no formal excavation report, it is left to Joseph Bonomi to preserve the details of this momentous find:

> In the winter of 1824 a discovery was made in Sakkara, of a tomb
> enclosing a mummy entirely cased in solid gold (each limb, each
> finger of which, had its particular envelope inscribed with
> hieroglyphics), a scarabaeus attached to a gold chain, a gold ring,
> and a pair of bracelets of gold, with other valuable relics.[9]

Today the location of this important tomb is unknown. Drovetti retired in 1829. His first collection, which contained many valuable papyri, including a royal canon or king list, and a series of legal papyri that may have formed part of the New Kingdom state archives, had been sold to the King of Sardinia for over £13,000. It now forms the basis of the Turin collection. His second collection was acquired by France and is now in the Louvre. Drovetti eventually lost his mind; he died in the Turin asylum in 1852.

WILLIAM BANKES finally erected the Philae obelisk on his estate at Kingston Lacy, Dorset, in 1839, with the Duke of Wellington attending. He died in Venice in 1855.

GIOVANNI D'ATHANASI now worked for Henry Salt. Never an easy man to get on with, he found himself in dispute with the Trieste-born Giuseppe Passalacqua, a former horse-trader turned archaeologist, who, in 1823, had discovered the intact Theban burial of the Middle Kingdom steward Mentuhotep. Soon their men too were quarrelling and even fighting over the ownership of the tomb contents. Passalacqua would eventually sell the contents to Berlin Museum, where, in 1827, he became curator in charge of the Egyptian collection. That same year d'Athanasi correctly identified artifacts from the Theban tomb of Nubkheperre Intef – the first intact burial of an Egyptian king. The tomb had, unfortunately, been discovered by local antiquity traders, who were reluctant to share their knowledge, and the collection had quickly been dispersed:

> The moment that the Arabs saw that the case was highly ornamented and gilt, they immediately ... knew that it belonged to a person of rank. They forthwith proceeded to satisfy their curiosity by opening it, when they discovered, placed around the head of the mummy, but over the linen, a diadem, comprised of silver and beautiful mosaic work, its centre being formed of gold, representing the asp, the emblem of royalty. Inside the case, alongside the body, were deposited two bows, with six arrows.[10]

Salt's retirement saw d'Athanasi first employed by his successor, John Baker, then working as a freelance collector. He sold his personal collection of antiquities in three auctions held at Sotheby's in

London (1836, 1837 and 1845), and set up in business as a picture dealer. But his new business failed, and d'Athanasi died in poverty in 1854.

JOSEPH BONOMI travelled extensively throughout Europe and the Near East. Maintaining his interest in Egyptology, he worked alongside the British traveller turned Egyptologist John Gardner Wilkinson. Bonomi revisited Egypt with the German expedition led by Richard Lepsius (1842–5), before returning to Britain, where he designed the Egyptian Court at the Crystal Palace. In 1861 he took up the position of curator at Sir John Soane's Museum, assuming direct responsibility for the care of Belzoni's alabaster sarcophagus. He died in 1878.

JOHN GARDNER WILKINSON had visited Egypt in 1821 and, smitten with the country, had stayed for 12 years. He sailed twice to the second cataract, excavated in and around Luxor, and produced significant scholarly work which contributed to the understanding of hieroglyphics. But it is for his surveying and numbering of the tombs in the Valley of the Kings that Wilkinson is best remembered. In 1833 he returned to Britain and, newly knighted, published *The Manners and Customs of the Ancient Egyptians* (1837), a hugely influential text, with woodcuts by Joseph Bonomi. Wilkinson died in 1875.

CHAPTER SIX

➤—≺

THE PYRAMIDOLOGISTS

GYPT HAS MORE THAN 30 kings' pyramids in varying states of repair. Associated with these is a series of smaller-scale queens' pyramids and satellite pyramids, which take the pyramid total up to over 60. The earliest Egyptologists focused their attentions on three of these pyramids.

The 4th Dynasty kings Khufu (Cheops to the Greeks), Khaefre (Chephren) and Menkaure (Mycerinus) each built a pyramid tomb in the desert outside their capital city, Memphis. These pyramids were intended to remain sealed until the end of time. After each funeral builders blocked the internal passageways, then covered the doorway in the same smooth casing stones that covered the rest of the pyramid. Now all four sides had the same, polished exterior with no sign of any way in. Herodotus, visiting Giza 20 centuries after the workmen had laid down their tools, marvelled at the size of the pyramids and, like almost everyone else, wondered exactly what could be inside:

> Cheops reigned for fifty years, or so the Egyptians say, and was succeeded after his death by his brother Chephren. Chephren was no better than his predecessor; his rule was equally oppressive and, like Cheops, he built a pyramid, but of a smaller size (I measured them both myself). It has no underground chambers, and no channel was dug, as in the case of Cheops's pyramid, to carry

water from the Nile. The cutting of the canal, as I have already said, makes the site of the pyramid of Cheops into an island, and there his body is supposed to be.[1]

His belief that the second Giza pyramid had no internal chambers was to influence archaeological thinking for many centuries. Herodotus was in fact wrong in much of his archaeology, including his denial of the chambers in the second pyramid, but he did understand one crucial fact: that the pyramids had been built as tombs. The first Europeans to visit Egypt, lacking this vital knowledge, thought that they were perhaps the granaries built by the prudent Old Testament Joseph against the predicted years of famine.

Today we know that Khufu's pyramid, the oldest and largest of the three, consists of three chambers linked by a system of passageways.

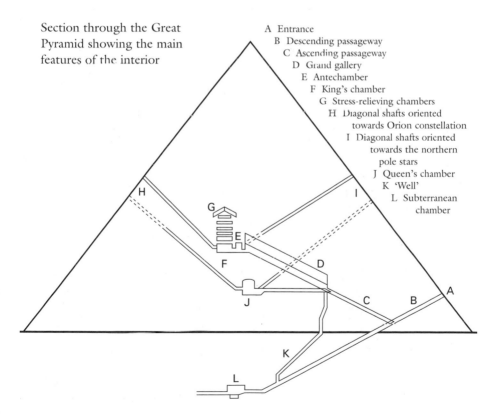

Section through the Great Pyramid showing the main features of the interior

A Entrance
B Descending passageway
C Ascending passageway
D Grand gallery
E Antechamber
F King's chamber
G Stress-relieving chambers
H Diagonal shafts oriented towards Orion constellation
I Diagonal shafts oriented towards the northern pole stars
J Queen's chamber
K 'Well'
L Subterranean chamber

It took many years of intrepid, and occasionally dangerous, exploration for archaeologists to reach this understanding. We have already encountered the enterprising Caliph el-Mamun, the first explorer to make his way into the Great Pyramid and follow the ascending passageway into the burial chamber. The Caliph left the pyramid open to subsequent visitors, allowing the astronomer John Greaves to offer his British readers the first semi-scientific survey of a pyramid's internal structure in 1646:

> Having passed with tapers in our hands this narrow straight [the descending passageway], though with some difficulty (for at the farther end of it we must serpent-like creep on our bellies), we laid in a place somewhat larger and of a pretty height, but lying incomposed [disturbed]; having been dug away, either by curiosity or avarice of some, in hope to discover an hidden treasure; or rather by the command of Alamoun [el-Mamun] the deservedly renowned Caliph of Babylon. By whomsoever it were, it is not worth the inquiry, nor does the place merit describing, but that I was unwilling to pretermit [neglect] any thing; being only an habitation of bats, and those so ugly, and of so large a size (exceeding a foot in length), that I have not elsewhere seen the like.[2]

He made his way to the burial chamber, where the sight of the lidless sarcophagus affected him deeply:

> ... within this glorious room (for so I may justly call it) as within some consecrated oratory, stands the monument of Cheops, or Chemmis, of one piece of marble hollowed within, and uncovered at the top, and sounding like a bell ... A narrow space, yet large enough to contain a most potent and dreadful monarch, being dead, to whom, living, all Egypt was too streight and narrow a circuit ...[3]

Greaves made it quite clear to his readers that the pyramid was neither a granary nor an astronomical observatory, but a tomb:

> That the priests might, near these pyramids, make their observations, I in no way question; this rising of the hill being, in my judgement, as fit a place as any in Egypt for such a design; and so fitter by the vicinity of Memphis. But that these Pyramids were designed for Observatories (whereas by the testimonies of the ancients I have proved before, that they were intended for sepulchres) is in no way to be credited.[4]

In 1763 the British diplomat and explorer Nathaniel Davison discovered the lowest of the relieving chambers in the ceiling above the burial chamber. Next he investigated the 'well'. Dangling dangerously from a rope held by his guides, Davison allowed himself to be lowered down until he found himself standing on a heap of sand, stone and rubbish, surrounded by bats whose fiercely beating wings threatened to extinguish his candle. The bottom of the shaft was blocked and he could go no further. Over half a century later Captain Giovanni Battista Caviglia, a Genoese mariner turned archaeologist working for Henry Salt, emptied the well and connected it to the descending passageway. In so doing, he cleared the pyramid of the foul atmosphere that caused his own nose to bleed and his unfortunate workmen to faint.

The internal architecture of the pyramid was now revealed. Most considered it to be fairly disappointing, and many simply refused to accept that there were no more rooms – a treasury perhaps? – hidden within the bulk of the masonry. Explorers continued to search for lost chambers, and their lost treasures, and it was not until 1837–8, when Colonel Richard Howard Vyse conducted a survey of the pyramid, filling the subterranean chamber with stone and rendering it temporarily inaccessible for further study in the process, that the truth was more or less accepted. Vyse discovered the upper relieving chambers, which he named, with patriotic fervour, after the celebrities of his age: the Duke of Wellington, Admiral Nelson, Lady Anne Arbuthnot and the diplomat Patrick Campbell (the latter two proving, if proof were needed, that celebrity can indeed be fleeting). His aims may have been laudable – his ultimate goal was to prove the truth of the Bible – but his vigorous survey methods left a lot to be desired:

> The mortar was nearly as hard as the stone itself, so that with Arab workmen, and common tools, it was a most tedious operation. To obliviate some of these difficulties I ordered the people to get up to twenty or thirty feet, and to cut perpendicularly behind the stones; but very little advantage was gained in proportion to the increased number which required to be removed. Towards the end of this work gunpowder was used with great effect ...[5]

Vyse had initially employed Captain Caviglia to help him with this survey, but the two soon had a major falling out. Vyse accused Caviglia of being more interested in the nearby 'mummy pits', the tombs of the nobles, than the pyramid that he was being paid to explore. Caviglia would later allege that Vyse had stolen his secret knowledge of the interior of the Great Pyramid. The row climaxed with Caviglia storming into Vyse's tent at breakfast time and throwing down his unused advance of £40 tied up in an old stocking. Vyse, unperturbed, extracted his money and returned the stocking to its unhappy owner. Caviglia was replaced by John Shae Perring, a civil engineer who worked happily alongside the irascible colonel for many years. Meanwhile, Caviglia left Egypt for good and went to live in Paris, where he came under the patronage of Lord Elgin.

THE GREAT PYRAMID had become a tourist attraction, and a series of distinguished visitors braved the heat, the dark, the dirt and the ever-present bats to crawl along the ascending passageway and visit the burial chamber. The French novelist Gustave Flaubert was one of them:

After breakfast we visit the interior of the Pyramid. The opening is on the north. Smooth, even corridor (like a sewer), which you descend; then another corridor ascends; we slip on bats' dung. It seems that these corridors were made to allow the huge coffins to be drawn slowly into place ... King's chamber, all of granite in enormous blocks, empty sarcophagus at the far end...

As we emerge on hands and knees from one of the corridors, we meet a party of Englishmen who are coming in; they are in the same position as we; exchange of civilities; each party proceeds on its way.[6]

In 1872 the British engineer Waynmann Dixon, who was in Egypt to oversee the transportation of the obelisk known as Cleopatra's Needle to London, discovered two 'air-shafts' hidden behind camouflage stones in the Queen's Chamber. The shafts are long, narrow passageways, too small to accommodate a human, oriented towards the northern pole star and the constellation of Orion. They extend only a short distance into the masonry before they are blocked. A similar pair of shafts leads from the King's Chamber; lacking any form of blocking, these run straight through the body of the pyramid and perhaps once pierced the pyramid's now-vanished casing. The purpose of the shafts remains a mystery, although as it is obvious that they would have supplied very little air to the pyramid builders, it seems likely that they had a ritual rather than a practical function.

KHAEFRE'S PYRAMID IS slightly smaller than Khufu's but, because he built it on slightly higher ground, and at a slightly steeper angle, it appears at first sight to be the larger. Inside, it has a simplified architecture. There are no chambers within the pyramid masonry. Instead a subterranean burial chamber was built and roofed in a large, open trench, and then the solid pyramid was erected on top. The entrance, again on the northern face, was so well hidden that many were agreed that the pyramid had no entrance. Belzoni, however, was not fooled. In 1818 he excused himself to Henry Salt on the grounds that he was conducting 'a little private business', borrowed some money, and headed for Giza in search of pyramid treasure. Here, the engineering skills that had helped him to locate the lost tombs in the Valley of the Kings were put to the test. He observed the open pyramid of Khufu, then scanned the surface of the north face of Khaefre's pyramid, looking for uneven or ill-aligned blocks. Eventually, after one aborted excavation, he realized that the entrance was not in the dead centre of the northern face, but slightly to the east. He removed the blocking stones to reveal a passageway running downwards through the masonry. Beyond a granite portcullis, which caused him considerable delay, the corridor opened into a horizontal corridor leading to the burial chamber:

> I reached the door at the centre of a large chamber. I walked
> slowly two or three paces, and then stood still to contemplate the
> place where I was. Whatever it might be, I certainly considered
> myself in the centre of that pyramid, which from time immemorial
> had been the subject of the obscure conjectures of many hundred
> travellers, both ancient and modern. My torch, formed of a few wax
> candles, gave but a faint light; I could however, clearly distinguish
> the principal objects. I naturally turned my eyes to the west end
> of the chamber, looking for the sarcophagus, which I strongly
> expected to see in the same situation as that in the first pyramid;
> but I was disappointed when I saw nothing there. The chamber
> had a painted ceiling; and many of the stones had been removed
> from their places, evidently by some one in search of treasure. On
> my advancing towards the west end, I was agreeably surprised to
> find, that there was a sarcophagus buried level with the floor.[7]

The plain, polished granite sarcophagus was already open, its heavy sliding lid broken in two. The few bones that Belzoni discovered in the sarcophagus turned out to be cattle bones – possibly the lunch left by earlier robbers. Frustrated and out of pocket, Belzoni scrawled his name and the date in the burial chamber that already bore an inscription in Arabic:

The Master Mohammed Ahmed, lapicide [stoneworker], has opened them; and the Master Othman attended this and the King Ali Mohammed at first from the beginning to the closing up.

The pyramid had been robbed in antiquity, resealed by the Saites, and then robbed again by the Arabs, who, failing to find the original entrance, made their own tunnel. Now, looking from inside the pyramid outwards, it became obvious that there had been a second, older entrance, also on the northern face, but this time opening at ground level, cut through the bedrock and starting outside the pyramid. This entrance was filled with granite blocks which Colonel Vyse first attempted to move manually, but which, thwarted by 'the unskilfulness of the Arabs', he soon blew to pieces. A passageway led downwards, through bedrock, into a horizontal corridor. A subsidiary chamber, perhaps a storeroom, opened off the passageway, which eventually connected with the first passageway leading to the burial chamber. The two entrances are unique and unexplained; they may reflect a change of plan, or the provision of access for the builders.

MENKAURE'S PYRAMID WAS built on a much smaller scale, establishing a precedent for all future pyramid builders, who would prefer to concentrate on their mortuary temples and statues. But, perhaps to distract from its size, the bottom layers of the pyramid were cased in expensive red granite. In antiquity it unfortunately attracted the attention of Caliph Malek al-Azis Othman Ben Youssef, who, for no good reason that we know, had determined to demolish all three Giza pyramids. Abd el-Latif of Baghdad preserves the story:

... He was prevailed upon by some persons of his court – people devoid of all sense and judgement – to attempt the demolition of the pyramids. He accordingly sent some miners and quarrymen, under the superintendence of some of the principal officers and emirs of his court, with orders to destroy the red pyramid, which is the least of the three. They encamped near it, collected labourers from all parts of the country at a vast expense, and endeavoured with great assiduity for eight months to execute the commission, with which they were entrusted, removing each day, with great difficulty, one or two stones, which were forced out of their places by levers and wedges, and afterwards drawn down by cords. When at last one of these enormous blocks fell, the tremendous noise was heard at an immense distance, and the concussion shook the ground, and made the mountains tremble.[8]

At least the Caliph had had the good sense to start with the smallest pyramid. After eight months' hard work, however, there had been little progress, and the Caliph was forced to abandon his scheme, leaving only a superficial wound in the pyramid masonry.

Giovanni Belzoni, recovering from his disappointment in finding Khaefre's pyramid empty, was tempted to try again:

Having thus finished my operation on the second pyramid, I felt a great inclination to have a cursory view of the third. I observed, that some one had made an attempt to penetrate it by excavations on the east side. I commenced my labours on the north side, and, after removing a great quantity of materials, found a considerable accumulation of enormous blocks of granite, which had evidently formed the coating. Proceeding yet lower, as I cleared away the rubbish I found, that part of the coating still remained in place down to the bases. The removal of these blocks would evidently have brought me to the entrance into the pyramid, but it required more money and time than I could spare.[9]

If only Belzoni had continued. Instead, the pyramid was left to the mercies of the explosive Colonel Vyse. Clearly, the only way to investigate such a solid building was with gunpowder. And this is exactly what Vyse and Perring did in 1837. The entrance, partway up the north face, was discovered (by simply removing a few blocks, as Belzoni had predicted) only after Vyse had driven a corridor right through the masonry, proving, by accident, that there are no hidden chambers in this part of the pyramid. From the entrance proper a corridor drops down into the bedrock before opening into a horizontal, decorated chamber. Beyond this a passage, originally blocked by three granite portcullises, leads to an antechamber. From the northern wall of the antechamber a corridor leads upwards through the bulk of the pyramid and opens into an unfinished upper chamber.

The burial chamber lies beneath the antechamber. Here Vyse found a beautiful dark basalt sarcophagus carved with elaborate palace façade panelling – the only decorated sarcophagus to be recovered from a Giza pyramid, and, just possibly, a Saite replacement for the Old Kingdom original. Vyse had determined to send the sarcophagus to the British Museum, but in 1838 it was lost at sea when the *Beatrice* foundered off the Spanish coast. Vyse himself returned to England in 1837, leaving all three Giza pyramids open. He considered that the pyramids had told all their secrets. The real archaeological work, however, had only just begun.

MEANWHILE, BACK HOME, an alternative and entirely theoretical form of pyramid studies was developing with an astonishing rapidity. In 1859 John Taylor had published *The Great Pyramid: Why Was It Built? And Who Built It?* This was the acknowledged inspiration behind Charles Piazzi Smyth's best-selling work *Our Inheritance in the Great Pyramid* (1866, later reissued as *The Great Pyramid: Its Secrets and Mysteries Revealed*) and its follow-up volume *Life and Work at the Great Pyramid* (1867). Smyth argued that Khufu's Great Pyramid was so perfect and so beautifully proportioned that it simply could not have been built by humans. Everyone knew that the world had been created in 4004 BC. Everyone knew that the Great Pyramid was built in 2400 BC (not too far out – today a date of 2550 BC is considered acceptable): how could mankind have progressed so far in a mere 1600 years? The whole thing was impossible. Clearly, the pyramid had been built, under divine guidance, by a lost race of God's chosen people. Far from being a pagan tomb, the pyramid was a record of man's destiny, built using the 'pyramid inch', (1.001 of an imperial inch), which those with the knowledge could use to predict the future. His argument is summed up in two rather lengthy, and often quoted, sentences:

> With many of the smaller and later pyramids there is little doubt about their objects; for, built by the Egyptians as sepulchres for the great Egyptian dead, such dead, both Pharaohs and their relatives, were buried in them, and with all their written particulars, pictorial accompaniments, and idolatrous adornments of that too graphic religion, which the fictile nation on the Nile ever delighted in. But as we approach, ascending the stream of ancient time, in any careful chronological survey of pyramidal structures, to the 'Great Pyramid', Egyptian emblems are gradually left behind; and in, and throughout, that mighty builded mass, which all history and all tradition, both ancient and modern, agree in representing as the first in point of date of the whole Jeezeh [Giza], and even the whole Egyptian, group, the earliest stone building also positively known to have been erected in any country – we find in all its finished parts not a vestige of heathenism, nor the smallest indulgence in anything approaching to idolatry; no Egyptology of the kind denounced by Moses and all the prophets of Israel; nor even the most distant allusion to Sabaism, and its elemental worship of sun, or moon, or any of the starry hosts of heaven.[10]

Smyth was wrong in his assumption that the smaller and later pyramids were heavily decorated with pagan images, wrong in his assumption that the Great Pyramid is the oldest and most significant pyramid (it is 'merely' the largest), and, as would later be proved, wrong in his identification of the pyramid inch. But, as Astronomer Royal for Scotland and professor of astronomy at the University of Edinburgh, he put up a persuasive argument, and there were many who believed him; there are many, indeed, who still believe him today. While his fellow academics remained highly sceptical, his work developed a large popular following, and the facts and figures that littered his book were accepted as totally accurate, even though the pyramid had never been subjected to a proper architectural survey. To many, it made perfect sense that the pyramid – undoubtedly a sophisticated and impressive structure – might be the indirect work of God. Indeed, many had been attracted to Egyptology in the first place because of their firm Christian beliefs. Captain Caviglia was one such literal believer, Colonel Vyse another. Vyse had perhaps the most intimate knowledge of the interior of the Great Pyramid of his generation, but absolutely no understanding of its true meaning, and he always hoped that he was exploring the extravagant tombs made by 'The Shepherd Kings [Second Intermediate Period Hyksos rulers], whose descendants ... after their expulsion from Egypt, built in Syria, Jerusalem ...'

The Christian certainties of the past were being assaulted from every direction, as scientists rather than priests took over the task of explaining the creation of the world. Charles Darwin had already published his *On the Origin of Species by means of Natural Selection* (1858), making it clear that the world could not have been created in 4004 BC. Mankind's long prehistory was becoming obvious and, rather than being God's deliberate creation – 'God made them high or lowly, and ordered their estate' – there was the uncomfortable possibility that all people, of all races, were an accident of evolution, the descendants of apes. The 'pyramid inch' must have seemed as believable, or as unbelievable, as the theory of evolution or the idea that light could be generated at the flick of a switch. Smyth's theories would inspire generations of alternative pyramid theorists: first those who attempted to connect the pyramids to Christianity, then later those who would see the pyramids as the tangible remains of otherwise lost or hidden civilizations, ranging from aliens from outer space to the vanished tribes of Atlantis.

THE ARCHAEOLOGISTS

>—<

... NOW THE PERIOD OF SUPERFICIAL SURVEY OF
THE WEALTH OF MATERIAL WHICH EGYPT OFFERS TO
THE STUDENT WAS DRAWING TO A CLOSE, AND WAS TO
BE SUCCEEDED BY THE PERIOD IN WHICH EXCAVATION,
CONDUCTED WITH CONSTANTLY GROWING SKILL AND
ATTENTION TO THE MOST MINUTE DETAILS, WAS TO DO,
AS IT IS STILL DOING, WHAT NO AMOUNT OF SUPERFICIAL
CATALOGUING OF THE MONUMENTS OF THE LAND COULD
EVER DO, AND TO GIVE US BACK, NOT ONLY PICTURES OF
THE LIFE OF THOSE ANCIENT DAYS, BUT THE TOOLS AND
WEAPONS WITH WHICH THE EGYPTIAN WORKED, FOUGHT,
AND HUNTED, THE VESSELS WHICH HE USED FOR ALL THE
PURPOSES OF LIFE, THE JEWELS WITH WHICH HE AND HIS
WOMEN-KIND ADORNED THEMSELVES, THE BOOKS WHICH
THEY READ, AND THE SONGS WHICH THEY SANG; ALL THE
MATERIAL FROM WHICH, IF WE HAVE THE VISION AND
THE INSIGHT, WE MAY RECONSTRUCT THE LIFE OF THOSE
FAR-OFF DAYS; AND TO CROWN ITS GIFTS BY CALLING
UP FROM THE TOMB THE VERY MEN THEMSELVES WHO
RULED AND WARRED IN THE LAND OF THE NILE IN THE
GREAT DAYS WHEN EGYPT WAS THE FIRST OF ALL EMPIRES,
AND HER PHARAOH A GOD INCARNATE, BEFORE WHOSE
GOLDEN SANDALS ALL THE LESSER KINGS OF THE WORLD
BOWED IN THE DUST 'SEVEN TIMES AND SEVEN TIMES'.

J. Baikie, *A Century of Excavation in the Land of the Pharaohs* (1923)

CHAPTER SEVEN

≻—≺

PROTECTING THE MONUMENTS

G RADUALLY THE WORLD was starting to realize that Egypt's antiquities were not, as had always been assumed, an infinite resource. It was no longer considered appropriate for an excavator to blast his way through a pyramid in search of secret chambers filled with gold and jewels, or for a museum-sanctioned collector to hack a painted scene off a tomb wall in order to 'conserve' it in his own museum. The monuments, a valuable asset for a developing country, needed to be protected against those who sought to exploit them.

Outside Egyptology there was a growing awareness of the true age of the world; the new disciplines of archaeology and geology were opening up unimagined possibilities. Within Egyptology the urge towards conservation was hastened by the decoding of hieroglyphics. The stone temples and empty tombs were no longer dumb. Readers could appreciate the complexities of dynastic life, while monuments that had been little more than intricately carved blocks of stone suddenly developed a context and meaning. Now scholars, rather than treasure seekers, could excavate with the hope of answering specific questions. The age of the great collectors was drawing to an end, and one man was to play an important role in its demise.

François Auguste Ferdinand Mariette was born in Boulogne-sur-Mer on 11 February 1821. After an early career teaching French and (curiously) designing ribbons in England, he returned to France, where he took up the study of Egyptology, teaching himself hiero-glyphics and Coptic from the texts published in the *Description*. By 1849 he had become a curator at the Louvre Museum, Paris. In 1850 his museum sent him on a six-month mission to Egypt to obtain as many Coptic manuscripts as possible. The British and the French were still quarrelling over Egypt's treasures, and it was felt that the French needed to keep up with recent British acquisitions. But once in Egypt, Mariette abandoned the quest for manuscripts – there was in any case, thanks to the British, now a dire shortage of Coptic texts – and turned to excavation. He started his work in the Sakkara cemetery, and it was here, in 1850, that he discovered the Serapeum – the catacomb designed by the 19th Dynasty Prince Khaemwaset to hold the burials of the sacred Apis bulls.

We have previously met Prince Khaemwaset in Chapter One, where he struggled to sweep the already ancient pyramids clean of sand. Archaeology was, however, only a hobby. Khaemwaset was a *Sem*-Priest of Ptah, a priest involved in the rituals associated with mortuary cults and funerals. Ptah of Memphis, his patron, was an immensely rich and influential creator god, a particular favourite of Ramesses II. His magnificent temple must have been the equal, if not the superior, of the temple of Amen at Karnak, but while the Karnak complex has survived more or less intact, there is today vir-tually nothing left of Ptah's domain. Now based at Memphis, Khaemwaset took a particular interest in the care of the Apis bull, the living representation of Ptah on earth, who lived in a palace sur-rounded by a harem of beautiful cows.

In Year 16 of Ramesses II, the Apis bull died. As his successor was chosen – the priests would recognize him by his distinctive markings – the old bull was given a funeral fit for a king. Embalmed and band-aged, his body was interred in a tomb in the bull cemetery. A deco-rated chapel covered the tomb. Fourteen years later his successor died. By now Khaemwaset was in charge of the funeral arrange-ments. Breaking with tradition, he interred the second bull next to the first, allowing the two to share a burial chamber and chapel.

Khaemwaset then made a radical decision. The old-fashioned individual tombs were to be abandoned, and instead the Apis bulls were to be buried in an underground gallery, or catacomb, today known as the Serapeum. Successive bulls would be interred in a series of side rooms opening off the main gallery, the rooms being sealed after each funeral. Above ground the individual chapels would be replaced by one magnificent temple. Khaemwaset recorded his plans in a lengthy inscription carved at the entrance to the gallery:

> ... the Osiris, the Sem-Priest and King's Son Khaemwaset, he says: 'I am a valiant heir, a vigilant champion, excelling in wisdom in the opinion of Thoth ... Never has the like been done, set down in writing in the Great Festival Court before this temple ... I have endowed for him [Apis] the sacred offerings; regular daily offerings, feasts whose days come on appointed dates and calendar feasts throughout the year ... I have built for him a great stone shrine before his temple, in which to repose in spending the day when preparing for burial. I have made for him a great offering-table opposite his great shrine, of fine Tura limestone ... It will indeed seem to you a benefaction when by contrast you look upon what the ancestors have done, in poor and ignorant works ... Remember my name ... I am the Sem-Priest, Khaemwaset.'[1]

Khaemwaset's gallery, known today as the Lesser Vaults, housed the Apis burials for many decades. Eventually, in 612 BC, King Psammeticus I ordered the building of the Greater Vaults. It is these, rather than the earlier vaults, which are today open to the public.

In the first century BC the classical author Strabo had visited Sakkara, and had noted the long avenue of sphinxes that led to the entrance to the Serapeum. In AD 1850 the antiquities market was flooded with sphinxes taken from Sakkara. Now Mariette, out walking with friends, put two and two together:

One day, walking across the necropolis, metre-rule in hand, seeking to disentangle the plans of the tombs, my eye fell on another of these sphinxes. It was a revelation. Although three-quarters buried, it was clear that this sphinx was in its original location. The avenue which had furnished the collectors of Cairo and Alexandria with so many monuments was therefore found.[2]

Mariette's workmen started to dig. Soon they had uncovered over a hundred further sphinxes. He had indeed discovered the lost processional way, and he was able to follow it as it led directly towards the temple of Apis. By November 1851 he had found the entrance to the Greater Vaults, housing 24 granite sarcophagi. All, unfortunately, were empty. The next year he found the Lesser Vaults built by Khaemwaset. Here the bulls had been housed in enormous wooden coffins, but once again their mummies had vanished. Only one body was discovered: a badly preserved mummy, wearing a gold mask and lying in half a gilded coffin, was found in the centre of the Lesser Vaults, hidden beneath rubble that had fallen from the collapsed ceiling. This body has become the focus of much archaeological debate. Mariette believed it to be human: Khaemwaset himself. Unfortunately, he used explosives to clear the gallery, and so we will never be sure of the body's original location. Had Khaemwaset really wanted to be buried here? It makes sense that he might have chosen a Sakkara burial, but less sense that he would actually be interred among the bulls. Had he perhaps been reburied here after building works had disturbed his original tomb? Could he have been blown into the gallery from another tomb? Or, as many Egyptologists now believe, had Mariette actually discovered the ill-preserved remains of a bull burial topped by an anthropoid mask? Unfortunately, the bones that could settle the debate once and for all have vanished.

Mariette subsequently discovered the paired bull burial made by Khaemwaset in Year 30 of his father's reign. This is the only Apis burial to have been recovered intact, and Mariette was moved by the sight of ancient footprints leading across the sandy floor of the tomb. The bulls still lay in their massive wooden sarcophagi. There was a set of enormous canopic jars, dozens of *shabti* figures (servant models who would work for the deceased in the Afterlife), two shrines, magic bricks and gold jewellery bearing the names of Ramesses and Khaemwaset. The bodies themselves were badly preserved, but it was obvious that they had been dismembered before mummification.

Mariette returned to Paris in 1854, but was then summoned back to Cairo in 1857 to prepare for the eagerly anticipated visit of Prince Napoleon, cousin of the Emperor of France. It had been decided that the prince was to be given every opportunity to discover antiquities: to save time, and embarrassment, Mariette was charged with first of all finding, then replanting, the antiquities that the innocent prince was to 'discover'. When the prince eventually cancelled his visit, Mariette took care to send him a selection of the prizes that he might otherwise have found. Meanwhile, his men had made an important discovery. A small, insignificant-looking tomb at Dra Abu el-Naga, Thebes, had yielded the badly preserved burial of the last king of the 17th Dynasty, Kamose. Two years later they would discover the intact burial of the contemporary Queen Ahhotep close by.

In 1858 Said Pasha, Khedive or ruler of Egypt, appointed Auguste Mariette Director-General of the newly formed Antiquities Service in Egypt. His duties were simultaneously very simple and highly complex: 'You will ensure the safety of the monuments; you will tell the governors of all the provinces that I forbid them to touch one single antique stone; you will imprison any peasant who sets foot inside a temple.'[3] The next year, Said Pasha agreed to establish a national museum in an empty mosque and collection of sheds in the Bulaq area of Cairo.

Mariette now found himself in the enviable position of being the only archaeologist authorized to license excavations in Egypt. His finds were to be reserved for the new national museum. Mariette was by no means an excavator above reproach. His list of faults is a long one. He worked too quickly, running far too many sites simultaneously; he excavated at an unprecedented 35 sites in total. He kept lamentably few records, paid no attention to stratigraphy, happily split up collections, allowed his unskilled men to work without supervision for weeks at a time, and occasionally used explosives – we have already seen him blowing open the chambers of the Serapeum. It was not unknown for his workmen, employed on unproductive sites, to buy and rebury antiquities that they would then 'discover' to keep their site operational. Nevertheless, Mariette's appointment was an important one. For the first time, someone was assuming responsibility for Egypt's vulnerable heritage. Unfortunately, the funding supplied to finance this worthy initiative was woefully inadequate.

Mariette was a man of firmly held beliefs. And one of his beliefs was in the 'silence' of the pyramids. No pyramid had yet yielded a formal text, and most Egyptologists believed that none ever would. Only the elite, those who could afford to build expensive stone or rock-cut tombs, carved autobiographies on their tomb walls for passers-by to read. To open up the pyramids and search for non-existent texts would therefore be a complete waste of time and money. Everyone knew that kings, like their poorer subjects, went silent to the grave.

Then, in the early 1890s, a chance find revolutionized pyramid studies. The 6th Dynasty King Pepi I had built his pyramid at south Sakkara. This pyramid, stripped of much of its stone, had been for many years a shapeless, spreading mound. Unexceptional from the outside, it was explored by John Shae Perring, who failed to notice anything unusual in the dark and rubble-filled interior. Then, one lucky day:

> ... a fox managed to penetrate into a cavity situated in the rubbish surrounding a ruined pyramid, and the animal was followed by an Arab head-workman who, passing into the cavern, arrived at the

funerary chamber of King Pepi I. The walls of the tomb were covered with hieroglyphic text ... Mariette did not hear of this until a long time afterwards, when he was on his deathbed. He authorised excavations to be carried out near this pyramid, and on January 4th, 1881, sent Heinrich Brugsch and his brother Émile – his German assistants – to verify the Arab's statement. It is doubtful whether, before he drew his last breath, the illustrious archaeologist wished to credit the statement of his assistants.[4]

The fox had discovered the Pyramid Texts. The earlier pyramids were, indeed, dumb. But the later Old Kingdom pyramids contained writings, a selection of spells and utterances that were provided to help the deceased 5th and 6th Dynasty kings be reborn within the pyramid. Over 700 spells are known, with different pyramid owners selecting a combination that addressed their own particular concerns. This would be a fleeting fashion. The kings of the Middle Kingdom would abandon the Pyramid Texts, perhaps because they favoured spells painted on their (now vanished) wooden coffins.

Mariette died in Cairo just two weeks after the Brugsch brothers' expedition, and is now buried in an imposing sarcophagus in the garden of Cairo Museum. He was succeeded by Gaston Camille Charles Maspero, professor of Egyptology at the Collège de France, Paris, and founder of the French School of Archaeology in Cairo. Maspero was to serve as Director-General of the Antiquities Service and head of the Bulaq Museum between 1881 and 1886, then again from 1899 to 1914. He was a man of intense enthusiasm and ability, who, as well as producing many scholarly publications, took on the difficult task of cataloguing the rapidly expanding museum collection.

But Maspero was working in difficult times. In 1879, almost bankrupted by the spending of the Khedive Ismail, Egypt had been placed under joint British-French rule, with the British exercising responsibility for finances, and the French for justice and culture. In 1882 Ahmed Orabi led a failed nationalist revolt that ultimately led to the imposition of British military rule. The French, meanwhile, retained their control over all cultural matters, including archaeology. By convention, the Director-General of the Antiquities Service would always be French, and this would inevitably lead to a conflict of interests with the British excavators. With little money available for official excavations, and an apparently insatiable demand for antiquities, unofficial excavations now threatened to strip Egypt of all her treasures.

Maspero was personally inspired by the discovery of the Pyramid Texts. Within three years he had cleared the chambers and copied the texts in the pyramids of Unas, Teti, Pepi I, Merenre and Pepi II, publishing them with a translation. Subsequently Kurt Sethe published *The Pyramid Texts* (1908), the foundation stone of Pyramid Text studies and the basis of R. O. Faulkner's *Ancient Egyptian Pyramid Texts* (1969), which will only be superseded when all the fragmented Sakkara texts have been restored, collated and translated.

In 1881 Maspero spent a holiday in France. In so doing, he missed the greatest Egyptological find of the nineteenth century: the discovery of a collection of New Kingdom royal mummies hidden in a private tomb at Deir el-Bahari, Thebes. In his absence, the find was investigated by Émile Brugsch, one of the two Brugsch brothers last seen crawling into the pyramid of Pepi I. Heinrich Brugsch, the elder brother, was a linguist of renown, respected and admired by all who knew him. He had been a good friend to Mariette, and had assisted at the excavation of the Serapeum. His younger brother Émile, however, acquired a bad reputation that has followed him to the grave. Unpleasant and uncouth in manner, Émile was suspected by many of being heavily involved in selling the Museum's antiquities to private collectors. His handling of the Deir el Bahari cache certainly left a lot to be desired.

By the late 1870s the Theban antiquities market was flooded with valuable Third Intermediate Period funerary papyri. Suspecting that the locals had found a new royal tomb, the Antiquities Service launched an investigation. The chief suspects were the el-Rassul brothers of the west bank village of Gurna. The residents of Gurna, living on top of the dynastic cemetery, were all accomplished tomb robbers – and proud of it! The large el-Rassul clan had, over the previous few years, grown unaccountably rich. Now their house was searched, but nothing untoward was found. So, on 6 April 1881, Ahmed el-Rassul and his brother Hussein were arrested and sent in chains to Qena, the provincial capital. Here they were interrogated by the governor, Daud Pasha. The brothers were tortured – Hussein would be left with a permanent limp – but in the absence of any proof, the trial had to be abandoned, and after a spell in jail to teach them a lesson the brothers returned home.

The Antiquities Service continued their close watch on the el-Rassul family. Eventually Mohammed, the eldest brother, felt that the time was ripe for a confession. In return for immunity from prosecution, a sizeable reward and a good job working for the Antiquities Service, he told the whole story. Ten years earlier, in 1871, Ahmed el-Rassul had been scrambling about on the cliff face near Deir el-Bahari, searching for a lost goat (or maybe a lost tomb – a lost goat makes a good cover for a would-be robber), when he stumbled across a concealed entrance. He told his brothers of his find and they, sensing a good business opportunity, dropped a dead donkey down the tomb shaft. The smell would certainly discourage others from investigating.

Ahmed had stumbled across the family tomb of Pinodjem II, which, as we saw in Chapter One, housed both the Pinodjem family burials and a collection of New Kingdom royal mummies. But the New Kingdom mummies, already stripped by the High Priests of Amen, had no valuables left to offer a modern robber. A hole, torn into the chest bandages of Tuthmosis III, should have revealed the heart scarab (the scarab provided to protect and if necessary replace the heart), but didn't. So, ignoring the older bodies, the brothers concentrated on the Pinodjem family. Slowly, so that they didn't lower the price, they sold an unprecedented series of illustrated papyri, bronze vessels, *shabti* figurines and at least one mummy.

On 6 July 1881 Mohammed led a group of officials along the steep mountain path winding behind King Hatshepsut's beautiful mortuary temple. Émile Brugsch was the first to be lowered down the shaft. Bent double and clutching a lighted torch, and ignoring the remains of the unfortunate donkey, he passed through a tiny doorway into a low corridor. Here he found his way almost blocked by an enormous coffin. Soon the corridor turned to the right, away from the light, and here it was possible to stand upright. The corridor led via a short flight of steps to a chamber packed with an unimaginable collection of coffins. A second chamber held the ransacked burials of the Pinodjem family.

To Brugsch it all seemed like a dream. He was standing in the presence of some of Egypt's greatest kings, including Ahmose, Tuthmosis I–III, Ramesses I, Seti I and Ramesses II:

> Collecting my senses, I made the best examination of them I could by the light of my torch, and at once saw that they contained the mummies of royal personages of both sexes ...
>
> Their gold covering and their polished surfaces so plainly reflected my own excited visage that it seemed as though I was looking into the faces of my own ancestors ... I took in the situation quickly, with a gasp, and hurried to the open air lest I should be overcome and the glorious prize, still unrevealed, be lost to science.[5]

Brugsch was worried about the effect of the discovery on the locals, who might well object to the Antiquities Service removing such a large and valuable find. He also seems to have worried that the tomb, with its tinder-dry mummies, was a firetrap. In a state bordering on panic, he made a remarkably bad decision. Although he was a conservator and a skilled photographer, there would be no attempt to record the mummies as they lay. No plans would be drawn, no photographs taken. There wouldn't even be a listing of the mummies. The tomb was to be cleared at once, and the mum-

ABOVE: Gaston Camille
Charles Maspero, founder
of the French School of
Archaeology in Cairo, and
Director-General of the
Antiquities Service between
1881 and 1886, and 1899
and 1914.

RIGHT: Miss Amelia
Blandford Edwards:
novelist, founder of the
Egypt Exploration Fund
and supporter of the work
of Flinders Petrie.

ABOVE: The Giza pyramids of Menkaure (left), Khaefre (middle) and Khufu (right) have attracted Egyptologists, theoreticians and treasure seekers from medieval times to the present day.

LEFT: Amarna – the now-ruined city of Akhetaten, built by the 18th Dynasty King Akhenaten as the centre of the cult of the sun god, the Aten.

RIGHT: The remains of the Amarna royal archives, discovered in 1887, have allowed Egyptologists an insight into the complexities of New Kingdom diplomatic life. This Amarna Letter is written in cuneiform script.

ABOVE: The Amarna artists, denied the usual Egyptian repertoire of gods and goddesses, produced stunning scenes of the natural world. This fragment of a painted plaster floor is displayed in Cairo Museum.

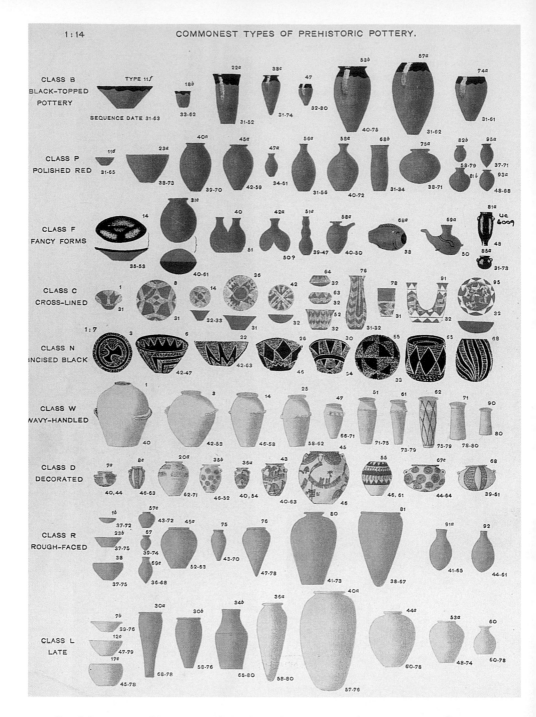

Petrie's system of 'sequence dating' used pottery typology to suggest dates for otherwise undatable prehistoric burials. A refined version of his system is still used by Egyptologists today.

RIGHT: The Narmer Palette –
a ceremonial cosmetic palette
dating to Dynasty 0 – shows
King Narmer in the act of
smiting an enemy. Facing
Narmer is an early version
of the hawk god, Horus.
Above him are two
representations of an early
form of Hathor.

BELOW: Ramesses II 'The
Great'. Ramesses' body was
recovered in 1881, a part of
the Deir el-Bahari mummy
cache. He was unwrapped
by Gaston Maspero in
Cairo Museum.

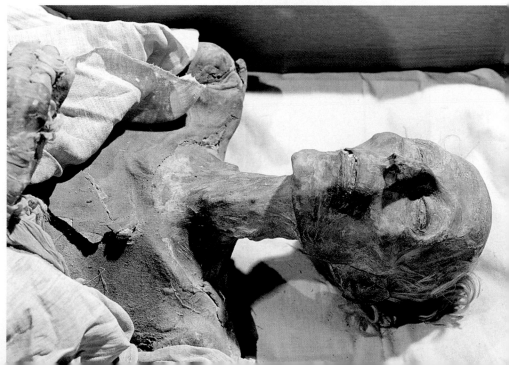

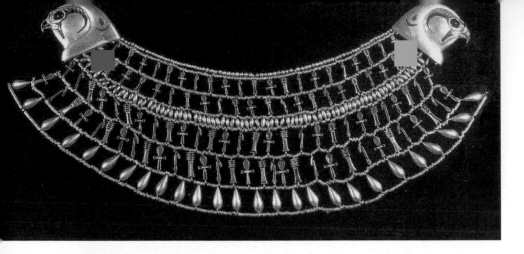

ABOVE: The Dahshur treasure, recovered by Jacques de Morgan between 1894 and 1895, included a series of exquisite Middle Kingdom pieces.

BELOW: The Valley of the Kings near Luxor: the hidden cemetery of the New Kingdom pharaohs.

mies were to be sent, for their own protection, to Cairo. Three hundred workmen set to work. The coffined bodies were snatched from their cool dark refuge, hauled up the shaft and laid out in the midsummer heat. Here they slowly baked and warped as they awaited their temporary wrappings. Two days later the first of the precious cargo was on its way north by steamer. As Egypt's kings made their last journey along the Nile, crowds gathered to watch. The women wept and tore their hair, while the men fired shotguns into the air. In Cairo a customs official, forced to register the cargo for tax purposes, famously classified the royal mummies as *farseekh*, or dried fish.

The Deir el-Bahari mummies were considered to be archaeological curiosities rather than important artifacts or, indeed, dead kings and queens. This was unfortunate; artifacts and the deceased would probably have been conserved with a degree of respect. The mummies, however, were considered to be of little archaeological importance, and were destined to be publicly unrolled at the first opportunity. The first king to come under the knife was Tuthmosis III, 'the Egyptian Napoleon', Egypt's greatest warrior king. His mummy had already been vandalized by the el-Rassul brothers, who had ripped open the wrappings on the left side of his chest, searching for his heart scarab. In July 1881 he was unwrapped by Émile Brugsch, and subsequently rebandaged. Gaston Maspero conducted a second unwrapping in 1886. Finally, the remains were examined by the distinguished anatomist Grafton Elliot Smith, who published his definitive *The Royal Mummies* in 1912.

Tuthmosis was not particularly well preserved, and not particularly pleasant to touch. His body was coated in a 'layer of whitish natron charged with human fat, greasy to the touch, foetid and strongly caustic'.[6] His head, arms, legs and feet had been broken off – presumably during a dynastic robbery – his arms were broken at the elbows, and his penis and testicles were missing. The priests who had restored his mummy had included wooden splints in the bandages to stiffen the corpse.

Chapter Seven

The Khedive Tewfik was present to watch Gaston Maspero unwrap Ramesses II on 1 June 1886. The autopsy took a mere quarter of an hour. Ramesses was in much better condition than Tuthmosis: 'the eyebrows are thick and white, the eyes are small and close together; the nose is long, thin, hooked like the noses of the Bourbons and slightly crushed at the tip by pressure of the bandages ...'[7] Maspero noted the king's firm, manly jaw, and prominent ears 'pierced, like those of a woman, for the wearing of earrings'. Later Elliot Smith, too, noted how the king's long, narrow, oval face was dominated by his prominent nose. Ramesses had been one of the few redheaded Egyptians, although at the time of his death, at over 90 years of age, his hair had turned completely white, and his face was heavily lined. He had also suffered from a series of painful ailments: he had severe arthritis in his hip, arteriosclerosis in his lower limbs, and badly decayed teeth.

Seti I, father of Ramesses II, was unwrapped by Maspero on 9 June 1886. Beneath the bandages was the best-preserved head of all the royal mummies: 'one of the most perfect examples of manly dignity displayed in a mummy that has come down to us from ancient Egypt'.[8] Unfortunately, his body had suffered considerable ancient damage, with the neck broken and the abdomen wall badly torn. A 'large, heart-shaped mass of stony consistency' found on the right side of the chest is probably his heart, accidentally removed and casually replaced during the packing process.

The other royal mummies proved to be less satisfactory. The 20th Dynasty Ramesses III was coated in hard black resin, and although scissors were used to chip his head free, his body remains wrapped to this day. Queen Ahmose Nefertari, consort of the 18th Dynasty King Ahmose, had gone bad and emitted a terrible smell. She was temporarily buried beneath the museum storehouse; when she was recovered a few months later the smell had vanished. The queen's right hand was missing – presumably stolen by thieves in search of bracelets and rings – and she had extensions woven into her own thin hair.

Two of the mummies had met unnatural deaths. The 17th Dynasty King Sekenenre Tao II had been killed on the battlefield, fighting against the northern King Apophis. His head clearly shows the distinctive wounds made by bronze Hyksos battleaxes. An anonymous mummy seems to have met an even more unpleasant end. A rolled sheepskin found in a plain wooden coffin yielded a male body whose face was twisted into an expression of suffering. The unnamed man had had his hands and feet bound, and all his internal organs were intact, leading to suggestions that he may have been buried alive in his sheepskin shroud.

IN 1869 THOMAS COOK SENT his first cargo of tourists down the Nile. The Prince and Princess of Wales had already enjoyed a Nile cruise in 1862, and Egypt suddenly found herself fashionable as she had never been before. Far cheaper than Europe, the warm climate was attractive to those who would prefer to avoid the damp and gloom of winter. Cairo already had a thriving, and entirely European, social scene. There were hotels, a sporting club, after-noon tea on the terrace, dinner dances and – as a nod to the antiq-uities – occasional picnics at the pyramids.

Among the new wave of visitors was Miss Amelia Ann Blanford Edwards, a lady novelist of some repute, whose recently published travel book, *A Midsummer Ramble in the Dolomites* (1873), had been very well received at home. Miss Edwards wrote in a lively, relaxed style, combining the story of her personal adventures with scholarly detail and standard tourist information. Now she was to write the story of her adventures in Egypt. Quite properly, Miss Edwards travelled with a companion, a Miss Lucy Renshawe, who appears simply as 'L' in her narrative. The two ladies started their adventure in Cairo, where they were struck by the sheer number of people wishing to enjoy the Egyptian experience:

It is the traveller's lot to dine at many table-d'hôtes in the course of many wanderings; but it seldom befalls him to make one of a more miscellaneous gathering than that which overfills the great dining-room at Shepheard's Hotel in Cairo during the beginning and height of the regular Egyptian season. Here assemble daily some two to three hundred persons of all ranks, nationalities, and pursuits; half of whom are Anglo-Indians homeward or outward bound, European residents, or visitors established in Cairo for the winter. The other half, it may be taken for granted, are going up the Nile. So composite and incongruous is this body of Nile-goers, young and old, well-dressed and ill-dressed, learned and unlearned, that the new-comer's first impulse is to inquire from what motives so many persons of dissimilar tastes and training can be led to embark on an expedition which is, to say the least of it, very tedious, very costly, and of an altogether exceptional interest.[9]

The two ladies hired the *Philae*: a *dahabiyeh*, or flat-bottomed houseboat with sails which, equipped with a crew of 20 (including two waiters) and a grand piano, would carry them in style as far as Abu Simbel. 'I may add that the whole cost of the *Philae* – food, dragoman's wages, boat-hire, cataract, everything included except wine – was about £10 per day.' Their journey was to be a long, fascinating and occasionally uncomfortable one – there were sandstorms, cataracts, visits to the monuments and day after day spent waiting for the wind to carry them south. Miss Edwards, 'the Writer', got to know and love Egypt well, although, isolated on her boat and constantly in the company of other tourists, she did not get to know the Egyptian people quite so well. Occasionally her comments jar the modern reader into remembering that she was a Victorian, with all the certainties of her race, religion and class. This is a very minor quibble, and *A Thousand Miles Up the Nile* (1877) remains essential reading for anyone with an interest in visiting Egypt.

At Abu Simbel they moored for 18 days beside the Great Temple:

... it was wonderful to wake every morning close under the steep bank, and without lifting one's head from the pillow, to see that row of giant faces so close against the sky. They showed unearthly enough by moonlight; but not half so unearthly as in the grey of dawn. At that hour, the most solemn of the twenty-four, they wore a fixed and fatal look that was little less than appalling. As the sky warmed, this awful look was succeeded by a flush that mounted and deepened like the rising flush of life. For a moment they seemed to glow – to smile – to be transfigured. Then came a flash, as of thought itself. It was the first instantaneous flash of the risen sun. It lasted less than a second. It was gone almost before one could say that it was there. The next moment, mountain, river, and sky, were distinct in the steady light of day; and the colossi – mere colossi now – sat serene and stony in the open sunshine.

Every morning I waked in time to witness that daily miracle. Every morning I saw those awful brethren pass from death to life, from life to sculptured stone. I brought myself almost to believe that at last there must sooner or later come some one sunrise when the ancient charm would snap asunder, and the giants must arise and speak.[10]

Back in the hustle and bustle of Luxor, they witnessed the officially sanctioned opening of a tomb, visited the west bank, and heard rumours of another, illegal tomb, which was said to have yielded a mummy and a wonderful papyrus:

Now, neither L. nor the Writer desired to become the happy proprietor of an ancient Egyptian; but the papyrus was a thing to be thought of. In a fatal hour we expressed a wish to see it. From that moment every mummy-snatcher in the place regarded us as his lawful prey. Beguiled into one den after another, we were shown all the stolen goods in Thebes. Some of the things were very curious and interesting ... Pieces of mummy-case and wall-sculpture and sepulchral tablets abounded; and on one occasion we were introduced into the presence of – a mummy! ... Meanwhile we tried in vain to get sight of the coveted papyrus. A grave Arab dropped in once or twice after nightfall, and talked it over vaguely with the dragoman; but never came to the point. He offered it first, with a mummy, for £100. Finding, however, that we would neither buy his papyrus unseen nor his mummy at any price, he haggled and hesitated for a day or two, evidently trying to play us off against some rival or rivals unknown, and then finally disappeared. These rivals, we afterwards found, were the M.B.s [friends of the Writer]. They bought both mummy and papyrus at an enormous price; and then, unable to endure the perfume of their ancient Egyptian, drowned the dear departed at the end of the week.[11]

For a long time Egyptologists speculated that the unfortunate mummy thrown into the Nile by the M.B.s may have been the missing mummy of Ramesses I, which had apparently been taken from the Deir el-Bahari cache by the el-Rassul brothers and sold. This mummy has, however, recently been rediscovered in Niagara, USA, and has been returned to Luxor Museum.

Miss Edwards and L had entered the murky world of the illegal antiquities trade. In spite of all Mariette's rules and regulations, locals were still earning a healthy income from selling a mixture of genuine and fake antiquities to foreigners. Increasing numbers of tourists simply increased demand; most were aware that they were breaking the law, but this merely added a frisson of excitement to the deal. Miss Edwards realized from the outset that this was wrong. Illegal excavations destroyed sites and dispersed collections that might have an important story to tell. An isolated artifact, such as a gold diadem, would, of course, have a high monetary value, but a gold diadem found in an untouched tomb, surrounded by other funerary objects, would be priceless to a scholar. Yet there was always the nagging feeling that purchasing an already excavated antiquity preserved it from a worse fate. And, of course, it provided an income for an otherwise desperately poor family. As the authorities could not cope with the sheer scale of the finds, was it not better to buy and export an antiquity that could then find a caring home in a European collection? As she looked at the crumbling sites, prey to increasing numbers of dealers and collectors, Miss Edwards started to wonder.

Her Egyptian experience altered the course of her life. *A Thousand Miles Up the Nile*, published two years after her return, was a huge success, sparking increased interest in everything Egyptian. But it was to be her penultimate book. In 1882, in association with Dr Reginald Poole, Keeper of the Department of Coins and Medals at the British Museum (who had spent a happy childhood in Egypt), and the eminent surgeon Sir Erasmus Wilson (who, having amassed a fortune on the Stock Exchange, had personally financed the transport of Cleopatra's Needle from Egypt to London, an indulgence that cost him almost £10,000), Amelia Edwards founded the Egypt Exploration Fund (EEF), a London-based society today known as the Egypt Exploration Society (EES). The Fund set out to finance properly conducted excavations by professionally competent excavators, with the approval of the Egyptian authorities. The first excavations would concentrate on the Nile Delta. A press announcement, published in several newspapers and journals, set out the aims in more detail:

> To raise a fund for the purpose of conducting excavations in the Delta, which up to this time has been very rarely visited by travellers and where but one site has been explored by archaeologists. Yet here must undoubtedly lie concealed the documents of a lost period of Biblical history – documents which we may confidently hope will furnish the key to a whole series of perplexing problems.

The Delta was chosen for the initial excavation for the simple, and clever, reason that no one else was interested in excavating in such a damp and unproductive area. Later, it was hoped, the Fund might be able to excavate further up the Nile. The mention of the Bible was another clever touch, guaranteed to attract backers. There were many who still believed that Egypt held the key to understanding the truth of the biblical stories, and the Delta featured heavily in the book of Exodus. Despite Poole's involvement, the British Museum was lukewarm in its support and Dr Samuel Birch, Keeper of Oriental Antiquities, wanted nothing to do with the Fund and its 'emotional archaeology'.[12] This was irritating, but didn't matter overmuch. Miss Edwards had the support of the grievously sick Mariette and, more importantly, of his successor, Gaston Maspero, who was a keen, if unlikely, admirer of her novels. Maspero knew from first-hand experience that Egypt did not have the finances to protect her own heritage. If the monuments were to be preserved through survey and excavation, outside help would be needed.

Who would head the first excavation? There was a shortage of British Egyptologists. The Fund's first choice, the German Heinrich Schliemann, fresh from his triumphs at Troy, was not to Maspero's liking; the Fund would be the first foreign organization to be granted official permission to excavate in Egypt, and the political situation was simply too sensitive for so flamboyant a character. Maspero's views on the appointment of Schliemann are worth quoting at some length, as they provide us with an insight into the difficulties facing excavators at this time:

> ... national vanity – if the word national means anything in Egypt –
> has been violently excited by recent events. It is taken for granted
> that Egypt is the premier country of the world, the mother of
> civilization both ancient and modern, and that foreigners in
> spending money for the benefit of the Egyptian Government are
> doing no more than to render due homage to Egypt's superiority:
> the money is accepted as an act of grace, nothing more. You will
> appreciate that, holding such views, the minister in office and
> those who will succeed him have sensitive skins. An imprudent
> word, a slip in the manner of presenting the case, might frustrate

everything at the last moment. M. Schliemann, amongst his other virtues, has not that of discretion. He loves publicity and controversial newspaper articles, and never lets an opportunity slip of speaking of himself ... at the slightest difficulty we should receive the order to suspend everything, and everything would indeed have to be suspended, and at least the English Government would be very reluctant to stir up diplomatic difficulties over excavations directed by a German, such as Schliemann, and a Frenchman, who would be myself.[13]

And so the exuberant German was rejected, and instead the Swiss Egyptologist Édouard Naville was chosen chosen to head Britain's first official excavation at the Delta site of Tell el-Maskhuta. The appointment seemed an ideal one. Naville was a calm and diplomatic man, a keen biblical scholar and a close personal friend of Maspero. Unfortunately, he was not, and never would be, a dedicated excavator. First and foremost a theoretician – a linguist and an expert on Egyptian religion – Naville regarded excavation very much as a means to an end. He had no interest in small-scale finds, and no experience of, or interest in, conservation. A site without texts and large-scale buildings was, to him, hardly worth investigating, and he was happy to delegate site supervision to others if, in so doing, it enabled him to work on his own interests. This approach would lead to problems in the future, but for now all went well. Naville was able to confirm that Tell el-Maskhuta was indeed the biblical city of Pithom (the Ramesside town of Per Atum), and he returned home with two impressive statues, a personal gift from the Khedive for Sir Erasmus Wilson, who in turn presented the statues to the British Museum.

The next year's excavations were scheduled to begin at biblical Zoan (San el-Hagar, ancient Tanis), but Naville was too busy to participate, and a new excavator had to be found. Maspero had always believed that the Fund should employ a novice who could be trained in the appropriate techniques:

I do not know by what mischance England has not yet produced a young Egyptologist: the school is dying out without renewing itself. I have therefore thought of asking you for a young man who has made proficient classical studies, who is interested in the history and the languages of the East, and who, with a little goodwill, could soon become something of an Egyptologist. I should then be able to give him some teaching ... [14]

The Fund agreed. They chose the relatively inexperienced and self-educated Flinders Petrie, a practical young man who had already proved his dedication to ancient Egypt by single-handedly surveying the Great Pyramid. The results of his survey, *The Pyramids and Temples of Giza*, had just been published, and had impressed Fund members most favourably. This was to prove an inspired appointment. Amelia Edwards died of bronchitis on 15 April 1892. In her will she left her extensive library, as well as £2400, to University College London. The money was to be used to finance 'a Professorship of Egyptian Archaeology and Philology including the deciphering and reading of Hieroglyphic and other Ancient Egyptian scripts or writings'. This was to be the first British Chair in Egyptology, and Miss Edwards had privately expressed the wish that the first professor would be Flinders Petrie. He was. Professor Petrie was to hold the post for the next 40 years.

CHAPTER EIGHT

>—<

FLINDERS PETRIE: FATHER OF POTS

WILLIAM MATTHEW FLINDERS PETRIE, known as Flinders throughout his professional career, was born on 3 June 1853, the son of William Petrie and his wife Anne Flinders. The happy couple were exceptionally talented, but slightly unusual in their backgrounds and habits. Anne, the only child of Captain Mathew Flinders, explorer of Australia, had learned German and Italian at school before teaching herself Hebrew, Greek, Spanish and Portuguese. As an adult she had published an impressive assortment of stories, novels and poems. William was a chemist with a deep interest in electricity, magnetism, maps and diagrams. He had numerous ingenious inventions to his credit but little business acumen, and so condemned his family to a life of genteel poverty. A member of a strict fundamentalist Christian sect, he was, unusually for his time, a vegetarian, an enthusiastic homoeopath and a strict teetotaller. Anne tolerated, but did not share, his views. She insisted that her only child eat meat, and she ensured that he was secretly baptized into the Church of England.

The young Flinders, an asthmatic, was considered too delicate for school. He was to be educated at home by governesses. It would be a thorough, if unconventional, education. His father would teach him chemistry and a literal interpretation of the Bible, while his mother taught him about minerals, fossils and ancient coins, and his great-aunt (who had also taught his mother) would teach him languages and mathematics. At the age of eight, his small head a muddle of ancient languages and arithmetic, Flinders had a break-down. On doctor's orders, all formal lessons were forbidden for two years. With outdoor games also banned – his chest was not consid-ered strong enough – Flinders grew up an isolated but by no means unhappy child; a voracious reader, passionately interested in coin collecting, music and chess. At the age of 24 he would attend a uni-versity extension course in algebra and trigonometry, and this would represent his entire formal education. Meanwhile, archaeology was becoming an increasingly important part of his life.

In his late teens Flinders had determined to record the prehistoric earthworks in his home county of Kent. Soon after, he had widened his ambitions and set about recording all the prehistoric monuments in southern England. Next he and his father decided to make a detailed survey of Stonehenge; the end result was the most accurate plan of Stonehenge so far. Indoors, in the galleries of the British Museum and in the British Museum Library, Flinders continued to measure and read about measurements. The results would be pub-lished in 1877 as *Inductive Metrology: or the Recovery of Ancient Measurements from the Monuments.*

Finally, the Petries, father and son, determined to apply their sur-veying techniques to the Great Pyramid. Their interest in ancient Egypt had been sparked by a chance find on a bookstall:

... One day I brought back from Smith's bookstall, in 1866, a volume by Piazzi Smyth, *Our Inheritance in the Great Pyramid.* The views, in conjunction with his old friendship for the author, strongly attracted my father, and for some years I was urged on in what seemed so enticing a field of coincidence. I little thought how, fifteen years later, I should reach the 'ugly little fact which killed the beautiful theory'; but it was this interest which led my father to encourage me to go out and do the survey of the Great Pyramid ...[1]

It comes as little surprise that the theory of the 'pyramid inch', a convincing blend of fundamental Christianity and mathematics, would have a strong appeal to the deeply religious, and deeply mathematical, Petries. By a curious coincidence they were already well acquainted with its author. Many years previously William Petrie had courted Henrietta Smyth, sister of Piazzi. Her parents had considered the match unsuitable – by anyone's reckoning the impecunious William was not much of a catch – and Henrietta had subsequently married the elderly Professor Baden-Powell. In so doing she became the mother of the founder of the Boy Scout movement. The two families had remained close friends, and it was at the Smyth family home that William Petrie had first met Anne Flinders.

Now William and Flinders entered into lengthy correspondence with Piazzi Smyth, questioning and even suggesting improvements to his mathematical calculations. Not surprisingly, Smyth's friendship cooled somewhat under the barrage of queries. Meanwhile, the Petries grew increasingly disenchanted with his methodology, until eventually they determined to test his theory – a theory which, being totally dependent on the measurements and ratios of the pyramid structure, could be subject to rigorous scientific assessment. They would measure the pyramid inside and out and, once and for all, determine the truth of the 'pyramid inch'. But William, always indecisive, kept delaying their departure until eventually, in 1880, Flinders lost patience with his father and set off for Egypt alone.

At Giza he quickly settled into an empty tomb. With the addition of some shelving, a new door and a petroleum stove, it made a comfortable and inexpensive base. Cheapness was important because Flinders was entirely self-funded. Much of his equipment, including his rope ladders and many of his surveying instruments, were home-made to save money. Now he had just one workman: Ali Gabry, an experienced excavator who had already worked with Vyse, Dixon and Smyth, was his sole assistant. Working conditions within the pyramid were not good; it was dirty and hot, and unwanted visitors could be a nuisance. It made sense to work as much as possible at night, when the plateau was deserted and unnecessary clothing could be removed without causing offence:

> It was often most convenient to strip entirely for work, owing to the heat and absence of any current of air, in the interior. For outside work in the hot weather, vest and pants were suitable, and if pink they kept the tourist at bay, as the creature seemed to him too queer for inspection.[2]

Petrie developed a complicated set of triangulations which extended over the entire pyramid site. This work was painfully slow; it took several hours each morning to set out the survey points, and all measurements had to be double-checked. At the same time, he collected information on the construction of the pyramid, determined to remove, once and for all, the lingering suspicion that the pyramid could not have been built by the dynastic Egyptians. After two seasons of survey and structural examination, including some limited excavation within the pyramid, his figures were collated in England. The end result was so accurate that Petrie's survey is still used by archaeologists today. His figures flatly contradicted the measurements that underpinned Smyth's work – the 'pyramid inch' simply didn't exist – while his structural examination showed that the pyramid could, indeed, have been made by human hands:

> ... Instead of a pyramid measuring 9140 inches, as was supposed, it measured only 9069 inches.
> Hence all theorising about the days in the year being represented was entirely erroneous. The size of the pyramid was ruled by being 7 × 40 Egyptian cubits (20.6 inches) high and 11 × 40 cubits wide. This is strongly confirmed by the pyramid of Meydum, which preceded it in date, being 7 × 25 cubits high and 11 × 25 cubits wide; it shows the use of the same system of a large number of cubits, 25 or 40, as a unit, multiplied by 7 or 11 for the dimensions. The angle of the slope required for this 7 and 11

proportion is within the small uncertainty (two minutes) of the actual remains.[3]

Khufu had built himself a pyramid of exceptional and certainly unprecedented precision. It stood 480.93 feet (146.59 metres) high, with a slope of 51° 50'40". Its sides, with an average length of 755.67 feet (230.33 metres), varied by less than 1.9 inches (5 centimetres) and were orientated almost exactly towards true north. Its base was almost completely level, varying by less than 1.2 inches (3 centimetres) from north to south side. Inside there were the three chambers already discussed in Chapter Six. Outside, the pyramid was surrounded by a narrow courtyard paved with large limestone slabs, which had once been defined by a tall limestone wall. There had also been a mortuary or memorial chapel, a causeway, and a valley temple opening onto a small harbour, although these had almost entirely disappeared. A tiny satellite pyramid lay outside the enclosure wall, to the southeast of the main pyramid; this was a part of the king's own mortuary provision, its purpose unknown. Three small-scale pyramids on the eastern side of the Great Pyramid, each with its own small mortuary chapel, provided a final resting place for the three most important royal women.

How, if we are to discount divine intervention, could such precision have been achieved on a Bronze Age building site? The Egyptians don't tell us much about their construction industry, but it is obvious from their surviving buildings that they were accomplished, practical builders. Measurements would have posed little difficulty – tax collectors had been measuring the fields accurately for years. The location of true north, too, was easy for a people whose priests regularly studied the heavens; north could be determined at night by studying the stars, or by day using the shadow cast by a vertical pole. Wooden set squares, and the use of the 3–4–5 right-angled triangle method, would ensure that all right angles were true.

It is usually estimated that Khufu's pyramid contains up to 2,300,000 blocks, but this is likely to be an exaggeration; we cannot see beneath the outer stones, and so cannot tell how much sand and rubble was incorporated into the bulk of the masonry. The cut blocks were dragged from the nearby limestone quarry. As they were laid in higher and higher courses, it became increasingly important to maintain the correct angle of slope. If the diagonals rising from the four corners did not remain true, the pyramid would appear to twist. Masons' marks scrawled on individual blocks show that the slope was recalculated as successive courses were laid. A shortage of working space meant that the blocks destined for the uppermost courses had to be cut before they were raised. As building work progressed, the outer face of the expensive casing stones was left untrimmed. Only when the pyramid was complete, and the ramps were being dismantled, would the casing be cut back, working from top to bottom.

Ramps leave little archaeological evidence; the one thing that we do know about Egyptian ramps is that they were not all the same. Builders, naturally enough, tailored their ramps to suit local conditions. It seems likely, but cannot yet be proven, that the Great Pyramid was built using a single, straight ramp stretching up to a third of the height of the pyramid, and then a smaller, wrap-round ramp, which would reach the summit.

His trips to Giza had made one thing very clear to Petrie. Egypt's monuments, even monuments as well known as the pyramids, were under dire threat. Those charged with their preservation were sometimes the worst offenders:

> I hear that Mariette most rascally blasted to pieces all the fallen parts of the granite temple [Khaefre's mortuary temple] by a large gang of soldiers, to clear it out instead of lifting the stones and replacing them by means of tackle. The savage indifference of the Arabs, who have even stripped the alabaster off the granite temple since Mariette uncovered it, and who are not at all watched here, is partly superseded by the most barbaric sort of regard for the monuments by those in power. Nothing seems to be done with any uniform and regular plan, work is begun and left unfinished;

no regard is paid to future requirements of exploration, and no
civilized or labour-saving appliances are used. It is sickening to see
the rate at which everything is being destroyed, and the little
regard paid to preservation.[4]

Gaston Maspero was of the same mind. Something had to be done
to save the pyramids. Eventually it was agreed that professional
Egyptologists should be invited to apply for permission to work at
Giza. Three teams responded: an Italian team led by Ernesto
Schiaparelli, a German team led by Ludwig Borchardt, and an
American team led by George Reisner. After much animated discussion, the cemetery was split in three, with the Italians receiving permission to work on Khufu's pyramid, the Germans Khaefre's, and
the Americans Menkaure's. Today work continues at Giza, but is
concentrated less on the pyramids and more on the surrounding
cemeteries, temples and settlements.

In October 1883 Flinders Petrie was again preparing to travel to
Egypt, this time at the request of the Egypt Exploration Fund. He
was to excavate at San el-Hagar (ancient Tanis), receiving £250 a
month to finance the excavation, as well as his own personal
expenses. The site was a huge mound that had been transformed, in
the rainy season, into a muddy morass; partially excavated by Lepsius
and Mariette, it had been abandoned without any thought to the
preservation of its antiquities. The first days were spent camping as
Petrie, undaunted by personal discomfort, but requiring dry storage
for his discoveries, built a suitable dig house. Then a mixed workforce of men, boys and girls was recruited, and, with the loyal Ali
Gabry by his side, work started in earnest. Petrie was able to clear
and plan the temple, excavate several Roman houses, and recover
over 200 demotic papyri. The season was an unqualified success, and
the EEF was delighted.

Everyone agreed that Petrie should head the Fund's next mission,
which would focus on the Delta site of Naukratis (modern el-Nibeira),
a Greek trading centre visited by Herodotus in the fifth century BC.

This time he was to have an assistant. The young Francis Llewellyn Griffith, inspired by Belzoni's book, had written to Petrie seeking advice on a career in Egyptology. Petrie had referred the matter to Miss Edwards, and she, with her usual efficiency, had found enough sponsors to endow a scholarship fund to support him in his studies. One condition of the scholarship was that Griffith had to spend part of each year in Egypt. The money would be well spent – Griffith was destined to become the first professor of Egyptology at Oxford University. Now, as a novice, he helped Petrie with his excavations.

Meanwhile, back in London, the EEF was in trouble. Sir Erasmus Wilson had died in 1884, before he could change his will to benefit the Fund. Money, which had always been taken somewhat for granted, became a matter of paramount importance. Miss Edwards, living in Bristol, and Dr Poole, living in London, were running the society in their spare time, and both were stressed and exhausted. Petrie, never one to suffer fools gladly, was growing increasingly exasperated over the lack of communication, the muddles and the squandering of precious funds. He himself had always struggled to save money – eating the most basic and unpalatable of rations, making his own equipment and packing cases, and never hiring a donkey when he could walk, even if it meant a stroll of 18 miles or more. In 1886 Petrie severed his connection with the Fund. He had also quarrelled with Wallis Budge, Assistant Keeper of Egyptian and Assyrian Antiquities at the British Museum, and was on bad terms with Émile Brugsch, representative of the Antiquities Service in Cairo. The future, even to one used to scrimping and saving, must have looked bleak:

> The work for the Fund having now ceased, I was left to my own resources, and it was needful to plan accordingly. From my great-aunt, and supplemented by a small share of family property, I had £110 a year; of that about £40 was due at home for my living while in England, leaving £70 in all to face work in Egypt, and I had no more fixed income till I was forty.[5]

Petrie did, however, have some work lined up. The geneticist Francis Galton had commissioned him to take photographs of the heads of the enemies and allies of Egypt, who could be seen processing across the walls of the New Kingdom temples. Galton needed the photographs for his work on racial types, and had obtained a grant of £20 to pay for them. Petrie joined forces with Griffith. They hired a small boat in Cairo and embarked on a trip to Aswan. It was to be a working holiday. By day they examined sites, copied inscriptions and collected pottery and bone samples. At night they read, wrote and tried to relax in the one cramped cabin, which served as bedroom, living room, study and dining room.

Back in Luxor, where he camped in the temple and recorded his heads, Petrie received good news. An anonymous benefactor was prepared to finance, up to a limit of £500, excavations in the Western Valley. But, as Eugène Grébaut, Maspero's replacement as Director-General of the Antiquities Service, refused point-blank to grant Petrie permission to excavate in or anywhere near the Valley of the Kings, the project had to be abandoned before it had started. Grébaut's appointment was to prove a disaster for British Egyptology. Lazy and ill suited to the demands of his post, he showed a consistent anti-British bias. Even Wallis Budge, not a natural supporter of Petrie and his fellow archaeologists, noted that 'all those who had at heart the progress of Egyptology, and the welfare of the national collection in Egypt, regretted the appointment'.[6] Grébaut's major achievement was to supervise the transfer of the collection from the old, cramped museum at Bulaq to new and rather unsatisfactory quarters at Giza. Unfortunately, but predictably, several valuable items went missing during the move.

Petrie's journey back to Cairo was memorable only because it was undertaken in the company of half a dozen convicted prisoners, all chained together and sleeping alongside Petrie on deck. There was just time for a partial survey of the Dahshur pyramids before it was time to return to London. Petrie brought with him an anonymous mummy, purchased for £20, which had been ordered by a friend of Miss Edwards. Genuine mummies were all the rage in the West, and

Petrie was not such an archaeological purist that he would refuse to bring home a present for his benefactor. Many of these exported mummies would, when their owners tired of them, make their way into local museums.

Petrie's anonymous benefactor was the Lancashire businessman Jesse Haworth, a friend of Amelia Edwards with a strong interest in the Bible and its links with ancient Egypt. Another backer, too, was preparing to step forward. Martin Kennard, another friend of Miss Edwards, had already given generously to the EEF. Unlike Haworth, Kennard had his own private collection of antiquities, and he was happy to pay Petrie to expand it. Financially secure at last, Petrie set off for the Faiyum site of Hawara, home of the Middle Kingdom pyramid of Amenemhat III and the 'labyrinth' already investigated by Belzoni.

On the north side of the Hawara pyramid Petrie found a large Roman cemetery. Initially he was disappointed; he would have much preferred a Middle Kingdom necropolis to match the pyramid. But this was no ordinary cemetery. Many of its mummies were equipped with lifelike, beautifully painted wood-panel faces. The spectacular mummies soon attracted a series of prestigious visitors to the site:

> From all the pottery and occasionally dated papyri, also a Flavian name on a head cover, the dating of all these portraits was pretty well fixed to AD 100–250 ... Sometimes we found portraits on alternate days, but occasional rushes poured in, of five in twenty-four hours. A boy came with a report of a portrait, and, before I could reach it, a party arrived. Schliemann, short, round-headed, round-faced, round-hatted, great round-goggle-eyed, spectacled, cheeriest of beings; dogmatic, but always ready for facts ...
>
> Then a report of another mummy ... a procession of three gilt mummies is seen coming across the mounds, glittering in the sun. Painted portraits, but the head covered with bright red-brown varnish, and scenes in relief gilt all over ...[7]

Sometimes the mummy bandages hid distressing secrets:

> One coffin that I opened contained a tiny child's figure; I wished
> to preserve the painted cartonnage, but on pulling away the
> dummy sandals, I found no infantile toes, but a man's knee joint.
> It seems that the undertaker had not troubled to mummify the
> little brat at all, but had picked up three old leg bones, and an old
> skull full of mud, and the rascal had done them up tidily to satisfy
> the parental feelings, and put on a little gilt headpiece and sandals
> to look proper.[8]

Not all the mummies in the cemetery had portrait faces; Petrie estimated that maybe 1–2 per cent of the mummies, of both sexes and
a wide age-range, were so decorated. He personally recovered 60
mummy portraits in varying condition. The mummies themselves he
discarded, but, perhaps mindful of Galton's work, he retained their
heads so that they might one day be compared with their portraits.
The grave goods buried with the mummies included pottery, clothing, toys, trinkets and papyri; there were socks with a separate 'finger' for the big toe so that they might be worn with sandals (these
fascinated Petrie, who himself frequently neglected to wear socks on
the questionable grounds that they were unhygienic), and there was
even a papyrus scroll of the second book of the *Iliad*. There was
also, nearby, a crocodile cemetery dedicated to the crocodile-headed
god Sobek. Here Petrie found mummified crocodiles in all stages of
development, from fully grown adults to eggs.

As work progressed in the Roman cemetery, Petrie turned his
attention to the pyramid. This was not Amenemhat's first pyramid.
Early in his reign he had started to build at Dahshur, and by Year 15
his mud-brick, stone-lined pyramid had been substantially complete.
Then disaster struck. The bedrock was not strong enough to support the weight of the superstructure, and the internal walls started
to crack and buckle. Amenemhat was forced to start all over again.
This time he decided to build at Hawara. As time was now running

out – it was essential that the tomb be substantially complete before the king died – his second pyramid would have to be smaller than his first.

Internally his pyramid was complicated by a series of doglegged passageways and hidden doorways designed to fool robbers. In this it failed – the pyramid was thoroughly emptied in antiquity. But it did fool Petrie, who, unable to detect an entrance on the north face (the usual face for pyramid entrances), decided to tunnel his way through the masonry, aiming for the burial chamber. This was a dangerous, difficult and unnecessarily destructive task that was to take two seasons of hard work to complete. But eventually Petrie reached the burial chamber and, unable to locate its door, was preparing to enter via the ceiling:

> By January 6, we got through into the upper chamber. There I wriggled head down into a forced hole which opened into the actual burial, and saw two sarcophagi in the water; I had to be dragged out by the heels. After enlarging the hole a little, I could enter. The chamber was one solid block of quartzite, twenty-two feet long, eight feet wide, and six feet deep inside, polished and cut so clean at the corners that I did not realize that it was not built, until I searched for a joint and found none. The water was up to one's waist, so the chips could only be searched by pushing them with the feet on to the blade of a hoe, and so lifting them up. I promised half a piastre for every hieroglyph found, and a dollar for a cartouche. This ensured a thorough search. The next day the name appeared, Amenemhat III, as was expected; the surface being half decayed by the water there could not be any doubt of its age.[9]

No wonder Petrie had failed to find a doorway. The burial chamber had been hollowed out of one enormous block of quartzite which, Petrie estimated, must have weighed 110 tons. It had been roofed with three large quartzite slabs so that the entire room might serve as a gigantic stone sarcophagus. Now, with the burial chamber breached, Petrie was able to work backwards and find the proper pyramid entrance that lay, unexpectedly, on the south face.

From Hawara, Petrie moved on to Illahun (Lahun), close by the opening to the Faiyum. Here the 12th Dynasty king Senwosret II had raised a mud-brick pyramid with a high-quality limestone covering. Once again, there was no obvious way into the pyramid. Petrie, baffled and reluctant to repeat his tunnelling experience, spent months hunting for a doorway. Eventually, when Petrie himself was absent from the site, the secret was revealed:

> Fraser employed a few men, including two old plunderers. When digging along the pyramid they found a shaft on the south side, forty feet deep, and on cleaning it they got into the pyramid before Fraser. The alabaster altar of Senusert [Senwosret] was secured, and there was no rumour of anything else being found by them in the pyramid.[10]

The plundered burial chamber still housed the king's red granite sarcophagus; when Petrie revisited the site a quarter of a century later, he would also discover a gold uraeus (the serpent headdress worn by Egypt's kings) and some fragments of leg bone.

The main pyramid was surrounded by an unprecedented nine queens' pyramids, and enclosed by two walls. The inner wall was built of stone, and the outer wall of mud-brick. To the south of the mud-brick wall there were four shaft tombs. Here, in 1914 Petrie and his young colleague Guy Brunton were to discover the 'Illahun treasure': five boxes of jewellery and cosmetic items hidden in a plastered and mud-filled recess in the tomb of Princess Sit-Hathor-Iunet. Petrie's one regret was that, as he was suffering from 'a strain', Brunton had to do all the excavation work. Gaston Maspero, feeling that the jewellery mirrored the treasure that de Morgan had found at Dahshur, was happy for most of this jewellery to leave Egypt – but where was it to go? Petrie's first thought was to offer it to the British Museum, tentatively suggesting a price of £8000:

> The answer from the British Museum to my letter was that, if when they saw the things they thought they were worth it, they might be able to put their hands on a couple of thousand – a ludicrous treatment of the matter, which closed that door.[11]

The jewellery of Princess Sit-Hathor-Iunet is today displayed in the Metropolitan Museum of Art, New York.

Close by his pyramid, Senwosret had built a town to house the priests, scribes and labourers who would be needed to maintain his funerary cult for all eternity. This town, Petrie discovered, was still substantially intact beneath its blanket of sand. His journal entry for 24 February – 2 March 1889 reads as follows:

> The town beyond the temple (called Medinet Kahun, I hear) I now suspect to be of the age of the temple, 12th Dynasty, and to be almost untouched since then. If so, it will be a prize to work for historical interest of dated objects. I cannot be certain as yet of its age, but the pottery is quite unlike any that I yet know, except some chips of 12th Dynasty that I got at Hawara: and the walls of the town run regardless of natural features, over a low hill and back again but square with the temple.[12]

Domestic sites are extremely rare in Egypt. Built of mud-brick on the edge of the fertile Black Land, villages, towns and cities have almost all dissolved into mud, or been lost under subsequent rebuilding. Only sites such as Kahun, intended for a particular purpose and so built away from the Nile in the dry and inhospitable desert, had a chance of surviving. It is therefore fortunate that this precious site was discovered by Flinders Petrie, who both recognized the importance of domestic sites and had the archaeological skills to excavate them properly. At Kahun he was to excavate and plan some

1800 rooms. Much of the material recovered from Petrie's excavations – poignant daily items, including tools, clothing, furniture, toys, pottery, jar sealings and even grain – found its way, through the generosity of Jesse Haworth, into the collections of Manchester Museum; the remainder of Petrie's share of the finds was given to University College London, and is today displayed in the eponymous Petrie Museum.

After a short interlude working in Palestine, Petrie was ready to return to Egypt. He had decided to tackle the pyramid cemetery of Meidum. Here the 4th Dynasty King Snefru, father of Khufu, had built Egypt's first true pyramid, surrounding it with low, flat mastaba tombs that would provide permanent homes for his immediate family and most favoured courtiers. When his pyramid proved unstable, Snefru abandoned the cemetery and relocated to Dahshur, where he went on to build a further two pyramids and many more private tombs. His Meidum pyramid subsequently collapsed; today it looks like a square tower standing rather forlornly in an island of rubble. Gaston Maspero had entered the pyramid in 1882, but no further work had been done at the site. Petrie, uncovering the remains of the mortuary temple that lay on the north side of the pyramid (then Egypt's earliest known temple), was able to confirm the name of the pyramid builder. He noted, to his own personal satisfaction, that this early pyramid, so similar in design and intent to the Great Pyramid, reinforced his own disproving of Piazzi Smyth's book which, to his intense irritation, was still a best-seller:

> The tombs at Meydum [Meidum] – the earliest then known – had been entirely neglected. Vassali had hacked away much fresco to get out the celebrated group of geese; after removing the figures of Rahetep [Rahotep] and Nefert [Nofret], the tombs had been re-opened, and visited by the boys of the place, who bashed the faces with stones. Mariette had taken wet squeezes off the painted sculpture, and left it pretty bare of colour.[13]

Petrie was to wage a lifelong campaign against 'wet squeezes': the common practice of pressing moist paper against carvings and drawings, which left the archaeologist with a faithful reproduction of the scene that could be outlined in pen, but which stripped the colour disastrously from fragile painted walls. He himself used 'dry squeezes', which, as their name suggests, used no water and relied on finger pressure alone to record the carved outlines.

Mariette had already investigated the nobles' cemetery, discovering the statues of Prince Rahotep and his wife Nofret, which today are among the highlights of the Cairo Museum collection. Now Petrie was able to discover Rahotep himself, one of Egypt's earliest mummies 'marvellously plumped out and modelled in pitch and resin, and coated with the most exquisitely fine linen', lying at the base of his mortuary shaft. The precious body was sent to London for autopsy, but was lost when the Royal College of Surgeons took a direct hit during the Second World War.

Petrie's next site would be Tell el-Amarna (ancient Akhetaten), the Middle Egyptian city built by the heretic king Akhenaten (formerly known as Amenhotep IV; known to Egyptologists in Petrie's day as Khuenaton). Amarna has given its name to an entire period in Egyptian history: the period when, during the late 18th Dynasty, the certainties of previous ages were overturned as the pharaoh decided to reject the multiple gods of Egyptian theology in favour of one all-powerful deity. Akhenaten's god was the light of the sun, known to the faithful as the Aten. Today the Amarna Period is perhaps the most intensely studied period in Egypt's long history. But at the time that Petrie was working very little was known about the so-called Amarna heresy, while Queen Nefertiti, who has since gained world-wide recognition, was just one among Egypt's many shadowy queens.

Amarna had never been officially excavated, although the city had been planned and briefly explored by John Gardner Wilkinson and Karl Lepsius. However, it had already yielded one extremely important find. In 1887 a peasant woman, illegally digging for *sebekh* or fertile soil (actually, degraded mud-brick – the remains of Akhenaten's city), stumbled across a series of curious clay tablets bearing strange, wedge-shaped marks. She sold the tablets to a canny neighbour for 10 piastres each, and slowly they made their way onto the antiquities market. The experts were not impressed, and declined to buy. The tablets, which as Egyptologist Nicholas Reeves has observed, 'are not dissimilar [in appearance] to stale dog biscuits',[14] seemed to be obvious, worthless forgeries. In fact, they were the remains of the royal archives of Amarna – copies, in cuneiform script, of the letters sent to and by the court. It was Wallis Budge, an Egyptologist able to read both hieroglyphs and cuneiform, who first realized the true value of the find: 'I felt certain that the tablets were both genuine and of very great historical importance.'[15] But Budge's recognition came too late. The archive had been split up, and many of the tablets had been destroyed.

Akhenaten's purpose-built city lies on the east bank of the Nile, almost equidistant between the traditional capitals of Thebes and Memphis. It occupies a wide semi-circle of desert, 7 miles long and 3 miles wide, sandwiched between the Nile to the west and an arc of steep cliffs to the east. This is not the most obviously suitable site for a capital city; it is isolated, water can be a problem, and there is a shortage of good agricultural land. This very unsuitability has, however, preserved the site for archaeologists for, unlike Thebes and Memphis, no other king was tempted by the delights of Amarna. Once the city had been abandoned early in the reign of Tutankhamen, it would never be reoccupied.

Amarna can be divided into three distinct elements. The city proper housed the palaces, the temples and the leafy green suburbs, where lived the courtiers, soldiers and tradesmen who serviced the city. The Amarna workmen's village, tucked into a little valley in the cliffs to the east of the main city, was a self-contained settlement of terraced houses, built for the labourers who worked in the elite cemeteries – the third element of Amarna life. The natural geography of the cliffs meant that the rock-cut tombs of the nobles fell into two distinct groups on either side of the royal wadi, the valley that held the great royal tomb. Locals had discovered the royal tomb sometime during the early 1880s, but its location had been kept a closely guarded secret until it had been thoroughly stripped of all valuables. When archaeologists finally came on the scene, there was very little left to record. The cemetery provided for the less important members of Amarna society who were buried, as they were at other cities, in simple graves dug into the desert sand, has only just been discovered by Egyptologist Barry Kemp.

Petrie had hoped to work in the tombs, but was denied permission and had to stand by as the royal tomb, officially discovered in late January 1892, was cleared by representatives of Cairo Museum, who, irritatingly, failed to publish their work. Instead he set to work in the city proper. Here, in a building known as the Great Palace, he uncovered a beautiful painted gypsum pavement. He spent an inordinate amount of time preserving the floor, painting it with a weak solution of tapioca applied using the side of one finger (a process that made the finger bleed), then building a raised walkway so that visitors might inspect the floor without damaging it. As word of his find spread, more and more visitors made their way to the site. Eventually a large shed was donated to protect the floor from sand and the elements, but there was no official path through the fields to the site, and the local farmers grew increasingly irritated as, year after year, thoughtless tourists trampled their crops. Petrie describes how, on 1 February 1912, at a time when a German expedition led by Ludwig Borchardt held the Amarna concession, the inevitable happened:

> ... in later years tourists stopped regularly to see it. The department provided no path for them, and the fields were trampled; so one night a man went and hacked it all to pieces to prevent visitors coming. Such was the mismanaged end of a unique find. I was never even informed and allowed to pick up the pieces.[15]

This was the official explanation of events. An alternative interpretation – that the pavement had been attacked by the guards paid to supervise the other, less obviously impressive parts of the site, who resented the *baksheesh* earned by their colleagues in charge of the floor – is perhaps more convincing. The fragments of the pavement were collected and reassembled in Cairo Museum. Here we may still see the calm blue pool filled with fat fish and surrounded by assorted animals, birds and plants.

Petrie's work at Amarna coincided with a tightening of the antiquity laws. Now everything officially belonged to Egypt, but excavators might, in acknowledgement of their work, receive a part of their finds at the discretion of the authorities. To modern readers, this at first seems entirely reasonable – the antiquities of a country obviously belong in that country, they are a part of its heritage. Petrie, however, was dismayed, and with good reason. He and all the other foreign excavators relied on private funding, which was, to a certain extent, dependent upon returning home with an assortment of impressive antiquities to share out. Why would benefactors like Haworth or Kennard pay to excavate anonymously for the benefit of the overcrowded Bulaq Museum – a museum that already had far more finds than it knew what to do with, and that was unable to look after the finds it did have? Petrie was still smarting under the treatment meted out to the unique wooden sarcophagus recovered from the Graeco-Roman Hawara cemetery, which had been left outside at the museum and had quickly dropped to pieces. The museum was so over-full that it was selling unwanted antiquities to tourists in the museum shop.

The obvious solution – leaving Egypt unexcavated, her finds naturally preserved under her sand – was no longer an option. There was a thriving black market in antiquities, and as the Antiquities Service could not afford to pay for guards at every unexcavated site, any site not officially investigated was under threat from enterprising locals. Today the issue has been resolved; all finds belong in Egypt, and there is a proper system in place to make sure that there are no unauthorized excavations. The overcrowding in Cairo Museum is another matter, soon to be solved by the building of a more spacious museum. But to Petrie, reliant on external funding, the new rules were a bitter blow.

In April 1892, only a month after Petrie lost his beloved mother, Amelia Edwards died. She left enough money to fund a Chair of Egyptology at University College London – an institution specifically chosen because it admitted women as well as men to its classes. The new professor was to teach for part of the year, but was to be left free over the winter to excavate in Egypt. Miss Edwards did not specifically mention Petrie in her will, but she stipulated that the new appointee should be less than 40 years of age, and could not be an employee of the British Museum. It was obvious to everyone that she had one specific Egyptologist in mind. With a guaranteed annual salary of £140, Professor Petrie had obtained his first professional appointment.

Excavations continued year after year, with only the occasional break when pressures of work or ill health proved too great. At the southern Egyptian site, usually known by its Greek name, Koptos (ancient Gebtu, modern Quft), Petrie discovered a series of statues: a colossal head of the Roman emperor Caracalla, a Ramesses II triad, and three very early – prehistoric or predynastic – colossal sculptures of the sexually aroused fertility god Min. Koptos had been the centre of the ancient cult of Min, and Petrie had discovered the remains of what was then Egypt's oldest temple. The statues and, indeed, any image of Min, posed a delicate problem for anyone of Victorian sensibilities, and the Petrie Museum in University College London would for many years display an image of Min with a large oblong label – written by Egyptologist Margaret Murray – stuck rather obviously over his offending member! The Egyptian authorities kept one of the Min statues. The Egyptian department of the British Museum turned down the other two, rejecting them on the bizarre grounds that it was 'advised that the figures were unhistoric rather than prehistoric' (the prehistory department was interested in the statues, but negotiations stalled), and so two of Egypt's earliest known cult statues are today displayed in the Ashmolean Museum, Oxford. This inexplicable stupidity rankled with Petrie, who would from now on offer his finds to the Ashmolean rather than the British Museum.

Petrie next chose to work at Tukh, close by the southern town of Nagada. This site had been chosen for a special reason: he had determined to investigate Egypt's beginnings, and to fill in the blank Dynasties 1–3 which the classical writers skipped over. The area was known for its extensive cemeteries, and Petrie was to find and clear many hundreds of graves – the graves of ordinary people, rather than royal personages. These ordinary people had been buried in a flexed position with a range of grave goods including pottery, but without coffins and without any evidence of writing. The whole cemetery was curious and most un-Egyptian; so much so that Petrie believed for several years that he had found evidence for a band of invaders whose dominant culture had wiped out the local Egyptian culture. Tentatively, he dated his 'New Race', the 'Falcon Tribe', to the ill-recorded period between the Old and Middle Kingdoms. He was wrong. With obvious embarrassment, he admitted his mistake in his autobiography:

The great surprise of the place [Nagada] was the immense prehistoric cemetery, from which that age is commonly called in France the Naqada [Nagada] period. Gradually we extended our work until we had cleared nearly two thousand graves. As the pottery and other products were different from what we knew in Egypt, they were provisionally referred to a 'New Race', and some indications here and at Ballas suggested that these people were invaders in the dark period after the VIth dynasty. De Morgan, who found similar graves, put them to predynastic times, though by a happy guess without any evidence.[16]

Jacques de Morgan, the enthusiastic new Director of the Antiquities Service, was a qualified mining engineer with a background in

European prehistory. He had much in common with the equally enthusiastic and equally practical Petrie, but was French (or, as Petrie rather sneeringly tells us, half-French and half-Welsh), and so would always be a colleague rather than a close friend. His one redeeming feature, in Petrie's eyes, was that he was far more efficient than the despised M. Grébaut. De Morgan was quite correct in his rejection of the 'New Race' theory, and this did not endear him overmuch to Petrie, who was not accustomed to being proved wrong. Petrie and de Morgan had together stumbled across Egypt's lost prehistory – the peoples who lived in the Nile Valley before Egypt became one unified country under King Narmer, the first king of the 1st Dynasty.

But how could the many hundreds of graves, each subtly different in content, be dated in the absence of writing? This was a challenge that appealed to Petrie's mathematical brain. By listing the contents of every grave on a separate slip of paper, he was eventually, after six years' hard work, able to develop Sequence Dating – a new method of pottery typology, or classification, which could be used to divide the Nagada graves and, by inference, the Nagada culture into three successive chronological phases: Nagada I, Nagada II and Nagada III (which is also known as Dynasty 0). His system, slightly modified in the light of subsequent archaeological discoveries, is still used by archaeologists today. We now know that the entire Nagada cultural phase lasted for approximately 1000 years from 4000 to 3050 BC. Petrie explained his methods to a non-mathematical audience at the annual general meeting of the EEF in November 1899:

> If in some old country mansion one room after another had been
> locked up untouched at the death of each successive owner, then
> on comparing all the contents it would easily be seen which rooms
> were of consecutive dates; and no one could suppose that a
> Regency room belonged to Mary and Anne, or an Elizabethan
> room to come between others of George III. The order of the

rooms could be settled to a certainty on comparing all the furniture and objects. Each would have some link of style in common with those next to it, and much less connection with others which were farther away from its period. And we should soon frame the rule that the order of the rooms was that in which each variety or article should have as short a range of date as it could. Any error in arranging the rooms would certainly extend the period of a thing over a longer number of generations. This principle applies to graves as well as rooms, to pottery as well as furniture.[18]

It was from this work, and from his insistence that humble pot sherds (broken pottery fragments) could be as informative to the initiated as formal inscriptions, that Petrie was affectionately dubbed the 'Father of Pots'.

Excavations at Luxor, Qurna, Deshasha and Dendera followed. By now Petrie was back working for the EEF, and he was married. Hilda Urlin, beautiful, spirited, adventurous and not at all interested in domestic matters, made the ideal wife for a dedicated archaeologist. Rather than keep house for the men, she preferred to don bloomers and work on site as an artist and planner. Flinders was in full agreement with this unusual arrangement. He had always scorned any attempt at domestic comfort on his digs: frugality was still his watchword, and he expected others to be as careful as he was. As archaeologist Arthur Weigall famously remarked: on Petrie's excavations 'you lived on sardines, and when you had eaten the sardines you ate the tin'.[19] Meals were invariably taken from tins, and it was not unknown for visitors to be offered an already open, half-eaten tin left over from the day before. Unused tins might even be buried in the desert for retrieval the next year. Those that bulged excessively were thrown against a wall; any that burst open were rejected. The heat, the dirt and the flies meant that upset stomachs were an unavoidable fact of life in Petrie's camp. Occasionally this could have an unexpected outcome; rumour held that the British

Egyptologist James Quibell grew romantically attached to his future wife, Miss Annie Pirie, when both were suffering from an unpleasant bout of ptomaine poisoning, the result of an incautious dinner with Petrie. Quibell, who remained a firm friend, was to gain international recognition through his excavation, with Frederick Green, of the ancient city of Hierakonpolis and his discovery of the Narmer Palette. But not everyone could cope with Petrie's spartan regime – the trick was to identify those who could survive before they left Britain. Back in London Petrie would select team members by inviting potential candidates out to lunch at the local Express Dairy. Those who picked a cheap meal made it through to the next test – a brisk run up several flights of the college stairs. The greedy and breathless had no hope of accompanying him to Egypt.

Petrie's next major excavation would be at Abydos, an extensive cemetery site, and cult centre of the god of the underworld, Osiris. Generations of Egyptians had built temples and tombs at Abydos throughout the dynastic age, but Petrie was principally interested in the earliest remains – the mud-brick tombs of the 1st and 2nd Dynasty kings, which lay on the most ancient part of the burial ground known as the Umm el Qa'ab, or 'Mother of Pots'. These tombs had already been investigated by Émile Amélineau, but his work had been shoddy and incomplete – it perhaps goes without saying that it would never be properly published. Amélineau was first and foremost a Coptic scholar with little feel for, or real interest in, excavation. He had hacked his way into all but one of the tombs, then, according to Petrie, deliberately smashed any artifact that he could not carry away, so as to increase the market value of his own finds, which he would later sell at auction. Maspero had heard enough to grow concerned over the rumours of malpractice at Abydos and, with one year of his concession still to run, Amélineau was replaced. Petrie was able to reinvestigate 13 royal tombs, piecing together the evidence left by Amélineau. Using today's terminology, these tombs are assigned to Nagada III/Dynasty 0 (Iri-Hor, Ka and Narmer), 1st Dynasty (Aha, Djer, Djet, Den, Queen Merit-

Neith, Anedjib, Semerkhet and Qaa), and 2nd Dynasty (Peribsen and Khasekhemwy). Petrie was delighted. The Abydos tombs had allowed him to join his prehistoric Nagada graves to the beginning of Egyptian history, which now ran in unbroken sequence from the pre-unification Neolithic to the conquest of Alexander the Great.

Petrie made many important finds at Abydos, including a mummified arm with four gold bracelets found hidden in a wall in the tomb of the 1st Dynasty King Djer. Petrie assumed, for no good reason bar the presence of its jewellery, that the arm belonged to a queen. It was to meet a sad fate, confirming Petrie's mistrust of museums and their employees:

> ... the arm of the queen of Zer [Djer] was found, hidden in a hole in the wall, with the gold bracelets in place. The lads who found it saw the gold, but left it untouched and brought the arm to me. I cut the wrappings apart and so bared the bracelets all intact. Thus the exact order could be copied when my wife rethreaded them next morning.
>
> When Quibell came over on behalf of the Museum, I sent up the bracelets by him. The arm – the oldest mummified piece known – and its marvellously fine tissue of linen were also delivered at the Museum. [Émile] Brugsch only cared for display; so from one bracelet he cut away the half that was of plaited gold wire, and he also threw away the arm and linen. A museum is a dangerous place.[20]

No longer working for the EEF, Petrie continued his fieldwork. At Giza he investigated the one small part of the site that had not been allocated to the Americans, the Italians or the Germans, and discovered the 2nd Dynasty tombs which confirmed the use of Giza as a cemetery long before Khufu built his pyramid. In the Tarkhan cemetery he found amazing quantities of textiles.

In 1914, at the age of 68, Gaston Maspero retired for the second time, dying in Paris two years later. His successor as Director-

General of the Antiquities Service, the respected French scholar Pierre Lacau, was welcomed by all concerned as a true Egyptologist. But Lacau had very different ideas from the easy-going Maspero, and he was an astute politician. He recognized the obvious: that Egypt was a rapidly changing land. In March 1922 Fuad I would be crowned King of Egypt. In April 1923 a new constitution would be put forward. With the protectorate abolished, the Egyptians naturally wanted to take control over their own affairs, and that included their own antiquities. Inspired by the wave of post-war nationalism, Lacau decreed that all future excavations should be under strict state control, with all finds, whatever the circumstances, automatically remaining in Egypt unless the authorities chose to make an exception. The old practice of splitting finds on a more or less 50:50 basis was to be abolished. Suddenly Sudan and the Near East, with their laxer antiquities laws, seemed an attractive alternative to those excavators, Petrie included, who relied on private finance. This change in excavation protocol goes a long way towards explaining why, after the First World War, Petrie seemed happy to abandon Egypt and turn his attention instead to Palestine, 'Egypt over the Border'.

Petrie retired from University College London in 1933, after 41 years as professor, and died Sir Flinders Petrie in Jerusalem on 29 July 1942. His body was buried in the Protestant cemetery on Mount Zion, but his head was preserved in a jar in the hospital laboratory. Petrie's last wish had been that it should be sent back to London for study, but the war made this impossible. Eventually his head was shipped home – classified, appropriately, as an antiquity – but to date, no study has been made of his brain.

When he came to write his autobiography, the 78-year-old Flinders Petrie estimated that he had spent 'seventy years in archaeology'. During those 70 years he did more than anyone else to turn Egyptology from a glorified form of treasure hunting into a reputable science. He had left a rich legacy. Egyptologists revere his name, his publications remain standard reading for archaeologists, and he has a permanent memorial in the Petrie Museum, part of

University College London. Yet to the general public his ground-breaking achievements have been eclipsed by the work of one man – a man who had the good fortune to make one spectacular find. The time has come to look at the extraordinary discoveries being made in and around the Valley of the Kings.

CHAPTER NINE

>—<

THE VALLEY OF THE KINGS

JACQUES DE MORGAN spent 1894–5 working intermittently at the pyramid site of Dahshur. In the Middle Kingdom cemetery he cleared several elite tombs, recovering jewellery – the 'Dahshur Treasure' – belonging to the queens and princesses of the 12th and 13th Dynasty royal courts. He moved on to excavate at Nagada, where he uncovered the spectacular mastaba tomb of Queen Neithhotep, wife of the first king of the unified Egypt, Narmer. Then he decided to abandon Egypt for the chance of excavating in Persia. He resigned from the Antiquities Service in 1897, and was replaced by Victor Loret, a man who inspired little confidence in non-French archaeologists. Many feared that the new regime would be a throwback to the bad old days of Grébaut. The Reverend Sayce, a respected Assyriologist who wintered each year on a houseboat on the Nile, offers us a flavour of Loret's crude management style:

> Soon after [Loret's] appointment, Brugsch Bey [Émile Brugsch], the curator of the Museum, came to me saying 'Yesterday I had occasion to see the new Director on a matter of business and accordingly knocked at the door of his room. When I entered he said: "In future, Monsieur, I must ask you to send a note or a card to me first of all when you wish to see me." I replied: "Monsieur le Directeur, *my* shadow shall never darken your threshold again."' And it never did.[1]

Loret turned his attention to the Valley of the Kings, which had been more or less neglected since Belzoni's spectacular discovery of the tomb of Seti I. On 12 February 1898 he found the tomb of the 'Egyptian Napoleon', the 18th Dynasty warrior king Tuthmosis III (KV34). The tomb had, of course, been emptied in antiquity, and the body of the king had already been recovered in the Deir el-Bahari cache and was now lying in Cairo Museum, but there was enough of the king's original burial equipment left – broken wooden statues, damaged models, and a beautifully carved quartzite sarcophagus – to generate public interest.

Less than a month later, on 9 March, Loret discovered the tomb of Tuthmosis's son and heir, Amenhotep II (KV35). The new tomb was long and dangerous, with steep, rubble-strewn stairways dropping from level to level, low ceilings and a potentially lethal open well-shaft (a combined burglar trap and rainwater sump) that had to be crossed by ladder. Candles and torches provided the only light. Straight away there were indications that this might be an atypical tomb. In the corridor that led away from the entrance there was a small-scale wooden boat. Lying across the boat there was a horrible sight that stopped the imaginative Loret in his tracks:

> ... a body lying there upon the boat, all black and hideous, its grinning face turning towards me and looking at me, its long brown hair in sparse bunches around its head. I did not dream for an instant that this was just an unwrapped mummy. The legs and arms seemed to be bound. A hole exposed the sternum, there was an opening in the skull. Was this a victim of a human sacrifice? Was this a thief murdered by his accomplices in a bloody division of the loot, or perhaps he was killed by soldiers or by police interrupting the pillaging of the tomb?[2]

This tomb had obviously been opened and ransacked in antiquity, and almost all the grave goods had vanished – some had already appeared for sale on the antiquities market. But in the burial chamber there was an open sarcophagus, and in the sarcophagus was a wooden coffin. Loret had found Amenhotep himself, the only pharaoh at that date to have been found lying in his own tomb in the Valley. It was clear that this was not the king's original burial. The king had been 'rescued' by the priests of Amen, who had stripped him of his original bandages and any remaining jewellery, rewrapped him, and replaced him in his own painted quartzite sarcophagus. He had not been left to lie alone. A sealed side chamber leading off the main pillared hall yielded three unwrapped and uncoffined mummies lying neatly side by side, each with a hole in the head and a damaged abdomen:

We approached the cadavers. The first seemed to be that of a woman. A thick veil covered her forehead and left eye. Her broken arm had been replaced at her side, her nails in the air. Ragged and torn cloth hardly covered her body. Abundant black curled hair spread over the limestone floor on either side of her head. The face was admirably conserved and had a noble and majestic gravity. '

The second mummy, in the middle, was that of a child of about fifteen years. It was naked with the hands joined on the abdomen. First of all the head appeared totally bald, but on closer examination one saw that the head had been shaved except in an area on the right temple from which grew a magnificent tress of black hair ... The face of the young prince was laughing and mischievous, it did not at all evoke the idea of death.

Lastly the corpse nearest the wall seemed to be that of a man. His head was shaved but a wig lay on the ground not far from him. The face of this person displayed something horrible and something droll at the same time. The mouth which was running obliquely from one side nearly to the middle of the cheek, bit a pad of linen whose two ends hung from a corner of the lips. The half closed eyes had a strange expression, he could have died choking on a gag but he looked like a young playful cat with a piece of cloth ...[3]

A neighbouring side chamber held an even more exciting discovery: nine dusty coffins bearing a series of royal names. Here, amongst others, lay the lost 18th Dynasty kings Tuthmosis IV and Amenhotep III, the 19th Dynasty kings Seti II and Siptah, and the 20th Dynasty kings Ramesses IV–VI.

Unlike Émile Brugsch, Victor Loret was well aware of the need to keep accurate records of his work. The bodies were photographed, detailed plans were drawn, and each of the finds (and there were over 2000 of them) was listed and plotted on the plan. Unfortunately, these records were never published, and today they are lost.

The mummies were left in the tomb, just as they had been found. Here, inevitably, they attracted both tourists and potential thieves. And so the decision was taken to transfer the coffined royal mummies – mummies that everyone agreed were not a part of the original burial – to the Giza Museum. In 1931, with increased concerns over tomb security, Amenhotep II was also sent to the museum. He made his final journey by steam train travelling, appropriately enough, in a first-class sleeper.

The three unwrapped mummies, which were not considered to be royal, were left sealed in their side chamber, arranged much as they had been when discovered. Who are they? The 'elder lady' with the abundant hair is now thought by many to be the long-lived Queen Tiy, influential mother of Akhenaten, although there are some who would classify her as the female King Hatshepsut. The 'child' is believed to be a royal prince. The third body, today generally known as the 'younger lady', has been variously identified as an Amarna princess, or even as Queen Nefertiti herself, although the most recent DNA analysis, conducted by the Egyptian authorities, indicates that the body may well be male after all. The body in the boat is now lost and so is difficult to identify, but many experts believe it may have been the remains of the young 20th Dynasty king Sethnakht.

Loret went on to discover KV38, the tomb that Tuthmosis III

had built for his grandfather, Tuthmosis I, plus a further 14 private tombs. But in 1899, much to everyone's relief, he was persuaded to retire from the Antiquities Service, and Gaston Maspero was lured back from France as his replacement. Maspero demanded, and got, an exorbitant salary of £1500 a year plus expenses; everyone agreed that he was worth it. During this second period of office he was to oversee the transfer of the national museum from its unsatisfactory quarters at Giza to the building in central Cairo where it remains today. Determined to improve administration within the Antiquities Department, he decided that there should be two European Chief Inspectors: one based in the north, at Cairo, and one in the south, at Luxor. Each would take full responsibility for excavation and conservation in his own area.

Meanwhile, back at the Valley of the Kings, there was a new mission waiting to dig. Theodore Monroe Davis was a retired, and very wealthy, American lawyer intent on striking archaeological gold in the form of an untouched royal tomb. He was happy enough to spend considerable sums of money funding excavations conducted by employees of the Antiquities Service, and to pay for their lavish, if woefully inadequate, publications. In 1902 Davis agreed to fund Howard Carter's work in the Valley of the Kings. Carter, then Chief Inspector of Antiquities for southern Egypt, was determinedly looking for the missing tomb of the 18th Dynasty pharaoh Tuthmosis IV. In 1903 he found it.

KV43 was a beautifully decorated tomb at the southern end of the Valley. The king's body was, as Carter knew it would be, missing from his tomb – it had been found by Loret five years previously in the tomb of Amenhotep II. But there were still some of the original grave goods. No metal, of course – that had gone long ago – but the floor was crunchy with broken vessels, the burial chamber yielded the remains of a war-chariot and a quartzite sarcophagus, and there was a body. Propped against a wall in a side chamber, the damaged mummy of Prince Webensenu, his abdomen torn open, was a satisfyingly horrible sight.

After a brief investigation in KV60, Carter turned his attention to the more promising KV20, a tomb with a complicated history and, when Carter set to work, no known owner. In fact, the tomb had had two royal owners. Originally it had been designed and used for the burial of Tuthmosis I. A decade or so later Tuthmosis's daughter, Hatshepsut, had extended the tomb so that she could be interred alongside her father. During his original funeral Tuthmosis had been laid to rest in a traditional wooden sarcophagus housed in the original small burial chamber. Now, in the improved tomb, he lay in a splendid quartzite sarcophagus in the new lower burial chamber. Eventually his daughter joined him, and the two lay side by side as she had wished. But her successor and nephew, Tuthmosis III, was not happy with this situation. He provided his grandfather with an entirely new tomb (KV38) and a new yellow quartzite sarcophagus. Here Tuthmosis I rested for several centuries until he was removed by the High Priests of Amen. His mummy was eventually recovered as part of the Deir el-Bahari royal cache.

KV20 had been known since the time of the Napoleonic Expedition, but it had attracted little attention. In 1804 a gentleman named C. H. Gordon carved his name on the entrance; in 1817 Belzoni recorded the tomb on his map of the Valley; in 1824 James Burton explored an upper chamber; and in 1844 Lepsius investigated the upper passage. Now Carter could understand why they had gone no further. The corridors were completely blocked by a solidified mass of rubble, mud and small stones, which had been washed into the tomb by floodwaters. After two seasons of hard work the corridors were clear, and Carter was able to make his way into the double burial chamber. Here the ceiling had collapsed, showering debris onto the floor. The men set to work with picks and shovels. It was not the easiest of workplaces:

... the air had become so bad, and the heat so great, that the
candles carried by the workmen melted, and would not give
enough light to enable them to continue their work; consequently

we were compelled to install electric lights, in the form of hand wires ... As soon as we got down about 50 metres, the air became so foul that the men could not work. In addition to this, the bats of centuries had built innumerable nests on the ceilings of the corridors and chambers, and their excrement had become so dry that the least stir of the air filled the corridors with a fluffy black stuff, which choked the noses and mouths of the men, rendering it most difficult for them to breathe.[4]

With the passageways and chambers finally clear, Carter could see that the tomb followed a simple plan. Four stepped passages, linked by three rectangular chambers, led down to a rectangular burial chamber and three very small storerooms. There were two yellow quartzite sarcophagi, both of which had originally been inscribed for Hatshepsut, although one had subsequently been reinscribed for Tuthmosis – an unmistakable indication that the female king had been happy to bury her father in one of her rejected sarcophagi (we should not blame her for her thriftiness; stone sarcophagi were both extremely expensive and time-consuming to produce). There was also Hatshepsut's matching canopic box, the box that would have held her preserved entrails. However, the tomb had been ransacked long ago. There were no mummies, and the floor was littered with broken pottery, fragments of stone vessels and burnt pieces of wooden coffins, statues and boxes. It was obvious that Hatshepsut had died before her tomb could be completed. Fifteen polished limestone slabs, inscribed in red and black ink with chapters from the funerary book known as the *Amduat,* had been intended to line the ceiling, but had been abandoned on the floor when time ran out.

When Howard Carter was transferred to northern Egypt, Davis continued to excavate with the assistance of the replacement southern Inspectors – first James Quibell, then Arthur Weigall, both of whom had been well trained by Flinders Petrie. On 5 February 1905 Quibell discovered the double burial of Yuya and Thuyu, the elderly parents of the 18th Dynasty Queen Tiy, wife of Amenhotep III.

Their tomb (KV46) had been ransacked in antiquity, but the robbers had been disturbed before they could make serious inroads into the grave goods. Yuya and Thuyu were still surrounded by a remarkable collection of artifacts, including furniture, household provisions and a full-sized chariot for Yuya, a cavalry officer, to use in the Afterlife. The deceased couple each lay in a nest of gilded coffins. Their white-haired mummies are two of the most lifelike mummies to have been found. Here, if not exactly the royal tomb that Davis sought, was the next best thing.

The official opening of the tomb saw Davis, accompanied by Maspero and Weigall (who had recently replaced Quibell as Inspector), groping his way along a dark, hot, dusty passageway nervously clutching a pair of candles. The passageway dropped steeply to the door of the burial chamber. Here a small hole left by the ancient robbers allowed access to the burial. Maspero, who was rather stout, stuck like a cork in a bottle, and had to be pushed through by his fellow archaeologists. Once inside the chamber, he was the first to read the name on the coffin: 'Yuya'. Davis takes up the tale:

> Naturally excited by the announcement, and blinded by the glare
> of the candles, I involuntarily advanced them very near the coffin,
> whereupon Monsieur Maspero called out 'Be careful!', and pulled
> my hand back. In a moment we realised that, had my candles
> touched the bitumen, which I came dangerously near to doing,
> the coffin would have been in a blaze. As the entire contents of
> the tomb were inflammable, and directly opposite the coffin was a
> corridor leading to the open air and making a draught, we
> undoubtedly should have lost our lives ...[5]

In late 1905 Davis stopped financing the Inspectors of the Antiquities Service, and instead employed Edward Ayrton, a free-lance Egyptologist, to excavate on his behalf. The Inspectors, who were finding it increasingly difficult to fit Davis's excavations in with their many official duties, welcomed this separation from the Antiquities Service. But it marked a downturn in the standard of Davis's archaeological work. Ayrton was a competent enough Egyptologist, but he had a living to earn, and found it very hard to resist his employer's demand for rapid results at the expense of scientific accuracy. Davis, still intent on finding a complete royal tomb, had little patience with either recording or conservation. It is therefore very unfortunate that, on 6 January 1907, the new team stumbled across the uniquely complex and highly significant burial in tomb KV55. Archaeologists ever since have bemoaned the lack of official plans, photographs and records, while breathing a loud sigh of relief that Davis, who came very close, never found the tomb of Tutankhamen.

At first sight the new tomb seemed simple, almost unimportant. An outer door opened into a sloping, rubble-filled corridor that led in turn to a single burial chamber. Wedged on top of the rubble in the corridor, however, was a dismantled wooden shrine coated with gold foil. The inscription on the shrine made it clear that this had been provided by the heretic pharaoh Akhenaten for the burial of his mother, Queen Tiy. Unfortunately, the wooden panels were in a highly fragile state and, with no attempt at conservation, they disintegrated before they could be properly recorded.

Beyond the corridor the burial chamber was a high, plain room. It too was in a state of disarray, with grave goods and equipment – more wooden panels, boxes, mud-bricks, stone chips, fallen plaster and tools – lying any old how on the floor. It was immediately obvious that these grave goods belonged to several different burials; they bore a series of 18th Dynasty royal names, ranging from Amenhotep II through Amenhotep III, Tiy and Akhenaten to Tutankhamen. As Tutankhamen's was the last name, archaeologists have always assumed that he was responsible for sealing the tomb. A recess cut into the right-hand wall held four delicately carved human-headed canopic jars. And an elaborately decorated anthropoid coffin lying on the floor, its face unaccountably ripped away, held a mummy. Mrs

Emma B. Andrews, who entered the tomb soon after its opening, recorded the scene in her diary:

> 1907, Jan 19. At the Valley ... I went down to the burial chamber and it is now almost easy of access; and saw the poor Queen as she lies now just a bit outside her magnificent coffin, with the vulture crown on her head. All the woodwork of the shrine, doors &c. is heavily overlaid with gold foil and I seemed to be walking on gold, and even the Arab working inside had some of it sticking in his woolly hair.[6]

The 'vulture crown' that Mrs Andrews so admired was nothing of the kind; it was a pectoral (necklace), as Ayrton should have known. The sealed tomb, already untidy, had suffered an unfortunate accident. The elaborate coffin had been left resting on a wooden bier, but a crack in the ceiling above had allowed flood-water to drip onto the burial and rot the wood. When the bier inevitably collapsed, the coffin was tipped to the ground, its lid slightly displaced. The mummy, now lying unprotected in a puddle, started to decay. Further damage was caused to both mummy and coffin when a rock fell from the ceiling. After Davis had stripped the mummy of its bandages, it was reduced to a skeleton. The autopsy was carried out in the tomb:

> Presently, we cleared the mummy from the coffin, and found that it was a smallish person, with a delicate head and hands. The mouth was partly open, showing a perfect set of upper and lower teeth. The body was enclosed in mummy-cloth of fine texture, but all of the cloth covering the body was of a very dark colour. Naturally it ought to be a much brighter colour. Rather suspecting injury from the evident dampness, I gently touched one of the front teeth (3,000 years old) and alas! it fell into dust, thereby showing that the mummy could not be preserved. We then cleared the entire mummy ...[7]

We would normally expect an inscribed coffin to tell us the name of its owner. But this coffin has a more complicated tale to tell. Experts are agreed that it was originally built for a woman – a lady who could be described as 'the beloved of Akhenaten', the words written on the coffin. As the head of the coffin wore a wig rather than a crown, it seems that this lady was not an immediate member of the royal family. But, some time after the coffin had been finished, the inscriptions were altered from feminine to masculine, while the name of the original owner was replaced by a royal name in a cartouche. At the same time the coffin was fitted with a beard and uraeus, making it more suitable for the burial of a royal male. Finally, some time after the burial, the gold facemask was torn away, while the name in the cartouches was erased.

Archaeologists have argued long and hard about who the body in this curious tomb might be. To Davis, it would always be Queen Tiy. But all experts who have since examined the body have agreed that it is male. Some believe that it is the lost body of King Akhenaten himself. But the most recent analysis of the bones indicates that it is the body of a young male in his late teens or early twenties rather than a fully mature man; Akhenaten is likely to have been at least 30 and probably nearer to 40 years old when he died. The shape of the skull is near enough to the shape of Tutankhamen's skull to indicate a very close family relationship; the KV55 body is either Tutankhamen's son, his brother or his father. As the KV55 male died too young to be Tutankhamen's father, and too old to be his son, he must be Tutankhamen's brother. It seems that Davis had found, but not recognized, Smenkhkare, elder brother of, and short-lived king before, Tutankhamen. How Smenkhkare, last king of Amarna, came to be buried amidst a jumble of second-hand grave goods in the Valley of the Kings, Thebes, we may never know.

Davis, flushed with his triumph in discovering 'Queen Tiy', went on to make more important finds, including KV57, the plundered royal tomb of Horemheb, last king of the 18th Dynasty. But there was a lingering feeling of disappointment; Davis had always hoped that he would find the missing tomb of the boy king Tutankhamen. The photographer Harry Burton tells us that he had come very close indeed:

> ... If Mr Theodore Davis, of Boston, for whom I was excavating in 1914, had not stopped his last 'dig' too soon I am convinced he would have discovered the present tomb of King Tutankhamun. We came within six feet of it. Just then Mr Davis feared that further digging would undermine the adjacent roadway and ordered me to cease work.[8]

Davis may not have found the tomb, but he had found several components of Tutankhamen's burial. In 1905–6 Edward Ayrton had discovered a faience [glazed] cup bearing the king's name. In 1907 Davis's team, again led by Ayrton, had found a small pit (KV54) housing the remains of Tutankhamen's embalming materials, which the undertakers, reluctant to destroy anything connected to a royal mummification, had buried. The smashed pottery that littered the floor of the pit probably represented the remains of Tutankhamen's funeral meal. Finally, in 1909, his team had discovered a small, undecorated chamber (KV58) which yielded a *shabti* (model servant) figure and the gold foil from a chariot harness inscribed with the cartouches of Tutankhamen and his successor, Ay.

Eventually Davis, now a sick man, abandoned his quest, convinced that the Valley had yielded all its secrets – 'I fear that the Valley of the Tombs is now exhausted'[9] – and that the small pit KV58 was in fact the lost tomb of Tutankhamen. Theodore Davis died in Florida on 23 February 1915.

As DAVIS'S CREW toiled in the Valley of the Kings, there were exciting discoveries being made in the nearby Valley of the Queens, or 'The Place of Beauty', the elite cemetery that served as the last resting place of many New Kingdom queens, princesses, princes and nobles. The Valley had been known ever since the traveller Robert

Hay first recorded it in 1826, but official excavations did not start until 1903, when Ernesto Schiaparelli, Director of Turin Museum, set to work. Schiaperelli was to open several tombs in the Valley, but his most important discovery was made in 1904, when he discovered QV66, the empty, beautifully decorated tomb of Queen Nefertari.

Queen Nefertari, first consort of Ramesses the Great, is one of the most enigmatic figures from ancient Egypt. We know her name, and we can recognize her beautiful face, yet we understand very little of her personal life. Her origins are obscure although, as she never uses the title 'King's Daughter' (the Egyptian equivalent of our 'princess'), we can guess that she was not a member of the immediate royal family. Many experts believe that she may have had links with the noble family of King Ay, successor to Tutankhamen. This well-respected family had already provided the commoner-born 18th Dynasty Queens Tiy (wife of Amenhotep III), Nefertiti (wife of Akhenaten) and Mutnodjmet (wife of Horemheb).

We do know that Nefertari was married to Prince Ramesses before he inherited his throne. She was to give him as many as ten children, including his eldest son Amenhirwenemef, his third son Prehirwenemef and one of his favourite daughters Meritamen, but none of her children outlived their nonagenarian father.

We think that we know what Nefertari looked like. Contemporary images show the queen to have been as beautiful and graceful as all New Kingdom queens invariably were. It is difficult to know how realistic these images are, although common sense suggests that not all the queens can have been quite so beautiful and, in fact, we know that the Egyptians placed very little importance on realism in their portraiture. Images, be they statues, drawings or paintings, were intended to convey the essence of the subject, and cannot be read as the ancient equivalent of our photographs. Nevertheless many modern observers, Amelia Edwards included, have been smitten by Nefertari's innocent charm. Miss Edwards, a writer of romantic Victorian novels, was eager to believe in the romance of Ramesses and his bride:

On every pillar, in every act of worship pictured on the walls, even in the sanctuary, we find the names of Ramesses and Nefertari 'coupled and inseparable' ... We see, at all events, that Ramesses and Nefertari desired to leave behind them an imperishable record of the affection which united them on earth, and which they hoped would unite them in Amenti. What more do we need to know? We see that the Queen was fair; that the King was in his prime. We divine the rest; and the poetry of the place at all events is ours. Even in these barren solitudes there is wafted to us a breath from the shores of old romance. We feel that Love once passed this way, and that the ground is still hallowed where he trod.[10]

We know that Nefertari was alive in Year 24 of her husband's reign, when the royal family travelled south to inaugurate the Abu Simbel temples, as she appears in the images that commemorate this joyous occasion. She is, however, absent from the jubilee celebrations of Year 30. It therefore seems that she died sometime between Years 24 and 30. Her cause of death is unknown. The meagre human remains recovered from her tomb – part of a mummified leg that has been variously described as a foot or a pair of knees – are of little help here and may not, of course, have belonged originally to the queen.

Nefertari's tomb was a simple one. Beyond the entrance a stepped passage with a central sarcophagus slide led into a small, square antechamber and a side chamber, from which a second stepped passage dropped to a large, four-pillared burial chamber and three small storage rooms. The queen's pink granite sarcophagus had vanished, but Schiaparelli was able to find fragments of its smashed lid. The whole tomb, walls and ceiling, was covered in a thick layer of plaster, which had first been carved in raised relief and then painted in vibrant colours. The carving throughout the tomb is of an extraordinarily high standard, while the use of shading – darkening folds of garments and skin, and the use of red to emphasize the contours of the face and arms – makes the scenes extraordinarily lifelike. Nevertheless, and perhaps inevitably, there are some areas where the workmanship is less than perfect. Paint splashes, misplaced guidelines and smudged edges all testify to the differences in skill of the various gangs who painted the tomb simultaneously.

The ceiling of the tomb is a deep blue night sky spangled with vivid golden stars – curiously, this was painted last, and so occasionally the sky rains down on the walls. The walls themselves chart Nefertari's final journey, as she transforms from an inanimate mummy and is reborn to eternal life. In the antechamber we see her embalmed body lying on a bier, protected by the divine mourners Isis and Nephthys, who take the form of birds. The jackal-headed god Anubis, and the Four Sons of Horus, the divine beings most involved with the preservation of the body, listen as Osiris grants the queen eternal life. Here, too, we see Nefertari seated alone at her *senet* board. *Senet* was a chess-like board game very much enjoyed by the living, but it was a game with strong religious undertones which, it was believed, might help the deceased negotiate the perils of the road to the Afterlife.

The entrance to the burial chamber is guarded by the goddess Maat, the personification of the concept *maat* (truth, order, justice and rightness), who stretches out her winged arms to embrace and protect Nefertari. Inside the chamber are five of the gateways leading to the Kingdom of Osiris, each guarded by three evil spirits. This is a test. In order to progress, Nefertari must name each of the gates, each of the gatekeepers, and each of the guards who squat, armed with large knives, in Underworld caverns. Fortunately, hieroglyphic inscriptions provide the correct answers. When all ordeals have been successfully completed, the four columns surrounding the sarcophagus represent the resurrection of the queen. Here the divine Horus, king of the living Egypt, brings life to the deceased.

To his great credit, Schiaparelli immediately recognized that his discovery was in a highly fragile condition. The tomb occupied a low-lying position in the valley, and its plaster-coated walls had been badly affected by long-term damp. Salt was crystallizing on the surface of the limestone, pushing the plaster off the walls and destroying the paintings. Ancient earthquake damage had done nothing to improve the situation. After decades of debate, recording and experimentation, the Nefertari conservation project, a joint enterprise conducted between the Egyptian Antiquities Organization and the Getty Conservation Institute, has been able to stabilize the tomb, restoring many of the paintings, while avoiding the use of modern paint.

THE LONG-LIVED architect Kha worked in the royal cemetery, serving four generations of 18th Dynasty pharaohs: Tuthmosis III, Amenhotep II, Tuthmosis IV and Amenhotep III. When the time came he was buried alongside his wife Meryet in the cemetery associated with Deir el-Medina, the walled village built to house the workmen, scribes and supervisors who worked in secret in the Valleys of the Kings and Queens. In most cases the Deir el-Medina elite topped their rock-cut tombs with conspicuous tomb chapels, where their families could visit and leave offerings to the cult of the deceased. But Kha had learned something from his long association with the royal tombs. Just as the pharaohs had decided to separate their mortuary or memorial temples from their tombs, so he would physically separate his mortuary chapel from his final resting place. Kha's decorated chapel, topped with a small pyramid, had been discovered by Bernardino Drovetti many years before. Now, in 1906, in the hillside facing his chapel, Schiaparelli was about to discover his tomb (TT8).

The tomb was approached via a flight of steps leading to a passageway blocked by a stone wall. Beyond the wall there was a long, low tunnel with a second blocking wall. Excitement grew as it became obvious that this wall had never before been breached. Beyond the wall Schiaparelli and Weigall, the local Inspector, found themselves standing in a rough entrance passage, the left-hand wall of which was lined with furniture, including a bed. Beyond this, a locked and sealed wooden door offered the promise of an intact elite burial. Schiaperelli had no key – he was forced to cut the lock open. Stepping inside, he found himself in a room neatly packed with everything that a prosperous couple could possibly need in the Afterlife. There was furniture, linen, cosmetics, Meryet's bed, Kha's tools, food, drink and even, in the passageway, a portable toilet. Meryet, who had predeceased her husband, lay in an anthropoid coffin within a rectangular shrine. Kha had two anthropoid coffins within one rectangular one.

If Kha, a relatively minor official, had been interred with so many splendid grave goods, how much richer would a royal burial be? On the Theban west bank Egyptologists were desperately seeking the ultimate prize: an intact royal tomb. There were some who thought that all the royal tombs must have been robbed many years ago, but at least one man believed he knew otherwise. Howard Carter had determined to find the lost tomb of an insignificant boy pharaoh: Tutankhamen.

CHAPTER TEN

≻—≺

WONDERFUL
THINGS

HOWARD CARTER, when asked to compile his own entry for *Who's Who*, famously stated that he was born in Swaffham, Norfolk. He also claimed, throughout his adult life, to have been born on 9 May 1873. In fact, he was mistaken on both counts. Howard Carter had been born in Brompton, London, exactly a year later, on 9 May 1874, to the fashionable animal painter Samuel John Carter and his wife, Martha Joyce Sands.

The Carter family did, however, own a house just outside the village of Swaffham. Here the sickly baby Howard was sent to be raised by his aunts, Fanny and Kate. Howard, considered far too delicate for public school, was taught quietly at home. His lack of formal education would cause him some embarrassment in later life, as would his endearingly erratic spelling. From a very early age Howard, like his six surviving brothers and his sister, showed an aptitude for drawing that was encouraged by regular lessons with their father. Four of the Carter children would grow up to be professional artists, while Howard's colourful archaeological illustrations are a continuing delight to readers more used to the stark plans and black and white photographs that ornament modern publications.

In Swaffam the Carter family were acquainted with the Amhersts of Didlington Hall. William Amherst Tyssen-Amherst MP, later

Baron Amherst of Hackney, had a strong interest in all things ancient. He was wealthy enough to indulge his passions, and his private museum of Egyptian antiquities included a series of important papyri, plus the most significant collection of monumental sculpture to be found outside the British Museum. Visiting the house with his father, who painted several animal portraits at Didlington Hall, Howard was fascinated by the monuments. So when the Egyptologist Percy Newberry happened to mention to his good friend William Amherst that he was looking for a young, artistically talented assistant to help with his Egyptian survey work, it was almost inevitable that Howard's name should be put forward. Howard was excited by the prospect; he had already decided that the life of an animal painter, although lucrative, was not for him. He spent the summer and autumn of 1891 studying manuscripts in the British Library, and drawing the Egyptian collections in the British Museum. Then, in the autumn of 1891, aged 17, he said goodbye to his family and set sail for Egypt.

In Cairo there was just enough time to visit the Giza Museum before Newberry whisked his new assistant away to the Middle Egyptian site of Beni Hassan. Here the local dignitaries of the 11th and 12th Dynasties had cut their tombs deep into the rocky cliffs. Following local tradition, they had decorated the plastered walls of their tomb chapels with not only the usual religious, agricultural and hunting scenes, but with a series of lively vignettes of daily life, including children at play, dancers, acrobats and wrestlers. Now the EEF was financing the recording of these decorated tombs. It was intensive, but satisfying, work. Carter slept in a cool tomb at night, and traced tomb scenes from seven in the morning until nightfall. His tracings, carefully recorded in pencil, would be finished off in London; as the draughtsmen never saw the originals, the end result would be less than accurate. Carter, as an artist, would have much preferred to copy the originals freehand, but time and finances did not allow this and, as Newberry reasoned, any copy of the walls, no matter how crude, was better than none at all. Moving on to the neighbouring rock tombs of el-Bersha the team, now camping in tents, resumed their tracing. When Christmas came the camp dispersed, and Carter went to stay with Flinders Petrie at Amarna.

William Amherst, hoping to add some Amarna pieces to his collection, had offered to finance Petrie's work – a generous gift with just one, not too onerous, string attached:

> Mr Tyssen Amherst wishes to do a little here under my
> permission; and so Mr Carter is to come here and work, not
> exactly with me, but on parts of the ground which I may assign
> to him. I having no responsibilities about his work except to the
> Government here.[1]

Petrie may well have had his reservations; he needed a competent field archaeologist, not an artist. Certainly the two were an ill-matched couple. Petrie was famously careful with money, and scornful of anything that smacked of unnecessary luxury or comfort. Carter, who freely admitted to enjoying his luxuries, could never understand why anyone would choose to waste valuable time building his own mud-brick hut (the frugal Petrie would sell off the bricks to his workmen at the end of the dig), or walking vast distances across the desert when donkeys were both plentiful and cheap to hire. But each was prepared to accommodate the other. Carter good-naturedly built his own hut, heated his own tins, and completed a competent survey of the Amarna road system, and Petrie soon came to recognize his young colleague's worth. Soon Carter was learning the techniques of excavation from the Master himself.

The 1892 season saw Carter briefly back copying Middle Egyptian tombs with the EEF survey team before being transferred to the Delta to conduct a rescue excavation at Tell Timai el-Amdid (ancient Mendes). Here Édouard Naville, working for the EEF, had come across a collection of fragile and badly charred Greek scrolls that he had been unable – and, many suspected, unwilling – to conserve. In a lecture, reported in *The Times*, he officially regretted his failure: 'What treasures we probably have lost, by the destruction of the library of Mendes', but seemed happy enough to move on. The local antiquities dealers, who had known about the 'library' for several years, continued to plunder the site unchecked. Petrie, in particular, was incensed by this casual approach, and the long festering rivalry between Naville, always the EEF's preferred excavator, and Petrie, undoubtedly the better field archaeologist but usually the second choice, burst open.

Petrie had a series of questions that demanded answers. Why had the EEF not sent a proper conservator to the site? Why had he found relatively well-preserved rolls, obviously from Mendes, in a dealer's shop in Cairo? And why was Naville, having proved himself incompetent in matters of excavation, to be allowed to investigate the Deir el-Bahari temple, one of the most important and challenging monuments in the whole of Egypt? Naville was deeply offended. To Petrie's suggestion that he should have at least planned the position of the scrolls in the 'library' he revealingly replied: 'you might as well make a plan of the raisins in a plum pudding'.[2] The EEF responded by sending Howard Carter – still in his teens but by now considered an experienced excavator – out to Mendes to salvage what he could. But the situation was already hopeless. By the time Carter arrived the 'library' had vanished (Naville having left no detailed plan) and the irreplaceable papyri along with it. Carter returned, depressed, to el-Bersha.

Naville, meanwhile, went to work at Deir el-Bahari, Thebes. Here, in a natural bay set in the Theban cliff of the west bank, the female King Hatshepsut had built her mortuary or memorial temple to ensure that her cult lived for ever. Hatshepsut's temple had been designed as a multi-functional building with a series of shrines dedicated to different gods. In addition to the mortuary temples of Hatshepsut and her father Tuthmosis I, there was a chapel dedicated to the goddess Hathor, a chapel dedicated to Anubis, the jackal-headed god of the cemetery, an area dedicated to the memory of Hatshepsut's ancestors, and a sun temple dedicated to the worship of the sun god Re-Herakhty. The main shrine, cut deep into the Theban rock, was dedicated to Amen. Hatshepsut's mortuary cult had been abandoned soon after her death, but the cults of Amen and Hathor had survived at her temple until the end of the 20th Dynasty. In the Graeco-Roman period the temple, now badly ruined, became the cult centre for the worship of two deified Egyptians: Imhotep, the 3rd Dynasty architect and builder of the Step Pyramid, and Amenhotep, son of Hapu, an 18th Dynasty sage and architect. The site then fell again into disuse until the fifth century AD, when it was taken over by a Coptic monastery. It was finally abandoned sometime during the eighth century.

The temple had never been lost. It had been visited by many travellers, and had even been intermittently excavated, most recently by Auguste Mariette in 1858, 1862 and 1866. But two-thirds of the temple remained covered in sand, while the remains of a Coptic monastery perched uncomfortably on the ruins. Naville was the first, after several seasons of hard work (1893–6), to reveal its unique design. A limestone wall had once surrounded the temple complex. Beyond this lay a peaceful garden area complete with pools, plants and incense trees. The white limestone temple rose against the cliff in three terraces linked by a central stairway. The lower porticoes were decorated with scenes depicting significant events from Hatshepsut's life and reign; here we can see Hatshepsut's workmen transporting obelisks from the Aswan quarries to the Karnak temple, and Hatshepsut's soldiers travelling to the far-away, mysterious land of Punt. Twenty-four colossal statues of Hatshepsut in the form of Osiris had dominated the uppermost level, the most important part of the temple. A further ten Osiride statues stood in niches at the rear of the upper court, four more stood in the corners of the sanctuary, and four truly enormous ones – each 26 ft tall – stood at either end of the lower and middle porticoes. Unfortunately, these statues had been torn down and smashed in antiquity. Today they are slowly being replaced, as the Polish Centre of Mediterranean Archaeology completes the restoration of the temple.

Chapter Ten

Carter was sent to help Naville at Deir el-Bahari. He was to over-see the copying of the reliefs that decorated the porticoes. Drawing on his experience of tomb-tracing, Carter devised a thorough system of tracings, freehand drawings and scale grids, which allowed him to produce the astonishingly accurate drawn record of the temple scenes published in Naville's six-volume work *The Temple of Deir el Bahari* (1895–1908). When it became obvious that Carter needed some help covering the vast wall area, his older brother Vernet joined the team. Vernet, a professional artist, was as skilled with a pencil as Howard, and the finished work of the two brothers is indistinguishable. But Vernet Carter found Egypt far too hot for comfort, and this was to be his first and last season working alongside his brother. Howard, working with a series of talented assistants, remained at Deir el-Bahari until 1899, when he was offered a permanent position with the Egyptian Antiquities Service.

Gaston Maspero, now back in his old job as Loret's replacement, had acquired enough funding to appoint two Antiquities Inspectors. One, James Quibell, would be based in Cairo and would assume responsibility for all the northern sites, as well as the Delta. The other, Howard Carter, would live at Luxor and supervise all the southern sites. The Inspectors would be responsible for everything archaeological; they would ensure that the sites were properly excavated, properly guarded and properly conserved, and they would investigate any thefts or acts of vandalism. Given Egypt's vast size, and the number and extent of her antiquities, this was always going to be an impossibly large challenge. But Carter set to work with relish.

His first task was to fit doors on the open tombs of the Valley of the Kings. Wooden doors were tried and quickly rejected; they did nothing to deter the determined thief. So iron gates and grilles, even though ugly and incongruous, were installed instead. At the same time the more popular tombs were fitted with the new electric light, and a donkey park was provided for the convenience of the ever-increasing numbers of tourists. Carter well knew that the ugly tomb doors were a necessity. There had already been an unpleasant incident in the tomb of Amenhotep II. The story was a sad, if familiar, one. The guards had been overpowered or, as Carter suspected, paid to look the other way. Bribery had been the favoured method of the dynastic tomb robbers some 3000 years earlier, and it was still a major problem. The prince and his boat had been stolen from the entrance corridor, where, covered in chicken wire, they had been left to entertain tourists; the prince would later be found smashed to pieces, but his boat, purchased from an antiquities dealer, is now in Cairo Museum. Amenhotep II's body was undamaged, but had been expertly stripped of its bandages in a fruitless search for jewellery. Carter determined to solve the theft. He already had a suspect in mind – the notorious Mohammed Abd el-Rassul, who lived quite close to the tomb.

The thieves had been careless, and a trail of footprints led from the scene of the crime. Carter photographed the footprints, and then paid a professional tracker to follow the trail. To no one's great surprise, the prints led straight to the house of Ahmed el-Rassul; they were indeed the footprints of his brother, Mohammed. Mohammed eventually stood trial for robbery – Carter's photograph was submitted as evidence – but he was acquitted. Meanwhile, the mummy of Amenhotep II was temporarily replaced in his tomb. In 1931 it would be sent to Cairo.

In 1900 Carter started to excavate 'The Tomb of the Horse', a curiously large 11th Dynasty tomb or cenotaph not far from the Deir el-Bahari temple. The tomb yielded a mysterious wooden statue wrapped in linen, an empty wooden coffin, and a blocked burial shaft. Convinced that he had uncovered an intact burial, he impetuously invited Lord Cromer, the British Consul General, to attend the grand opening of the burial chamber. Unfortunately, when, in the presence of the great and the good, the chamber was opened, it proved to be disappointingly bereft of burials. This very public humiliation did nothing to dissuade Carter from excavation, and he soon started to work with Theodore Davis in the Valley of the Kings. But it did teach him a valuable lesson. Never again would he invite officials to a grand opening without checking first to make sure that there was indeed something in the tomb.

After five highly successful years based in Luxor, the northern and southern Inspectors swapped roles, and Carter found himself based at Sakkara, while Quibell now assumed responsibility for the Valley of the Kings. Carter, a proud and stubborn man, almost immediately became involved in a difficult situation that ultimately led to his resignation. Flinders Petrie, an equally proud and stubborn man, takes up the tale:

> For the first six weeks my wife excavated at Saqqareh [Sakkara] ...
> One Sunday, some drunken Frenchmen tried to force their way
> into her huts, and were stoutly resisted by the cook boy. They
> went on to the official house and began to smash furniture and
> fight the native guards. Carter, then inspector, was fetched, and he
> very rightly allowed the guards to defend themselves till the police
> could come.
>
> The indignity of letting a native resist a Frenchman weighed
> more than the indignity of being drunk and disorderly, in the eyes
> of the French Consul, who demanded an apology from Carter.
> With proper self-respect Carter refused to apologise for doing his
> obvious duty. For this he was, on demand of the French, dismissed
> from the Service. This was perhaps the dirtiest act of subservience
> to French arrogance.[3]

Petrie, a good friend and mentor to Carter, with an ingrained distrust of the French, was by no means an unbiased witness. Indeed, he was no witness at all, not having been present at Sakkara on 8 January 1905 when the unfortunate episode occurred. But Hilda Petrie was present, and presumably able to give her husband an accurate, if somewhat exaggerated, account of events. The official report of the incident lodged by the French tourists is, not surprisingly, very different from Petrie's tale: they claimed to have suffered an unprovoked attack when a mild dispute over tickets intensified into a near-riot. The accounts published in the Cairo newspapers varied in both content and dramatic style, although *L'Égypte* did include the not irrelevant fact that the French party had consumed a dozen bottles of red wine during their picnic luncheon.

The main error in Petrie's account, however, lies in his interpretation of what happened next. Carter was expected, whatever the rights and wrongs of his case, to drop his demand that the drunken Frenchmen be properly punished in the law courts. And that he absolutely refused to do. Maspero, exasperated, had Carter moved from Cairo to the Delta city of Tanta. But provincial Tanta was not to Carter's liking, and, despite his success in foiling a gang of robbers and recovering a valuable hoard of temple equipment, gold, silver and jewellery at the site of Tukh el-Qaramus, he was unhappy and in ill health. In October 1905 he resigned from the Service and started a new, and impoverished, life as an artist and part-time antiquities dealer.

GEORGE HERBERT, Lord Carnarvon, was an enormously wealthy man obsessed with speed. His devoted sister, Lady Winifred Burghclere, introduces us to the dashing and multi-talented earl:

> A fine shot, an owner of racehorses, a singularly well inspired art
> collector – his privately printed catalogue of rare books is a model
> of its kind – Lord Carnarvon was also a pioneer of motoring. He
> owned cars in France before they were allowed in England. In fact,
> his was the third motor registered in this country, after the repeal
> of the act making it obligatory for all machine-propelled carriages
> to be preceded on the high road by a man carrying a red flag.
> Motoring was bound to appeal to one of his disposition, and he
> threw himself with a passion into the new sport. He was a splendid
> driver, well served by his gift – a gift which also served him in
> shooting and golf – of judging distances accurately, whilst
> possessing that unruffled calm in difficulties which often, if not
> invariably, is the best insurance against disaster.[4]

On several occasions the earl was forced to appear before the magistrates for speeding (at approximately 20 mph), but when Winifred worried that her brother might be driving with too much exuberance, he soon put her straight: 'Do you take me for a fool? In motoring the danger lies round corners, and I never take corners fast.' It is therefore ironic that Lord Carnarvon was travelling along a perfectly straight and seemingly empty road in Germany when he swerved and crashed, trying to avoid a pair of bullock carts hidden in a dip in the road. His life was saved by his chauffeur, Edward Trotman, who dragged the car off his master and threw a bucket of water over him to restart his heart. But the accident, in 1901, left him weak, unable to gain weight and vulnerable to chest infections. His doctors, worried about the effects of a damp British winter, therefore recommended a visit to Egypt.

Like Theodore Davis before him, Carnarvon developed an immediate fascination with Egypt's past that he too was able to satisfy by funding private excavations. At first things did not go too well. Allocated a barren patch of land by the Antiquities Service, who doubted both his competence and his dedication, he found virtually nothing. Rather than abandon his new hobby, he hired a professional. In 1909 he started to excavate at Thebes with Howard Carter, who came with a glowing recommendation from Gaston Maspero, as his archaeologist. The partnership suited both men. With Carter at the helm, Lord Carnarvon's excavation was regarded as seriously as any other mission in Egypt, while Carter, for his part, was happy to abandon the uncertain life of the artist/antiquities dealer and earn a decent wage. For three years Carnarvon and Carter worked the Theban necropolis as a team, their enthusiasm undaunted by a steady stream of unspectacular, but archaeologically satisfying, results. In 1912 there was a brief excavation at the Delta mound of Xois (modern Sakha), before uncongenial living conditions and an intolerable number of snakes caused Carter to relocate to the Delta site of Tell el-Balamun. Here he found some silver Graeco-Roman jewellery, hidden in a pot, and a statue fragment.

ABOVE: Theodore Davis (centre right) standing in front of the entrance to the Valley of the Kings tomb of Ramesses IV, with Arthur Weigal (centre left) and his wife Corinna (left), and Edward Ayrton (right). The then-lost tomb of Tutankhamen was hidden close by.

RIGHT: The gilded cartonage mask of Yuya, father of the 18th Dynasty Queen Tiy. The tomb of Yuya and his wife Thuyu (KV 46) was discovered by Theodore Davis in 1905.

ABOVE: The beautifully decorated tomb of Nefertari, consort of Ramesses II, in the Valley of the Queens. Here we can see (from left) the goddess Hathor, the god Re-Herakhty and the god Horus.

LEFT: This reconstructed mummy case, recovered from tomb KV 55, held the bones of an anonymous male member of the Amarna royal family, now identified as Smenkhkare, elder brother of Tutankhamen.

ABOVE: Luncheon in the tomb of Ramesses XI. Seated round the table from the left: James Breasted, Henry (Harry) Burton, Alfred Lucas, Arthur Callender, Arthur Mace, Howard Carter and Alan Gardiner

BELOW: The anteroom in the tomb of Tutankhamen (KV 62). The plastered entrance to the burial chamber, guarded by life-sized figures of the king, is obvious in the far wall.

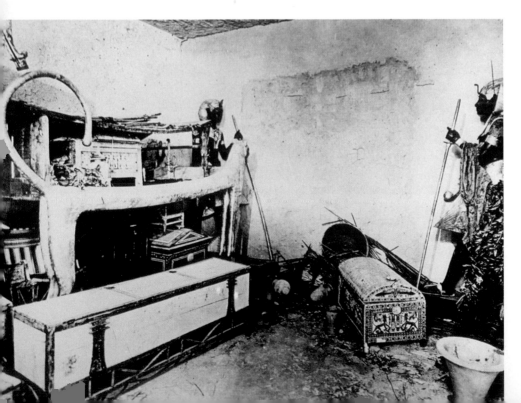

ABOVE: The gold funerary mask of King Tutankhamen.

OVERLEAF: The building of the Aswan High Dam in the 1960s threatened many monuments. In an unprecedented archaeological rescue mission, the twin Abu Simbel temples, built by Ramesses II, were dismantled and moved to a new, artificially created environment.

ABOVE: Abu Simbel: A coffer dam protected the vulnerable sandstone from the rising water as workmen cut the Abu Simbel temple into gigantic blocks and lifted it up the cliff face to safety.

BELOW: The mummy of the temple singer Asru has undergone a thorough medical examination as part of the Manchester Mummy Project, headed by Professor Rosalie David.

After that excitement there was a return to Luxor and the familiar comfort of the necropolis.

Carter spent his war years doing sporadic and unspecified work for the Intelligence Department of the War Office in Cairo, while continuing with small-scale excavation work financed by Lord Carnarvon. The most spectacular discovery of this fallow period occurred in 1916. In a lonely ravine known as the Wadi Sikkat Taka ez-Zeida, local robbers had discovered an almost inaccessible tomb carved high in a cliff face. Carter was soon on the scene:

> The tomb was discovered full of rubbish ... this rubbish having poured into it in torrents from the mountain above. When I wrested it from the plundering Arabs I found that they had burrowed into it like rabbits, as far as the sepulchral hall ... I found that they had crept down a crack extending half way down the cleft, and there from a small ledge in the rock they had lowered themselves by a rope to the then hidden entrance of the tomb at the bottom of the cleft: a dangerous performance, but one which I myself had to imitate, though with better tackle ... For anyone who suffers from vertigo it certainly was not pleasant, and though I soon overcame the sensation of the ascent I was obliged always to descend in a net.[5]

An entrance stairway dropped to a doorway that led in turn to a gallery, antechamber, second gallery and burial chamber. The tomb was unfinished and empty, but in one of the galleries there was a quartzite sarcophagus inscribed for 'The Great Princess, great in favour and grace, Mistress of All Lands, Royal Daughter and Royal Sister, Great Royal Wife, Mistress of the Two Lands, Hatshepsut'. Carter had discovered a second tomb, and third sarcophagus belonging to the female king. This tomb had been commissioned when Hatshepsut was a mere queen consort, and abandoned when she became king.

Carter was absolutely convinced that there was still an undiscovered royal tomb waiting to be found in the Valley of the Kings. Davis's discovery of Tutankhamen's embalming materials suggested to him that Tutankhamen's tomb proper could not be far away. And, as Tutankhamen's body had not been recovered in either of the royal caches, it seemed entirely possible that his tomb was undisturbed. Carter was prepared to clear the Valley down to the bedrock if necessary, in order to find the missing tomb, and he had the full support of his patron. But there was a snag. The one and only concession to excavate in the Valley had already been granted to Theodore Davis, and Carter and Carnarvon could only stand by and watch as Davis grew nearer and nearer to their prize. When, in 1914, Davis finally gave up the concession, Lord Carnarvon took it over, but the war years prevented any intensive digging campaign.

The clearance of the Valley finally started in 1917 and proved to be a slow and expensive business. The results were so meagre that Lord Carnarvon started to have serious doubts over the wisdom of pouring vast amounts of money into a potentially fruitless mission. Meanwhile, Carter fell ill while enjoying a holiday in London. It was not until January 1922, fully restored to health after the removal of his gall bladder, that he was able to resume his search. Another short, unproductive season followed, and Lord Carnarvon grew even more disillusioned. He wanted to admit defeat and agree with Davis that the Valley was indeed empty. Carter, who would be unemployed when the work did stop, strongly disagreed. He even went so far as to offer to pay the costs of a final season himself. Over a summer break spent at Highclere, Lord Carnarvon's country estate, it was agreed that there would be one last, short season, financed by Carnarvon. This would allow Carter enough time to clear the one part of the Valley, a heap of rubble and ancient huts beneath the entrance to the tomb of Ramesses VI, that had so far been left untouched. Why had this area been ignored? Not for any sound archaeological reason, but because it was feared that excavations in this area would disrupt the flow of tourists intent on viewing the tomb above.

On 1 November 1922 Carter's workmen started to dig away the rubbish that lay at the base of Ramesses's tomb. Just three days later they discovered a flight of 16 stone steps leading down to a blocked doorway, its necropolis seals still intact. A small portion of plaster had fallen away from the upper section of the doorway; with the aid of a new-fangled electric torch, Carter was able to peer into a descending corridor packed with stones and rubbish. This was obviously a find with huge potential. Demonstrating admirable self-control, Carter re-covered the stairwell to hide the tomb from thieves, swore his workmen to secrecy, and then crossed the river to the Luxor telegraph office where he sent a coded message to Lord Carnarvon who was still in England:

At last have made wonderful discovery in Valley. A magnificent tomb with seals intact. Re-covered same for your arrival. Congratulations. Carter

Three weeks later — three weeks of nail-biting inactivity for Carter, we must assume – Lord Carnarvon and his daughter, Lady Evelyn Herbert, had arrived, and the clearing of the stairwell and doorway was resumed. Soon it was possible to read the name of the tomb owner: Tutankhamen. It was also now possible to see that the tomb had been opened and resealed at least twice in antiquity. Carter must have feared the worst.

Archaeology confirms that the tomb had indeed been robbed twice. The first phase of thefts must have occurred soon after the funeral, and may even have been carried out by members of the burial party: it was by no means unknown for undertakers and grave diggers to rob those whom they were paid to protect. Thieves had made their way along the entrance corridor, which was empty except for jars containing the king's embalming waste as well as the remains of the funeral feast, and had entered the antechamber. Here they had ransacked the neatly stacked boxes and bundles, seeking the light and valuable items – precious metals, linen, oils and cosmetics –

which could be sold easily on the black market. Luckily, the necropolis guards realized that a robbery was in progress. Forced to flee, the thieves dropped some of their swag in the corridor. The guards carelessly repacked the boxes and chests – articles were simply stuffed in anywhere they fitted. The tomb was then reconsecrated and resealed, and the access corridor was filled with tons of debris and limestone chips in an attempt to foil future robbers. With the corridor blocked, the king's embalming waste was given a separate burial in a small, stone-lined pit close to the tomb (KV54 – excavated by Edward Ayrton and Theodore Davis in 1907).

The second robbery had been both more ambitious and more dangerous for the thieves. By tunnelling through the limestone chips that now packed the corridor to its ceiling, then cutting through the blocked doorways, they were able to gain access to all the chambers in the tomb. Fortunately, although the outer shrine was opened, they never reached the mummy itself. These thieves targeted the jewellery and amulets, which would have been easy to carry back through the narrow tunnel in the corridor; Howard Carter later estimated that they might have helped themselves to as much as 60 per cent of Tutankhamen's jewellery. Once again the thieves were discovered and the tomb was restored. The holes in the doorways were blocked and plastered over, the corridor tunnel was refilled with chips, and the entrance was resealed. Doubtless the whole sorry cycle would have been repeated again and again, until the depleted burial and stripped mummy were 'rescued' by the necropolis officials responsible for the two royal caches. But here fate stepped in. Tutankhamen had died suddenly, before his planned regal tomb was complete. He had been buried in an inconspicuous non-royal tomb, perhaps the tomb that his successor, the courtier Ay, was preparing for himself. This insignificant tomb entrance was easily overlooked, and Tutankhamen vanished off the necropolis map. The builders who worked on the tomb of Ramesses VI had certainly forgotten all about him. They allowed the rubble from their excavations to cover his tomb entrance, then built their huts on top of the mound. This, rather than official security measures, saved Tutankhamen's burial for Howard Carter.

The blocked doorway was quickly dismantled, and the entrance corridor cleared of its rubble and limestone chips. By 26 November Carter and Carnarvon were again standing in front of a sealed doorway: this, we now know, was the entrance to the antechamber. At this most exciting point in the history of Egyptology, it is appropriate that Howard Carter should take up the tale:

> Slowly, desperately slowly it seemed to us as we watched, the remains of passage debris that encumbered the lower part of the doorway were removed, until at last we had the whole door clear before us. The decisive moment had arrived. With trembling hands I made a tiny breach in the upper left hand corner. Darkness and blank space, as far as the iron testing-rod could reach, showed that whatever lay beyond was empty, and not filled like the passage we had just cleared. Candle tests were applied as a precaution against possible foul gasses, and then, widening the hole a little, I inserted the candle and peered in ... At first I could see nothing, the hot air escaping from the chamber causing the candle flame to flicker, but presently, as my eyes grew accustomed to the light, details of the room within emerged slowly from the mist, strange animals, statues and gold – everywhere the glint of gold. For the moment – an eternity it must have seemed to the others standing by – I was struck dumb with amazement, and when Lord Carnarvon, unable to stand the suspense any longer, inquired anxiously, 'Can you see anything?' it was all I could do to get out the words 'Yes, wonderful things.'[6]

The next day this second doorway was unblocked, and an electric light was connected to the Valley supply – the supply that Carter himself had brought to the Valley during his period as Inspector. The bright light showed that the antechamber was effectively a small warehouse packed, rather untidily, with everything that a king could want in the Afterlife; there were three large, animal-shaped beds, a heap of dismantled chariots, furniture, boxes filled with clothing and sandals, alabaster vessels, food, drink, bouquets of flowers and much, much more. A second undecorated chamber cut into the western wall, 'the annexe', held even more boxes and bundles. In the northern wall was the blocked and sealed entrance to the burial chamber, guarded by two life-sized statues of the king himself.

> Excitement had gripped us hitherto, and given us no pause for thought, but now for the first time we began to realise what a prodigious task we had in front of us, and what a responsibility it entailed. This was no ordinary find, to be disposed of in a normal season's work; nor was there any precedent to show us how to handle it. The thing was outside all experience, bewildering, and for the moment it seemed as though there were more to be done than any human agency could accomplish.[7]

Carter was facing a huge logistical headache. Regardless of what lay in the burial chamber – and the hole made by the ancient robbers was very obvious in the sealed doorway – he already had the most important collection of royal artifacts ever to be recovered from Egypt. Here was a microcosm of royal life, but it was all in desperate need of conservation. And everything would have to be sent to Cairo for its own protection. He needed vast amounts of packing and conservation equipment, workrooms, a motorcar (which must have pleased Lord Carnarvon), and steel grilles to protect the tomb chambers against unwanted visitors. And he needed help if the job was to be done correctly. Amongst the international team of experts who now gathered in the Valley, several of them loaned by the Metropolitan Museum, New York, were the conservator (and distant cousin of Flinders Petrie) Arthur Mace, the engineer and architect Arthur Callender, and the chemist Alfred Lucas. The architects Walter Hauser and Lindsley Hall were to plan the tomb. Meanwhile, KV55 (Davis's mysterious 'tomb of Queen Tiy') was converted into a darkroom for photographer Harry Burton, KV15 (the tomb of Seti II) was transformed into a workshop/laboratory, and KV4 (the tomb of Ramesses XI) became the essential luncheon tomb.

It was to take seven weeks of painfully slow work to empty the packed antechamber, a task that Carter likened to 'playing a gigantic game of spillikins'. The tomb as a whole would not be officially cleared until 1932. Each object had to be numbered, photographed, planned, recorded and drawn before it could be moved to the storage tomb. Fortunately, Carter had been well trained in the arts of conservation by Petrie:

> There were sandals, for instance, of patterned bead-work, of which the threading had entirely rotted away. As they lay on the floor of the chamber they looked in perfectly sound condition, but, try to pick one up, and it crumbled at the touch, and all you had for your pains was a handful of loose, meaningless beads. This was a clear case for treatment on the spot – a spirit stove, some paraffin wax, an hour or two to harden, and the sandal could be removed intact, and handled with the utmost freedom.[8]

Further conservation treatments were given in the storage tomb, before the artifacts were packaged in miles of wadding and bandages for transfer to Cairo.

It was not until 17 February 1923 that the sealed entrance to the burial chamber was officially opened in the presence of an invited audience of archaeologists and government officials. The next day there would be a far grander second 'opening', attended by Élisabeth, Queen of the Belgians, and her son, and Lord and Lady Allenby. The Belgian Queen was to become something of a nuisance to the excavators; fascinated by what she had seen, she paid a further three visits to the tomb, bringing all work to a halt each time, in the hope of seeing a box, any box, unpacked.

Carter had learned a harsh lesson at the humiliating opening of the Tomb of the Horse. Never again would he invite a prestigious visitor to watch as he demolished a sealed doorway to reveal – absolutely nothing. He was supremely confident that there was indeed something lying in Tutankhamen's burial chamber because shortly after the opening of the antechamber he, Lord Carnarvon and Lady Evelyn had breached the wall and crawled inside the burial chamber to inspect its contents. The ill-kept secret of this first visit to the burial chamber has since provoked intense debate. Unethical it may have been, although many would argue that an excavator should be fully aware of the extent of the treasures that he is required to protect, but deliberately dishonest it was not. There is absolutely no evidence, as some have since alleged, that either Carter or Carnarvon removed any objects on their earlier, clandestine visit.

Now Carter stood on a wooden platform and prepared, with a trembling hand, to knock down the partition wall that separated the burial chamber from the antechamber:

> My first care was to locate the wooden lintel above the door: then very carefully I chipped away the plaster and picked out the small stones which formed the uppermost layer of the filling. The temptation to stop and peer inside at every moment was irresistible, and when, after about ten minutes' work, I had made a hole large enough to enable me to do so, I inserted an electric torch. An astonishing sight its light revealed, for there, within a yard of the doorway, stretching as far as one could see and blocking the entrance to the chamber, stood what to all appearance was a solid wall of gold.[9]

As Carter and Mace levered blocks out of the wall with a crowbar, they were handed to Callender then passed along a chain of work-men and neatly stacked outside the tomb. Two hours later the 'solid wall of gold' was revealed in all its glory; an enormous and very frag-ile floorless gilt shrine decorated with blue inlay, its double doors bolted but not sealed, almost filled the burial chamber. Carter drew back the ebony bolts and swung open the doors to reveal – another gold shrine, this time both bolted and sealed and covered with a delicate linen veil spangled with golden flowers. It was obvious that the shrines – there were four in total – would have to be dismantled in order to reach sarcophagus.

The general public was fascinated by activities within the tomb. Those who could travel to Egypt did so, even though there was little for them to see. Those who could not manage a visit to the Valley had to content themselves with Egyptian-style clothing, accessories, biscuits and even buildings; many new cinemas in the West were designed with a distinct Egyptian twist. Luxor was swamped with visitors, and the expedition found itself living in siege conditions as a constant stream of sightseers and journalists traipsed out to the tomb each day, making the lives of the excavators a misery. In an attempt to reduce the number of reporters who now hounded his every move, and, of course, as a means of recovering some of the many thousands of pounds that he had spent excavating, Lord Carnarvon signed an exclusive deal with *The Times*. This proved to be a very bad decision – it incensed the other reporters, and did nothing at all to staunch their demands for information. Howard Carter, already under immense stress, was finding it difficult to cope:

> The tomb drew like a magnet. From a very early hour in the
> morning the pilgrimage began. Visitors arrived on donkeys, in
> sand-carts, and in two-horse cabs, and proceeded to make
> themselves at home in The Valley for the day. Round the top of
> the upper level of the tomb there was a low wall, and here they
> each staked out a claim and established themselves, waiting for
> something to happen. Sometimes it did, more often it did not,
> but it seemed to make no difference to their patience. There
> they would sit the whole morning, reading, talking, knitting,
> photographing the tomb and each other, quite satisfied if at the
> end they could get a glimpse of anything ... We were really

alarmed sometimes lest the whole wall should give way, and a
crowd of visitors be precipitated into the mouth of the tomb.[10]

Lord Carnarvon found it easier to handle his newfound celebrity,
but even he felt in need of a break. In late February 1923, soon after
the opening of the burial chamber, the excavation was closed down
for ten days. Closing the excavation was no simple matter – the
chambers had to be locked, then the entire tomb had to be reburied
to save it from thieves – but everyone felt that it was worth it.
Everyone needed some time off. While Carter chose to stay in
Luxor, Lady Evelyn and her father sailed south to spend a few peaceful days at Aswan.

While away, Carnarvon was bitten on the cheek by a mosquito,
an unremarkable, everyday occurrence on the Nile. But soon after
his return to Luxor, he accidentally sliced the scab off the bite while
shaving himself with a cut-throat razor. Although he treated the
wound with iodine, he soon started to feel unwell. Lord Carnarvon
refused to give in to his illness. With his condition worsening by the
day, he travelled with Lady Evelyn to Cairo and booked into the
Continental-Savoy Hotel. Here blood poisoning set in, and pneumonia soon followed. Lord Carnarvon's underlying weak constitution – the very reason for his presence in Egypt – made recovery
impossible. Lady Carnarvon arrived from England, and Lord
Porchester, Lord Carnarvon's son and heir, was summoned from
India. On 20 March Howard Carter travelled to Cairo to help Lady
Carnarvon and Lady Evelyn in any way he could. But there was
nothing to be done. At 1.45 a.m. on 5 April 1923, George Herbert
died of pneumonia. His body was embalmed in Egypt and then
returned to England for burial. Winifred Burghclere watched as her
beloved brother was interred in a simple ceremony on Beacon Hill,
part of the Highclere estate:

Organ, music, choristers, there were none at this burying. The
beautiful office, commanding 'the body of our dear brother to the

ground in sure and certain hope', had something of the stark grandeur of a funeral at sea. But the whole air was alive with the springtide song of the larks. They sang deliriously, in a passion of ecstasy which can never be forgotten by those who heard that song. And so we left him, feeling that the ending was in harmony with the life.[11]

She neglects to tell us that the beautiful song of the larks was almost entirely drowned out as an aeroplane, hired by a London newspaper, buzzed the ceremony. Lord Carnarvon's sudden death, extensively covered in all the newspapers, had stimulated an even greater interest in the drama unfolding in Tutankhamen's tomb. The whole story had become a drama on an epic scale, as Winifred most perceptively summarized:

> If it is true that the whole world loves a lover, it is also true that either openly or secretly the world loves Romance. Hence, doubtless, the passionate and far-flung interest aroused by the discovery of Tut-ankh-Amen's tomb, an interest extended to the discoverer, and certainly not lessened by the swift tragedy that waited on his brief hour of triumph. A story that opens like Aladdin's Cave and ends like a Greek myth of Nemesis cannot fail to capture the imagination of all men and women who, in this workaday existence, can still be moved by tales of high endeavour and unrelenting doom.[12]

Western Europe, in the aftermath of the First World War and the devastating flu epidemic that followed it, had lost the rock-solid certainty of unquestioning Christian faith. Instead there was an unfocused wave of interest in all things supernatural and occult, including Egyptian religion. It was now possible for everyone to read, in published translation, the hieroglyphic texts and spells decoded by Champollion, but there were no explanatory texts available, and misunderstandings over the true nature of Egyptian

Chapter Ten

theology abounded. Many believed, as the Theosophists did, that the Egyptians had been the possessors of strong magical powers, which students of the occult now sought to awake.

At the same time there was a growing unease over the archaeologist's automatic assumption that the dead had no rights. Lord Carnarvon had deliberately sought out Tutankhamen; he had been preparing to reveal him to the world. But surely it was fundamentally wrong to desecrate a grave, no matter how ancient that grave might be? Perhaps the Egyptians had untold powers which they would, of course, not hesitate to use to protect their dead?

Soon it became generally accepted that Tutankhamen had somehow killed Lord Carnarvon. Howard Carter found it necessary to repeat time and time again that Tutankhamen's tomb contained no biological booby traps, no poisons and no curse, but to no avail. The speculation simply grew and grew, with many choosing to believe that Carter was collaborating with 'the authorities' to hide the evidence. Conspiracy theories are notoriously difficult to disprove. Could Lord Carnarvon have been infected by a mosquito that had itself been contaminated by Tutankhamen's embalming fluids? No; before the Aswan High Dam raised the water table, there were no mosquitoes in the dry Valley of the Kings. Could he have been poisoned by inhaling the toxic bat dung heaped on the tomb floor? No, because there were no bats in the sealed tomb. Could he have been killed by the potent curse carved over the entrance? No, because, contrary to many reports, there was no such curse. Could he have been killed by an 'elemental', as Sir Arthur Conan Doyle, who also believed in fairies, suggested? No, because 'elementals' don't exist.

In 1934 the American Egyptologist Herbert Winlock attempted to disprove the theory of the curse by studying the facts. He found that a mere six of the 26 people present at the tomb opening had died within a decade, while only two of those present at the lifting of the sarcophagus lid had since died. Of those who had first crept into the burial chamber, only Lord Carnarvon – a man already in ill health – had died prematurely. Howard Carter would outlive Lord

Carnarvon by 16 years, and Lady Evelyn would not die until 1980. But still, rumours about the 'curse' of Tutankhamen persist.

The second season of work on Tutankhamen's tomb was scheduled to start in October 1923, with Lady Carnarvon now holding the permission to excavate and Howard Carter charged with liaising with the authorities and the press. Carter, not a natural diplomat, found himself facing many seemingly trivial bureaucratic problems. The press had complained about their restricted access to the tomb, the Antiquities Service had demanded a full list of those authorized to work on the site, with the right to veto anyone that they objected to, and there was a new requirement to have a government-appointed Inspector on site. This was a sign of things to come; the Egyptian government, via the Antiquities Service and Pierre Lacau, was preparing to take a more active role in events in the Valley.

By 3 January 1924 the team was ready to open doors of the innermost shrine surrounding the sarcophagus. Carter again takes up the tale:

> The decisive moment was at hand! What was beneath and what did the fourth shrine contain? ... With intense excitement I drew back the bolts of the last and unsealed doors; they slowly swung open, and there, filling the entire area within, effectually barring any further progress, stood an immense yellow quartzite sarcophagus, intact, with the lid still firmly fixed in its place, just as the pious hands had left it. It was certainly a thrilling moment, as we gazed upon the spectacle enhanced by the striking contrast – the glitter of metal – of the golden shrines shielding it.[13]

The shrine was dismantled and stored in the antechamber. On 12 February 1924, in front of an invited audience of officials and archaeologists, the cracked granite lid (the crack cemented and painted over by the ancient craftsmen), weighing 1.25 tons, was hoisted off its quartzite sarcophagus base. A shrouded figure was revealed. As the veils were drawn back, the audience let out a collective gasp of astonishment. Here was a gleaming golden coffin in the image of Tutankhamen himself. For the first time, it was absolutely certain that Carter was dealing with an intact royal burial.

The next day had already been planned. The tomb was to be opened to the press, then 'The Ladies', the wives of the archaeologists, were to be allowed a private viewing of the sarcophagus. But the Egyptian government sent a last-minute objection. The Ladies could not be admitted. Carter was horrified and furious. Surely he alone had the right to veto entry to the tomb that he himself had discovered and that his patron, Lady Carnarvon, herself now excluded, was financing? As we have already seen at Sakkara, Carter was no diplomat, and he was not a man to take what he perceived as an insult lightly. Backing down was never an option with Howard Carter. In fact, there was only one possible response – his workmen downed tools and he closed the tomb. The dispute worsened, and on 20 February Lady Carnarvon's concession was withdrawn. Work would not start again until January 1925, when Carter came to a grudging agreement with the authorities. Included in this new agreement was the stipulation that the Egyptian Government would take possession of all the finds from the tomb. Lord Carnarvon's estate would eventually receive £35,867 13s 8d as compensation for their excavation costs, and a quarter of this would be paid to Howard Carter.

Tutankhamen had been buried in three concentric anthropoid coffins. The outermost coffin was made of wood that had been coated in plaster and covered in gold decorated with inlays of semi-precious stone. Its lid had been fastened to its base by a series of ten silver pins. With these removed, it was a simple enough matter to lift the lid and reveal a second, linen-shrouded and garlanded golden coffin beneath. This too was a wooden coffin covered in gold and decorated with stone inlays. But its face was sufficiently different from the first coffin (and, as would subsequently be shown, from the third) to allow experts to suggest that this coffin was originally prepared for the burial of Tutankhamen's brother and predecessor, Smenkhkare.

All three coffins still lay inside the stone sarcophagus, and with the second coffin fitting very snugly inside the base of first, there was insufficient room to manoeuvre. The next stage had to be the extraction of the nest of coffins from the sarcophagus. This was done using lifting apparatus; the archaeologists were astonished at the weight of the coffin assemblage, which far exceeded their estimates. Then the entire second coffin was lifted from the base of the outermost coffin, which was replaced in the sarcophagus for storage. The lid of the second coffin was lifted on 23 October, revealing a third shrouded and garlanded golden coffin beneath. But unlike the other two, this coffin was made of solid gold.

The gold coffin, still in the base of the second coffin, was transferred to the antechamber. Here its lid was raised to reveal an amazing sight:

> At such moments the emotions evade verbal expression, complex and stirring as they are. Three thousand years and more had elapsed since men's eyes had gazed into that golden coffin ...
>
> Before us, occupying the whole interior of the golden coffin, was an impressive, neat and carefully made mummy, over which had been poured anointing unguents ... in great quantity – consolidated and blackened by age. In contradiction to the general dark and sombre effect, due to these unguents, was a brilliant, one might say magnificent, burnished gold mask or similitude of the king, covering his head and shoulders, which, like the feet, had been intentionally avoided when using the unguents.[14]

Carter estimated that at least two buckets of unguents and perfumes had been poured over Tutankhamen as part of his funeral ritual. Unfortunately, the resin-based fluids had both darkened and hardened with age, sticking the king into his bandages, the mask to the bandages, and the whole mummy firmly into the inner coffin. The body could not be easily separated from the coffin, so if the body was to be unwrapped in the near future, it would have to be unwrapped where it lay, inside the coffin in the tomb. On 11 November 1925, in the presence of officials from the Antiquities Service, including Pierre Lacau, Dr Douglas Derry and Dr Saleh Bey Hamdi started the autopsy:

> We had hoped, by removing a thin outer layer of bandage from
> the mummy, to free it at the points of adhesion to the coffin so
> that it might be removed, but in this we were again disappointed.
> It was found that the linen beneath the mummy and the body
> itself had been so saturated by the unguents which formed a pitch-
> like mass at the bottom of the coffin and held it embedded so
> firmly, that it was impossible to raise it except at risk of great
> damage. Even after the greater part of the bandages had been
> carefully removed, the consolidated material had to be chiselled
> away from beneath the limbs and trunk before it was possible to
> raise the king's remains.[15]

As for the golden mask, Howard Carter feared that 'it would require a hammer and chisel to free it'. Eventually he succeeded with the aid of hot knives.

The results were disappointing. Beneath the bandages, the king's body was in a far worse state of preservation than any of the bodies that had been recovered from the royal caches. This is perhaps understandable; the other bodies had been separated from their original, unguent-saturated bandages a mere century or so after burial. In Tutankhamen's case, it seemed that the unguents had had a corrosive and oxidizing (or combustive) effect on the skin, although Carter's incautious use of intense heat to separate the body from its surrounds may have been at least partially responsible for the signs of charring. The king's face had not been coated in unguents, and so was tolerably well preserved; even so, the skin was greyish in colour, brittle and cracked, and marred with white natron spots.

Tutankhamen's head was shaven, his ears were pierced and his lips had been glued shut with resin.

The autopsy showed that the king had died at approximately 18 years of age, and that he had stood approximately 5ft 6in tall. It was generally assumed that he had died of tuberculosis, although there was no specific evidence to support this assumption. More recently archaeologists, noting that part of the king's chest – the breastbone and the frontal ribcage – had gone missing before he was bandaged, have accepted that he might have met an accidental death; the racing chariots included among the burial equipment suggest a possible scenario.

In 1923 Arthur Mace had developed a more dramatic theory. The young and healthy Tutankhamen had perhaps been murdered by his successor, the ambitious courtier Ay:

> The rest is pure conjecture ... We have reason to believe that he
> was little more than a boy when he died, and that it was his
> successor, Eye [Ay], who supported his candidature to the throne
> and acted as his advisor during his brief reign. It was Eye,
> moreover, who arranged his funeral ceremonies, and it may even
> be that he arranged his death, judging that the time was now ripe
> for him to assume the reins of government himself.[16]

This theory, recently readopted and refined by Professor Bob Brier, is an intriguing one, but it is a theory that rests on very flimsy 'evidence'. In 1968 R.G. Harrison, professor of anatomy at Liverpool University, took an X-ray of Tutankhamen's head. In this X-ray it is possible to see a detached fragment of bone within the skull; it is generally agreed that this is the result of post-mortem damage, and nothing to do with the king's death. It is also possible to see an area of darkness or thickening at the base of the skull, just where the head joins the neck. While this thickening falls within the accepted normal range of skull thickness, there exists the possibility that it may indicate a haemorrhage caused by a blow to the back of the head.

An area of clouding in the region of the thickening may or may not be evidence for a calcified membrane formed over a blood clot. If this is membrane, it complicates the issue by suggesting that the king may have lived for at least two months after receiving a blow to the back of his head.

Today Tutankhamen rests once again in his coffin in the Valley of the Kings. He is the only one of Egypt's pharaohs – apart, of course, from those who remain undiscovered – to still lie in his original tomb.

The king's viscera (his stomach, intestines, liver and lungs) had been embalmed and stored in golden canopic jars shaped like miniature coffins. These jars stood in a beautiful alabaster chest housed in a gilt shrine in the 'treasury', a small storage chamber opening off the burial chamber. Here Carter found two further miniature coffins in a plain wooden box. These each yielded a smaller golden coffin holding a mummified foetus. The first mummy, a premature baby girl, wore a golden funerary mask. The second baby, also a girl, had died at or soon after birth. An autopsy conducted by Dr Derry showed that she had suffered from Sprengal's deformity, an illness causing spina bifida and scoliosis.

The discovery in 1922 of Tutankhamen's tomb saw the end of Howard Carter's career as an excavator. For the next decade he would dedicate himself to recording and preserving the tomb; his summer breaks would be spent lecturing on his work. When the tomb was finally empty, the full scientific publication of the results became his top priority. But his health was starting to fail – he had the beginnings of Hodgkin's disease – and the full publication would never be completed. Howard Carter died in London on 2 March 1939.

Carter had been both blessed and cursed by the discovery of Tutankhamen's tomb. Blessed because the discovery brought him worldwide recognition: his name would forever be linked with the name of the boy king. Cursed because the discovery effectively brought his career to a halt as he struggled to empty and record the tomb and its contents. Carter's reputation would always be based on his work in KV62. This work, at first appreciated as some of the most painstaking practical Egyptology ever undertaken, seems clumsy and even crude by today's standards. His treatment of the body of Tutankhamen, though acceptable in the early twentieth century, makes modern observers shudder. But before we condemn Carter for thinking and behaving like a man of his time, we should perhaps reflect what would have happened had Tutankhamen's tomb been discovered by some of his contemporaries.

THE
SCIENTISTS

≻—≺

THE EXCAVATOR GOES TO HIS WORK NOW, NOT WITH
THE HOPE OF FINDING SOME GREAT MONUMENT
WHICH WILL CONFIRM SOME DOUBTFUL STATEMENT OF
HISTORY OR DISPROVE SOME THEORY OF SUCCESSION,
NOT EVEN WITH THE HOPE OF DISCOVERING SOME
STORE OF TABLETS WHICH WILL LET NEW LIGHT IN ON
A DARK PERIOD. SUCH THINGS MAY OF COURSE BE
FOUND, AND ARE WELCOMED WHEN THEY ARE FOUND;
AND SUCH DISCOVERIES AS THAT OF THE TOMB OF
TUTANKHAMEN TELL US THAT THE ROMANCE OF
EXPLORATION IS BY NO MEANS A THING OF THE PAST.
BUT THE MODERN EXPLORER HAS LEARNED THE
INFINITE IMPORTANCE OF LITTLE THINGS, AND THE
RESULTS FOR WHICH HE MAINLY HOPES ARE SUCH
THINGS AS WOULD BE HEARTILY DESPISED BY THE
CASUAL AND UNINSTRUCTED BEHOLDER. PERHAPS
THE CHANGE MAY BE EXPRESSED MOST SIMPLY
BY SAYING THAT WHILE THE EXPLORER OF TWO
GENERATIONS BACK LOOKED FOR COLOSSI, HIS
PRESENT-DAY SUCCESSOR LOOKS FOR CROCKERY.

J. Baikie, *A Century of Excavation in the Land of the Pharaohs* (1923)

CHAPTER ELEVEN

>—<

OUTSIDE THE
VALLEY

THE DRAMATIC SEQUENCE of events unfolding in the Valley of the Kings drew the eyes of the world. Meanwhile, outside the Valley, a stream of important discoveries went almost unnoticed. There were major finds at the pyramid sites and at the Delta city of Tanis, while in Middle Egypt, the short-lived royal city of Amarna started to tell the complicated story of Nefertiti and Akhenaten.

We last visited Amarna during Flinders Petrie's 1891–2 season of excavation in the city-site. He was followed, in 1902, by an Egypt Exploration Fund expedition led by the Unitarian minister and brilliant tomb-copyist Norman de Garis Davies. Davies concentrated on making a detailed epigraphic (inscription) study of the elaborately decorated elite tombs in the Amarna cliffs. This was in many ways a rescue mission, and it was not pleasant work. Over the centuries the dark and dirty tombs had been used as houses, burial sites and even churches, had suffered from deliberate and accidental vandalism, and had filled with many layers of repulsive rubbish. To make matters worse, they were infested by large bats, whose droppings corroded the walls, destroyed the artwork and generated a peculiarly noxious smell. The intrepid explorer was forced to take drastic action to save the tombs:

The surface of the stone ... is most unsightly and sadly corroded; indeed in the upper parts the sculpture is almost effaced. This is

due to the countless bats that infect the tomb and make their
presence known to the nose as unpleasantly as to the eye ...
[A footnote adds] When working here I cleared the tomb of
them in an hour or two by a massacre of about a thousand
victims – a good proof of how easily the pests could be kept
down or exterminated.[1]

Davies was not exaggerating. The American Egyptologist James
Breasted had visited Amarna while enjoying a busman's honeymoon
in 1895, and had been shocked by the condition of the tombs:

> Unfortunately, and to the shame and disgrace of the French
> administration, I find the finest inscriptions in Amarna so
> mutilated by the fellahin that I can hardly use them. I told
> Brugsch of it at the museum today – he was greatly surprised,
> having known nothing of it. I am so filled with indignation against
> the French and their empty, blatant boasting, 'la gloire de la
> France', that I can hardly contain myself. I could have wept my
> eyes out in Amarna. Scarcely less indignant must one feel against
> the English who are here only for the commerce and the politics
> of it, and who might reform matters if they would. A combination
> of French rascality, of English philistine indifference & of German
> lack of money is gradually allowing Egypt to be pillaged and
> plundered from end to end. In another generation there will be
> nothing to be had or saved.[2]

Davies was to spend three seasons recording both the tombs and the
boundary stelae that defined the limits of Akhenaten's new city.
Although the bats are now a thing of the past, the tombs have continued to deteriorate, and his six-volume *Rock Tombs of Amarna*
(1903–8) has proved invaluable to modern Egyptologists.

In 1907 a team from the Deutsche Orient-Gesellschaft (German
Oriental Society), led by the experienced excavator Ludwig
Borchardt, were granted permission to excavate in the Amarna main

city. They started by conducting a site survey, dug a few exploratory trenches, then began to excavate in the ruined city suburbs. In December 1912 the team came across the mud-brick remains of the studio-workshop of the royal artist Tuthmosis, 'Chief of Works, the Sculptor'. Tuthmosis, like all the Amarna craftsmen, had been forced to abandon his studio early in the reign of Tutankhamen, when the boy king took the sensible decision to revert back to the old religion, and return the court to Thebes. Amarna was left more or less empty, as not only the courtiers, but also their servants, the army, the artists and craftsmen and the labourers from the workmen's village all sailed south. We must assume that Tuthmosis took with him all the artworks that he considered valuable, but that he left behind the broken, unfinished and redundant pieces. Among these were 23 heads and faces of the now discredited Amarna royal family, including the world-famous bust of Queen Nefertiti. Nefertiti's bust had been left sitting on a shelf but had eventually, as the shelf collapsed, toppled forward to be buried knee-deep in rubble.

Tuthmosis had carved Nefertiti's head from limestone, which he then covered with a layer of smooth plaster, and painted. He gave his queen a flawless pink-brown skin, deeper red-brown lips, a straight nose, arched black eyebrows and a universal beauty that transcends all boundaries of race and time. It seems almost churlish to point out that many other images of the Amarna queen show her in a far less flattering, even ugly, light. Egyptian art can never be assumed to be telling a literal truth. Tuthmosis's bust shows no hair under the queen's flat-topped blue crown, suggesting that she followed the elite custom of shaving her head. Nefertiti's right eye is inlaid with rock crystal and has a black pupil; it gleams softly in direct light. Her left eye, however, is missing. Borchardt ordered an immediate and intensive search of the workshop, but was unable to find the absent eyeball; as the socket shows no trace of any adhesive, it seems that it must have been missing when the head was abandoned. Theories about this lost eye abound. Could the bust simply be unfinished? But why stop work with only one eye to insert? Is it a teaching piece, used by Tuthmosis when instructing his pupils in the correct placement of an eyeball? Was the eye perhaps plucked out by Tuthmosis as the result of a personal vendetta against the queen?

The rules by which concessions were granted in 1912 dictated that there must be a 'division' at the end of each season, with all finds split 50:50 between the Egyptian Antiquities Service and the excavator. The excavator would then distribute his share of the finds amongst his sponsors. The Antiquities Service always had first pick of the finds, and it was accepted that they would choose the best pieces. But now, instead of the bust of Nefertiti, Inspector Lefebvre chose a painted relief of the royal family. This seemingly perverse choice has led to intense debate. Did Borchardt deliberately conceal the true beauty of the bust by coating it in grime so that Inspector Lefebvre would fail to spot its potential? Did Borchardt argue that Berlin already had a relief of the royal family, while Cairo had other royal statue heads? Was Inspector Lefebvre perhaps paid to make his irrational choice? More controversially, could Borchardt have smuggled the bust out of Egypt without ever including it in the division? The matter may be simpler than this. Today Nefertiti's head, clean and displayed to its best advantage in Berlin, is very obviously a uniquely beautiful piece. It is universally accepted that it is one of Egypt's best works of art. But is it really so much better than some of the other beautiful sculptures displayed in Cairo Museum? Sculptures that tend to go unnoticed, swamped as they are by so many other beautiful sculptures? How far does our understanding of Nefertiti's romantic history – a history unknown when Inspector Lefebvre made his momentous choice – influence our appreciation of the bust? Certainly, from an archaeological point of view, it can be argued that Lefebvre was quite correct in his choice; the painted relief is the more interesting piece.

Nefertiti left Egypt for Germany, and was given to Dr James Simon, the backer of Borchardt's expedition. It was not until 1920 that she was donated to the New Museum, Berlin. In 1924, not long after the glories of Tutankhamen had been revealed to an incredulous world, Nefertiti went on public display. She fitted well into the current craze for Nile style, and quickly became the museum's main exhibit. It was not long before the Egyptians asked for the return of the bust, claiming that it had been taken from Egypt under irregular circumstances. The Germans, however, were reluctant to cooperate, and Nefertiti remains in Berlin today.

The advent of the First World War had put an end to the German excavations. In 1921, the Egypt Exploration Society resumed their work at Amarna, where they have worked intermittently ever since under a series of distinguished directors, including T. Eric Peet, Leonard Woolley, Francis Newton (who was taken ill during the 1924 season and died at Asyut), Francis Llewellyn Griffith, Henry Frankfort and John Pendlebury. The present phase of work, which started in 1979, is directed by Barry Kemp of the University of Cambridge. His team has produced a detailed survey of the site, and has conducted a series of excavations focusing on the workmen's village. At the same time a team led by Geoffrey Martin and Ali el-Khouli has been engaged in recording and publishing the sadly neglected Amarna royal tomb.

Ludwig Borchardt died in Paris in 1938; his body was taken to Egypt for burial. He left an extensive and expensive archaeological library in Cairo. His widow, who spent the war in Switzerland, offered the library to the British Government on condition that she be offered British nationality immediately. The library would have formed the basis of the proposed British Institute of Archaeology in Cairo, but the British Government decided that it could not meet Madame Borchardt's terms and her offer was politely declined. Britain still lacks an archaeological institute in Egypt.

The discovery and eventual display of the Nefertiti bust thrust the hitherto shadowy queen into the limelight. So it was a matter of great archaeological excitement and interest when, in 1925, a team led by French archaeologist Henri Chevrier discovered a series of colossal statues of Nefertiti's husband, Akhenaten, in the precincts of the Karnak temple. Here at the very beginning of his reign, before he took the decision to relocate to Amarna, Akhenaten had built a series of temples dedicated to the sun god, the Aten. These temples were decorated inside and out with colossal statues of the king himself. When Akhenaten's successors restored the old religion they dismantled his Aten temples, burying his statues and reusing the valuable stone blocks as fill inside their own stone walls. Today over 35,000 disjointed, decorated and inscribed blocks have been collected from inside the walls and gateways of the Karnak Temple. Since the mid-1960s the Akhenaten Temple Project has been dedicated to the recovery – by computer analysis – of their lost scenes.[3]

Chevrier's discovery made obvious what archaeologists had already suspected: King Akhenaten was not afraid to experiment with his own image. For over 1000 years the kings of Egypt had presented themselves as perfect human beings with no obvious flaws or deformities. No matter what they really looked like – and the mummies of the New Kingdom monarchs show that some of them were by no means conventionally good-looking – they were invariably shown as ageless men with taut, muscled bodies and handsome faces. This was not simply a matter of personal vanity. The king was not to be regarded as an individual, but as merely the latest in a long line of identical rulers. By producing essentially the same portrait of successive monarchs, the royal artists confirmed the continuing presence of a traditional king on the throne, and this in turn confirmed the all-important presence of *maat* (order) in Egypt.

Akhenaten's earliest portraits show a slightly plump but otherwise unremarkable king of Egypt. But he soon develops a startling range of features. His head is narrow and elongated, his neck abnormally long and thin. His eyes too are narrow and almond-shaped; he has fleshy earlobes, a long nose, hollow cheeks, pronounced cheekbones and thick lips. In case this all sounds too repulsive, it has to be added that his knowing smile has a disturbing sensuality that many today find curiously attractive. His body is distinctly feminine, with underdeveloped shoulders, chest, arms and lower legs, but wide hips, heavy thighs, a narrow waist and obvious breasts. His swollen stomach bulges slightly over his tight-fitting pleated kilt.

When viewed as intended, from below and in profile lit by strong natural sunlight, Akhenaten's colossi must have been an arresting sight. But one of them, recovered by Chevrier from the open court-yard of the main Aten temple (*Gempaaten* or 'the Sun-Disk is found'), is more arresting than its fellows. The courtyard was sur-rounded by at least 24 colossal figures of Akhenaten dressed in a pleated linen kilt, carrying the crook and flail in his crossed arms and wearing a headcloth, as well as either the double crown of Upper and Lower Egypt or the feathered headdress worn by the god of the air, Shu. One unfinished and slightly damaged statue, however, had a naked torso lacking both kilt and genitalia.

How can we explain this aberration? The simplest explanation is that the statue is not of Akhenaten at all, but Queen Nefertiti appearing in the role of the goddess Tefnut, sister-wife to Shu. The face of the statue, however, appears to be pure Akhenaten. Alternatively, it is possible to argue that this is an unfinished statue, which would have eventually been carved or painted to show a kilt. However, given the shaping of the body, this seems unlikely. It may be that the sculpture would eventually have been dressed in clothing made from some separate material, perhaps a skirt of pre-cious metal or linen. Again, this is not a particularly convincing argument, as there are no known examples of colossal statues clothed in this way.

Maybe, then, the missing genitalia are intentional. Could it be that this is an accurate representation of an ill or deformed king? Unfortunately, we do not have Akhenaten's mummy, and so cannot comment with any authority on his medical condition. The evidence of the art alone suggests that he may have suffered from one of two feminizing conditions, either Marfan's syndrome or Fröhlich's syndrome. But either of these syndromes would have made him impotent, and Akhenaten claims to have fathered at least six chil-dren; if we include Tutankhamen and Smenkhkare, and the two daughters known to have been born to the Lady Kiya, he fathered at least ten. But, as we have already seen, there is no need to read Egyptian art as a literal portrait. Today the most widely accepted explanation is that this piece is a one-off experiment, designed to show Akhenaten as a genderless entity, a combined male and female who could serve as the earthly representative of the sexless creator god, the Aten.

It was accepted that the king of Egypt was the only mortal able to communicate with the gods. In theory, therefore, the king alone bore the responsibility of making all the offerings in all of Egypt's temples. But Egypt's gods needed regular, in some cases even hourly, offerings. As it was clearly impossible for the king to be present in every temple every hour of every day, he was allowed to appoint deputies who would make the offerings for him. Up and down the Nile, priests offered to the gods in the time-honoured rituals that would ensure the continuing presence of *maat*. But the scenes that decorated the temple walls invariably depicted kings, and kings alone, performing the rituals – until, that is, we come to the reign of Akhenaten. For in one of his Theban temples, the temple known as Hwt-Benben (Mansion of the Benben-Stone – the Benben being an ancient sacred stone connected with sun worship), Nefertiti, and Nefertiti alone, was allowed to make offerings to the Aten. As far was we can tell from the reconstructed scenes, Akhenaten never set foot inside the temple.

The Hwt-Benben was dismantled at the end of the 18th Dynasty, when many of its blocks were incorporated in Horemheb's Second Pylon (gateway) at Karnak. During the late 1940s Henri Chevrier rediscovered the blocks of Nefertiti's lost temple. Within the new pylon, Horemheb's workmen had carefully reassembled the old temple walls so as to make up partial scenes, but at least two of these scenes had been deliberately reconstructed upside-down. Many of the images of Nefertiti had been defaced within the pylon, and many of the hands on the end of the Aten's rays had been slashed across the fingertips.

A S CHEVRIER TOILED at Karnak, a team led by George Reisner, professor of Egyptology at Harvard University, was involved in a survey of the Giza plateau. Reisner, dubbed 'the American Petrie',[4] was a systematic and methodical archaeologist, whose exemplary work did a great deal to advance the science of excavation. He took particular care to make detailed records of all his surveys and excavations, and it is therefore both unfortunate and ironic that he was to die before he could complete the publication of his extensive and highly productive fieldwork. Already at Giza, in his 1908–10 season, he had recovered an astonishing series of statues of King Menkaure from the ruins of his valley and mortuary temples. The hard-stone statues, all of extremely high quality, showed the king alone, the king and his queen, and the king and his gods. As Reisner himself marvelled:

> Previous to the excavation of the temples of Mycerinus [Menkaure], only thirteen statues and statuettes were known of the kings of Dynasty IV ... In the temples of Mycerinus, the Harvard-Boston expedition found seventeen statues equal in preservation ... and in addition fifteen statuettes presenting eight stages in the creation of a statue ...[5]

Fifteen years later the American team was to make another spectacular discovery. On 2 February 1925, when Reisner himself was back home in the USA, the team was working to the east of the Great Pyramid. As the photographer set up his tripod, one leg sank deep into the desert sand. It had pierced the plaster covering to a blocked shaft. Reisner's British assistant, Alan Rowe, started to excavate. After weeks of hard work – the shaft proved to be 89 feet long, and was completely filled with limestone blocks – the team discovered a simple, undisturbed chamber.

Here, behind a blocked doorway, lay the neatly stored grave goods of Queen Hetepheres, wife to King Snefru, and mother to King Khufu. The archaeologists could see the queen's alabaster sarcophagus and a sealed niche in the wall that they hoped held her canopic chest. But the tomb was cramped, deep and uncomfortably hot, and many of the objects were in an extremely fragile condition. It was to take almost two years to empty the tomb with the help of a block and tackle. Among the goods recovered were thousands of fragments of pottery, a collection of wooden furniture, precious silver jewellery and personal cosmetic items, including perfume pots and a set of gold razors and knives.

Finally, on 3 March 1927, with the obligatory audience of dignitaries present, Reisner prepared to open the sarcophagus. Anticlimax is probably too mild a word to describe what happened next. Egyptologist Dows Dunham takes up the tale:

> At a nod from Reisner, the jacks that had been placed for the purpose began to turn. Slowly a crack appeared between the lid and the box. Little by little it widened until we could see into the upper part of the box; nothing was visible. As the lid rose higher we could see further into the interior and finally to the bottom of the box.[6]

Deflated, the party climbed back to the surface, where they consoled themselves with refreshments provided by Mrs Reisner.

Although the tomb held her funerary equipment and the sealed niche held her preserved internal organs, the queen's body was absent from her burial. How could this have happened? Reisner thought that perhaps his team had discovered the reburial of the remains of Hetepheres's looted tomb. More recently American pyramid expert Mark Lehner has suggested that this may have been Hetepheres' intended tomb – a small-scale pyramid substructure occupied before its superstructure could be built. Perhaps the queen's body was later retrieved for a more opulent reburial in one of the three queens' pyramids built by Khufu alongside his own much larger pyramid? Unfortunately, all three queens' pyramids were looted in antiquity.

Included amongst Hetepheres's burial equipment was a collection of rare wooden artifacts, including a sedan chair, a dismantled bed-canopy, a curtain box, a bed, two chairs, various wooden headrests and a series of wooden chests. Most of the wood was decayed beyond repair but its gold decorations had survived, allowing Hag Ahmed Youssef Mustafa, chief restorer with the Antiquities Service, to reconstruct the missing elements. Today Hetepheres's splendidly restored wooden furniture is displayed in Cairo Museum.

Hag Ahmed Youssef was to find himself re-employed at Giza, when, in 1954, the Antiquities Inspector Kamel el-Mallakh, carrying out routine survey work to the south of the Great Pyramid, discovered a pair of dismantled wooden boats in two stone-lined, airtight pits. One of the boats was left in its pit, where it remains in an unhappy state of decay today, but the other boat was excavated, restored and reconstructed. It took Hag Ahmed Youssef a decade to reassemble the 1224 pieces of cedar and acacia wood, as well as rope, and build a boat 140 feet long and almost 20 feet wide. Then, dissatisfied with the end result, he dismantled the boat and started all over again. The reconstruction that is today displayed in the specially built Giza Boat Museum is actually his fifth attempt. Experts are divided over the meaning of the two boats. Some think that they were ritual boats provided to allow the spirit of the dead king to sail off into the sky; others believe that they are the actual boats used in Khufu's funeral procession.

THE GREAT PYRAMID of Giza is without doubt Egypt's most famous pyramid, but Djoser's Sakkara Step Pyramid runs it a close second. Unlike the Great Pyramid, the Step Pyramid had been open and empty for many years. Its earliest modern investigators include Napoleon's soldiers, John Shae Perring and Colonel Vyse (1837), and Karl Richard Lepsius (1842). In 1877 Amelia Edwards paid a visit. She was clearly impressed with what she saw:

> As for the Pyramid in platforms (which is the largest at Sakkarah
> and next largest to the pyramid of Khafra) its position is so fine, its

architectural style so exceptional, its age so immense, that one altogether loses sight of these questions of relative magnitude. If Egyptologists are right in ascribing the royal title hieroglyphed over the inner door to Ouenephes, the fourth king of the First Dynasty, then it is the most ancient building in the world ... One's imagination recoils upon the brink of such a gulf of time ...

When a building has already stood for five or six thousand years in a climate where mosses and lichens, and all those natural signs of age to which we are accustomed in Europe are unknown, it is not to be supposed that a few centuries more or less can tell upon its outward appearance; yet to my thinking the pyramid of Ouenephes looks older than those of Gizeh. If this be only fancy, it gives one, at all events, the impression of belonging structurally to a ruder architectural period. The idea of a monument composed of diminishing platforms is in its nature more primitive than that of a smooth four-sided pyramid.[7]

The inner door – actually an inscribed door lintel and frame – mentioned by Miss Edwards had been discovered by Lepsius in 1842, removed and taken to Berlin Museum. It was carved with the royal name Netjerikhet, the ancient name of the first king of the 3rd Dynasty, who is today more commonly known by his alternative name, Djoser. Although at the time of her visit the true age of the Step Pyramid was unknown, Miss Edwards's gut feeling was correct. She was indeed standing before Egypt's most ancient stone building: a step pyramid some 4500 years old, designed and built by the vizier and high priest of Re, Imhotep, for the burial of his king.

Above ground, the pyramid has six flat, solid stone steps. Ninety feet below ground lies the king's tiny, granite-lined burial chamber, the heart of a warren of contemporary passageways and storerooms, as well as a tangle of tunnels made by determined tomb robbers, Late Period restorers, and early explorers who were prone to conduct their explorations using gunpowder. To the east of the burial chamber is the so-called 'king's apartment' – a set of underground rooms provided for the soul of the deceased. These rooms had been decorated with over 36,000 plano-convex, blue-green faience tiles, so that they resembled the reed walls of Djoser's Memphis palace. Already, when Miss Edwards visited in 1877, the underground galleries were considered dangerous, and were closed to visitors. The pyramid expert I.E.S. Edwards was allowed to inspect the substructure in 1943, and tells how during his visit:

> In one of the tomb-chambers on the east side of the pyramid, where there is a fine alabaster sarcophagus, the space between the sarcophagus and the rock wall of the chamber is very narrow, and one of us brushed against the wall. Immediately a thin surface-layer of the rock wall just collapsed to the floor.[8]

The underground chambers remain closed today.

Djoser's body has never been found but his pyramid has yielded some human remains. In 1821 the Prussian General Heinrich von Minutoli and his Italian engineer Geronimo Segato reported the finding of body parts but these, including a curious object described as a 'gilded skull', were lost at sea in a storm. All that are left are a mummified left foot wrapped in plaster-coated linen, a portion of an upper right arm and shoulder, and assorted bits of skin, chest and spine discovered on different occasions by various archaeologists.

Fortunately, Imhotep had had the foresight to provide his king with a substitute body. In the *serdab*, a small stone box leaning against the pyramid, he placed an almost life-sized painted stone Djoser. Eyeholes allowed the statue to look outwards and upwards towards the northern sky. But the statue's inlaid eyes were mutilated in antiquity, and are now empty sockets. The *serdab* statue was discovered by Dows Durham, who had been 'lent' to the Sakkara expedition by Reisner for the 1924–5 season. It is now on display in Cairo Museum. Meanwhile, a replica statue sits beside the pyramid and stares through blind eyes at the tourists who dare to peek through his eyeholes.

It was not until 1924, when Pierre Lacau and Cecil M. Firth started to excavate around rather than beneath the Step Pyramid, that the true extent of the ruined site was recognized. We now know that Djoser's pyramid was just one part of his mortuary provision. His complex, surrounded by an impressive stone wall about a mile long, originally included rooms, chapels, ritual courtyards, a small-scale subsidiary tomb and columned halls. In 1932 Firth was succeeded by Jean-Philippe Lauer, a French-architect-turned Egyptologist, who was to work at Sakkara for over 70 years. It is due almost entirely to his efforts that the Step Pyramid complex is today in a relatively good state of repair.

The Sakkara cemetery was already old when Djoser chose it as the site for his Step Pyramid. Here the nobles, the higher-ranking civil servants and at least two kings of the 1st and 2nd Dynasties had built their mud-brick tombs, the northern contemporaries of the royal tombs excavated by Amélineau and Petrie at Abydos. In 1931 Cecil Firth had started to investigate these most ancient tombs, but on leave in England he caught pneumonia and died at the comparatively young age of 53. Walter Bryan Emery took over, and in 1935 started to excavate mastaba 3035. It had generally been assumed that the superstructure of this splendidly large tomb was built of solid mud-brick. But Emery found, to his great delight, that it included some 45 rooms, each packed with grave goods. There was pottery, stone and metal vessels, and Egypt's oldest papyrus roll, which was, sadly, uninscribed.

We now know that this mastaba tomb belonged to Hemaka, a seal-bearer who lived during the reign of the 1st Dynasty King Den. Why did Hemaka feel that he needed so many grave goods when Queen Hetepheres, who had far more wealth at her disposal, was content with a relatively modest assortment? Hemaka was trying to respond to a theological crisis. He knew that as long as his body survived he would be able to live beyond death. But his spirit would not be strong enough to leave his tomb. Only kings, at this early date, were thought to be capable of travelling into the sky to enjoy eternal life with the gods. This meant that Hemaka needed to be buried with enough provisions to last for all eternity. He was not the only one to feel this way. The 1st and 2nd Dynasty elite tombs were crammed with necessities – garments, jewellery, toiletries and cosmetics, furniture, games, musical instruments, and even, in some cases, a toilet. Eventually, by the beginning of the 3rd Dynasty, it was realized that it would never be possible to provide an infinite amount of grave goods. Instead, the tomb builders turned to magic. A picture of a particular object, perhaps carved on a stone stela or on the tomb wall, would become both real and permanent for all eternity. This means that at the end of the 2nd Dynasty we find an abrupt decline in the number of grave goods, although, as the tomb of Tutankhamen shows, the elite never entirely lost the habit of being buried with vast quantities of goods.

A series of equally rich discoveries followed, leading Emery to conclude that Petrie had perhaps been wrong in his interpretation of the Abydos tombs. The kings of the 1st and 2nd Dynasties had not been buried at Abydos; they had been buried here, at Sakkara. The Abydos 'tombs', inferior in size, design and content to the Sakkara tombs, must be cenotaphs, or empty tombs. This theory was a logical and attractive one, but today we know that the Abydos tombs – which are indeed royal tombs – were just one part of the 1st and 2nd Dynasty royal mortuary provision. Close by the Umm el Qa'ab tombs, on the edge of the cultivated land, the kings built massive walled enclosures, housing shrines, sacred open spaces and in at least one case a 'proto-pyramid', a mound cased in mud-brick. Here, in their enclosures, the kings hoped that their cults would be celebrated for all time

In 1964 Bryan Emery, now Edwards professor of Egyptology at University College London, made his last spectacular discovery while excavating close by the Step Pyramid. He had high hopes of discovering the tomb of the architect Imhotep, who, he reasoned, must have been buried close to his greatest creation. Instead he found a Late Period sacred animal cemetery packed with mummified ibises. Later, as he excavated the 'Temple Terrace', he found the burials of the mothers of the Apis bulls, and galleries housing

baboon and falcon burials. Professor Emery died in 1971, still looking for the lost tomb of Imhotep.

THE DISCOVERY of Tutankhamen's tomb had sparked almost
uncontrollable media frenzy. But when, in 1939, French
archaeologist Pierre Montet discovered the lost tombs of the 21st
and 22nd Dynasty kings at the eastern Delta site of Tanis (modern
San el-Hagar), it seemed that no one was interested in the burials of
such 'unfashionable' kings:

> I had the earth and stones blocking the entrance removed, and
> went down into a square chamber with walls covered with figures
> and hieroglyphics; this led into another chamber with a large
> sarcophagus emerging from the earth which filled three quarters of
> two rooms. The cartouche is that of Osorkon ... I had
> Hassanaein's team come with all the carts so that we could clear
> this remarkable structure as quickly as possible ...[9]

The Third Intermediate Period kings ruled northern Egypt from the
Delta, far from the Valley of the Kings, which was by now dangerously unsafe for any form of burial. They built their tombs where
they could be guarded night and day: inside the precincts of their
temples. The kings were interred in limestone and granite-lined
chambers (the stone 'borrowed' from earlier dynastic buildings)
built in a large pit. The pit was then filled in and covered, during the
reign of Shoshenq III, by a low, flat, mastaba-like structure. A series
of shafts allowed access to the burials. Eventually the burials were
forgotten, the mud-brick structure was demolished, and a series of
Ptolemaic workshops was erected on top of the tombs. Only the
robbers remembered the lost kings – the tombs were plundered, but
by no means completely stripped, during the Ptolemaic Period.

Tanis had been explored by a series of excavators (Mariette
1860–80; Petrie 1883–6; Barsanti 1903–4) but Montet was the first
to conduct anything resembling a systematic survey of the strati-

graphically complex site. He had started work in 1921, and had already uncovered a series of interesting but far from spectacular finds. On 27 February 1939, excavating in what he believed to be the 'temple of Anta' (the smaller Mut temple), he discovered a tomb. Here, in a suite of four rooms, lay the burials of Shoshenq III, Takelot II (buried in a recycled antique sarcophagus), Osorkon II and his son Prince Hornakht. On 17 March he opened another tomb and discovered the burials of Heqakheperre-Shoshenq (lying in a spectacular falcon-headed silver coffin), Siamun and Pseusenes II. A false wall and granite plug concealed the entrance to the undisturbed burial of Pseusenes I, who still lay in his (or rather Merenptah's — Pseusenes too had 'borrowed' his funerary equipment) sarcophagus, surrounded by grave goods. A second chamber held the intact burial of King Amenemope. Two more chambers, housing the undisturbed burials of generals Ankhefenmut and Wendjebauendjedet, were subsequently discovered.

The coffins were opened in the presence of King Farouk, and then the treasures were transferred to Cairo Museum, where they are displayed today. Pierre Montet continued to work at Tanis until 1951. French survey work carried on at the site, first under Jean Yoyotte (1965–86), then Philippe Brissaud (1987 to the present). To date, nine royal tombs have been recovered.

There is now just one major set of Egyptian royal burials missing. The Saite kings of the 26th Dynasty have never been found, and it is left to Herodotus to tantalize us with the memory of their tombs:

> The Saites buried within the temple precincts all kings who were natives of their province, and so it even contains the tomb of Amasis as well as that of Apries and his family. The tomb of the former is farther from the sanctuary than the tomb of the latter, yet it is also within the temple. It is a great colonnade of stone, richly adorned, the pillars of which are carved in the form of palm trees. In this colonnade is a chamber with folding doors and the place where the coffin lies is behind these doors.[10]

CHAPTER TWELVE

>—<

EGYPTOLOGY TODAY

Two hundred years ago Egypt's monuments were little more than curiosities – the abandoned relics of a lost civilization appreciated for their beauty and scale, but by no means understood. The 1822 decoding of hieroglyphs made an enormous difference. Suddenly it was possible to read the words of the long dead, and Egypt's lengthy and complex history emerged with a startling rapidity from the sands. This was, at first, a history very much concentrated on royal and elite male culture, and the ordinary, illiterate members of society remained dumb in their unmarked graves. But it was a good beginning, and with the dynastic framework in place, social history soon followed. Egypt's monuments were no longer useless pieces of stone; they were the keys to understanding her past.

Running parallel to the growing understanding of Egyptian history has been a growing understanding of the need for accurate excavation, adequate conservation, and thorough recording and publication. It is now accepted that the excavator owes a duty of care to both the past and the future. Conservation has become the Egyptologist's first priority, while excavation is an extreme measure to be conducted either to answer a specific question, or to record a site that is under threat. When excavation does occur, it has to be properly recorded. To excavate a site, be it temple, town or tomb, is, after all, to obliterate it, while all too often to remove an ancient artifact from the sealed environment where it has rested for many centuries is to destroy it. When the sand has been cleared away and the surviving artifacts have been boxed and sent to Cairo, it is the excavator's record alone that will allow future generations to re-create the pristine site untouched by modern hands.

Egypt's most ambitious conservation project to date did not actually occur in Egypt itself. In the early 1960s the decision to build the Russian-financed Aswan High Dam meant flooding a large part of the Nile Valley to create a vast artificial lake extending over 300 miles southwards from the Egyptian town of Aswan to the Dal Cataract in Sudan. All the monuments standing in the way – including the Graeco-Roman temple of Philae and the two Abu Simbel temples built by Ramesses II and excavated by Belzoni – would be lost for ever beneath the water. The smaller temples, Philae included, could be dismantled and rebuilt on higher ground; this was done, with some of the less significant temples being rebuilt in foreign museums. But the Abu Simbel temples were massive and cut into the actual rock face. How could they be moved? A team of international experts offered a variety of suggestions, some more practical than others. Perhaps the temples could be encased in a see-through bubble that would protect them from the surrounding water. Or maybe they should be given their own curved dam to hold back the water. Eventually it was realized that the temples, as well as parts of the cliff face, would have to be moved to a new, artificially created environment. As work on the high dam had already started, the first step was to build a temporary coffer-dam to protect the temples. Then the temples were cut into huge blocks and hauled up the cliff face. Here they were reassembled inside two concrete domes, which were subsequently covered by an artificial hill. After a four-year operation, the temples were reopened to the public on 22 September 1968. It is a tribute to the thoroughness of the project that many tourists forget they are standing inside resited temples – until, that is, they wander round the back of the dome.

The great Egyptologists of the past were polymaths, who happily took responsibility for all aspects of their sites – survey, excavation, planning, photography, pottery analysis, bone identification, mummy unwrapping and so on. The discovery in 1922 of Tutankhamen's intact tomb made it clear that this approach was no longer appropriate. Today's excavators are team leaders who supervise a diverse collection of experts in both modern scientific and traditional methodologies. Local workmen are still used to excavate the monuments, but not in the vast numbers employed by Belzoni or Petrie. Work is far slower, far more careful and far better supervised, with the Supreme Council of Antiquities quite rightly insisting that only those with the appropriate training and experience be allowed to set foot on Egypt's sites.

So what kind of excavation work is being conducted in Egypt today? There are now hundreds of missions of all nationalities (Egyptian included) working in the Nile Valley and in the Delta. Many of these are involved in long-term conservation projects, or in the re-excavation of previously known but hastily excavated sites. The scrupulous Flinders Petrie would be mortified to learn that today's Egyptologists consider his carefully sieved waste dumps fertile hunting grounds, and it would probably be little comfort for him to realize that the dumps of other archaeologists have yielded even more finds. Many of today's missions are concentrated on the Theban area. We have already, briefly, seen the work of the Akhenaten Temple Project, led first by Ray Winfield Smith, then by Donald B. Redford. Since 1965 this project has been engaged in analysing and reconstructing the many thousands of inscribed blocks which once formed the walls of Akhenaten's Aten temples. These, dismantled during the reign of Horemheb and used as fill in the Karnak and Luxor temples, have been reassembled, jigsaw-like, to create virtual temples, whose scenes can be studied and whose words can be read: 'Through photography of the relief-carved faces of these blocks, and with the aid of a computer, we have matched thousands of stones and seen superb works of art take form again after thousands of years ...'[1]

Across the river, there has been ongoing conservation work at the Deir el-Bahari temple of Hatshepsut, where Naville's 1893–1904 work was followed by a mission from the Metropolitan Museum of New York (1911–31) led by Herbert E. Winlock. In 1961 a team from the Polish Centre of Mediterranean Archaeology of Warsaw University in Cairo resurveyed the temple, and their work led, in the 1990s, to alternating seasons of epigraphic work (Warsaw University, directed by J. Karkowski) and restoration (Polish-Egyptian Mission, directed by F. Pawlicky). Today, with the terraces again accessible, the temple has resumed some of its original splendour.

No one now expects the Valleys of the Kings and Queens to yield treasure as rich as that found in Tutankhamen's tomb, although Egyptologist Nick Reeves believes that Nefertiti, like Smenkhkare before her, may well have been buried or reburied somewhere in the Theban necropolis. And yet we know that there are many members of the New Kingdom royal family – not kings, but queens, princes and princesses – still unaccounted for. Attention has focused in recent years on the 100-plus children of Ramesses II. We know that Ramesses built tombs for his more important daughters – the daughters whom he married – in the Valley of the Queens. It seems logical to assume that their less important, unmarried, sisters were buried in the cemeteries attached to the rural harems where they spent their lives. But what about their brothers? Merenptah, as King of Egypt, had a suitably regal tomb in the main Valley. Khaemwaset may or may not have been buried close by the Apis bulls at Sakkara. What happened to the 40 or so others? The 1989 rediscovery of tomb KV5 provided the unexpected answer.

KV5 had been included on the earliest maps of the Valley, and had even been explored by the British traveller James Burton in 1825. He dug a tunnel through the debris that completely blocked the tomb, and examined its first three chambers, but found the whole experience highly unsatisfactory. The tomb was:

> ... all in a state of ruin ... Being full of mud and earth the descent from the pillared room to those underneath is not perceptible.

The catacomb must have been excavated very low in the valley or the valley much raised by the accumulation of earth stones and rubbish brought down by the rains ... It is possible that there is some passage leading from below the centre of the pillared chamber into that where the sarcophagus stood ...[2]

Lepsius, too, visited to tomb and recorded the cartouche of Ramesses II on its doorway. Then, in the early twentieth century, the entrance was buried beneath tons of rubble carelessly dumped by Howard Carter, who, having examined the tomb in 1902, clearly thought it to be of no importance. The tomb vanished, but was not forgotten. When, in 1985, it was realized that a scheme to widen the access road to the Valley might destroy KV5, the Theban Mapping Project, led by American Egyptologist Kent Weeks, set out to rescue and record the lost tomb.

The tomb was, as Burton had reported, completely blocked by a mass of compacted mud and rubble that had been deposited by successive floods. Since Carter's visit, a leaking sewerage pipe had also disgorged its noxious contents all over the entrance, adding greatly to the excavators' problems. Clearance work progressed at a rate of less than 7 cubic feet of rubbish removed per day, but gradually the true size of the tomb was revealed. First came anterooms and a large, 16-pillared hall, then a long passageway beyond the hall. Opening off this corridor were doorways, ten on each side, while the lowest two doorways in turn led to more passageways with yet more side chambers. The tomb – by far the largest tomb in the Valley – is a catacomb or mausoleum designed for the royal princes, and, as such, is highly reminiscent of the Sakkara Serapeum designed by their brother Khaemwaset. Work on the tomb is still very much in progress, but already more than 100 chambers built on different levels have been revealed. So far there have been no intact burials, although some human skeletal material (three skulls and a complete skeleton) has been recovered from a pit in one of the chambers. There have been no substantial artifacts, no sarcophagi or coffins, but a mass of debris, including pot sherds, *shabti* figures, beads, amulets and fragments of canopic jars, hints at series of rich but thoroughly robbed burials. This is not surprising. The Turin 'Strike Papyrus', a legal document detailing robberies in the royal cemetery during the reign of Ramesses III, specifically mentions thefts from the area around KV5:

> Now Usherhat and Pawere have stripped stones from above the tomb of Osiris King Usermaatre Setepenre, the Great God ... And Kenena son of Ruta did it in the same manner above the tomb of the royal children of King Osiris Usermaatre Setepenre, the Great God ...[3]

In northern Egypt, work is still in progress at the Giza pyramid site. But here the experts are concentrating not on the pyramids themselves, but on the 'pyramid city', the living quarters and graves of the many thousands of pyramid workers and their supervisors. All of Egypt's state building sites were manned by labourers who were conscripted for a few months, then released. For the duration of their service, these temporary workers lived close by the building site in state-provided accommodation. Here they were fed, clothed and given medical attention, should they need it. For a long time it was feared that the Giza workers must have been housed close by the Nile, and that their houses had been destroyed by the high water table. But this made little sense. The workers would surely be housed as close to the building site as possible. In 1880 Flinders Petrie suggested that a series of long galleries running behind Khaefre's pyramid might be the remains of barracks capable of holding approximately 4000 men. But these 'barracks' are entirely devoid of any settlement debris, and it is now generally accepted that they are more likely to have been workshops or storerooms.

Instead, it is now realized that the workmen, their supervisors and in some cases their families lived, and died, just outside the imposing limestone wall, known today as the Wall of the Crow, that defined the sacred limits of the Giza cemetery. The ancient houses are as yet undiscovered, and it seems that many must lie beneath the modern town of Nazlet el-Samman. But away from the modern town, in a project that started in 1988 and continues to the present day, American Egyptologist Mark Lehner has uncovered a large complex of mud-brick industrial units dating to the time of the pyramid builders. Here is evidence for mass production, and mass catering, on an unprecedented scale. Hundreds of thick, bell-shaped, pottery bread-moulds and many baking pits mark the site of two bakeries. A large building equipped with ankle-high 'benches' has been identified as a fish-processing unit, its floor covered by a thick deposit of hardened ash and organic material, including fish remains – gills, fins, heads and even bones. Another industrial unit has been identified as a copper workshop. The discarded animal bones and cereal grain – small-scale evidence that early Egyptologists almost invariably ignored – reveal the workers' diet. Not only did they eat the classic peasant foods of bread, beer and fish, but they also enjoyed duck, the occasional sheep and pig, and even some choice cuts of meat.

Meanwhile, in a parallel project Dr Zahi Hawass, currently Secretary General of the Supreme Council of Antiquities, has identified the tombs built by the pyramid workers, both overseers and labourers, in the dunes above and to the west of the industrial complex. He has so far uncovered over 600 burials arranged on two levels. The lower cemetery contains the more modest mud-brick tombs and graves, although there is a fair smattering of miniature step pyramids, small-scale mastabas and beehive-shaped tombs, some of which incorporate stone elements 'borrowed' from the pyramid site. Higher up the slope are the larger and more sophisticated limestone tombs, and a *serdab* housing four statues.

Hawass has estimated, based on the evidence from the tombs and the associated industrial complex, that Giza would have been home to approximately 5000 permanent elite workers (officials, supervisors and master-craftsmen), as well as 15,000 temporary manual workers with the total number working at the site at any given time being no higher than 20,000. The analysis of the skeletal material recovered from the tombs is still in progress, but already there have been some interesting results. There are very obvious differences between the labourers and their supervisors. As the manual labourers were a temporary workforce, their burials represent the unfortunate few who died while on site, and show, as we might expect, a high proportion of accidental deaths. The average age at death of the male manual workers is 30–35 years; their womenfolk, faced with the perils of childbirth, die even younger. The elite, full- or part-time salaried necropolis employees would have expected to live with their families on site until the pyramid complex was complete; their tombs are therefore far better prepared, and their burials include both the very young and the very old. Life expectancy for these elite males was ten years longer than the life expectancy of the workmen. Of over 600 skeletons examined, half are male and half are female, with children and babies making up over 23 per cent of the cemetery population. DNA analysis carried out by Dr Moamina Kamal of Cairo University Medical School has confirmed that these are families, with the DNA of the adult bones correlating closely to that of the children.

Zahi Hawass's 1990 discovery of the tombs of the Giza pyramid builders was the result of logical deduction and painstaking excavation. His discovery in 1996 of the Roman cemetery in the Valley of the Golden Mummies in the Bahariya Oasis, 230 miles to the soutwest of Giza, was the result of a lucky accident.

A ruined settlement site, close by the modern city of Bawit, has long been recognized as home to a sizeable Graeco-Roman community, while the nearby temple of Alexander the Great has been the subject of archaeological investigation. But generally speaking, this area had not furnished many important finds. Then one day a donkey tripped, its leg caught in a sand-filled hole. The donkey's owner was an antiquities guard attached to the temple. Peering into the dark hole, he could see interesting things. Zahi

Hawass was summoned, and it soon became obvious that the don-key had stumbled across the entrance to a multi-chambered tomb cut into the sandstone bedrock and filled with gilt-covered mum-mies. The tomb was part of a Graeco-Roman graveyard of between two and four square miles, each of its tombs housing anything up to 100 mummies in varying states of preservation. News of the discov-ery was kept secret for three years, but was finally announced to the world's press in June 1999. Excavation of the cemetery is still in progress, and it is estimated that it will take at least a decade for the multi-disciplinary team of archaeologists, conservationists, draughtsmen and artists to fully explore and publish the site.

Even further to the west, a team from the University of Liverpool led by Steven Snape has, since 1994, been engaged in excavating the Ramesside fortress site of Zawiyet Umm el-Rakham. During the reign of Ramesses II the mighty Egyptian empire stretched north-wards as far as Syria, where Ramesses fought a famous battle against the Hittites at Kadesh, and southwards into Nubia, where he erected the Abu Simbel temples. But Ramesses always had a niggling con-cern over the security of his western frontier, where the Libyan tribes were growing in strength and threatening to settle – invade is prob-ably too strong a word – in the eastern Delta. And so, to protect Egypt against any potential Libyan threat, Ramesses built a series of fortress-towns following the edge of the Delta and the Mediterranean coast. The largest of these fortress-towns was the most western: Zawiyet Umm el-Rakham lies on the Mediterranean coast almost 200 miles to the west of the Delta.

Zawiyet Umm el-Rakham was clearly built to offer protection against serious attack. The outer mud-brick wall of the fortress, a neat square with each side 150 yards long, was 5 yards thick and probably 10 yards tall. The single entrance-gate in the middle of its north side was heavily defended with massive towers. As yet, however, no sign has been found of any warfare within the fortress, and it appears that it was deserted peacefully during the early part of the reign of Merenptah, son and successor to Ramesses the Great.

This would give the fortress an active life of less than 50 years. After its abandonment by the Egyptians, the fortress was occupied by Libyan tribes.

About a third of the interior has already been excavated by the Liverpool team. They have discovered a substantial temple built of the inferior-quality local limestone, temple storerooms, a series of smaller chapels, and a kitchen area where there is evidence for the mass production of the bread needed to feed the 500 or so soldiers who Snape believes were garrisoned at the fort at any given time. The Governor's Mansion has been only partly excavated, but it is already obvious that this is the building where the fortress commander, Neb-Re, both lived and worked. The excavators have found his bedroom and his bathroom, complete with a pedestal toilet, and have recovered his private chapel, where they found a magnificent two-thirds life-size statue of the commander himself. Curiously, the name of the commander had been erased from his statue.

The temple storerooms have yielded large numbers of high-quality pottery vessels from a wide range of eastern Mediterranean countries, including mainland Greece, Crete, Cyprus, Syria and Canaan. This pottery offers very good evidence that Zawiyet Umm el-Rakham was an important link in the chain of trading posts that made possible large-scale, long-distance trade in the Late Bronze Age. It is likely that the location of the fortress was carefully chosen not only to protect Egypt from the Libyan tribes but also to protect Egypt's trade routes.

Alexandria, too, is a coastal site. Founded in the fourth century BC by Alexander the Great, the ancient city has attracted land-based archaeologists for many decades. Now, however, Egyptologists have realized that much of the city lies drowned beneath the waters of the harbour, and are starting to search the sea bed. The first underwater excavation was conducted in 1961, when Kamal Abu el-Saadat, helped by the Egyptian navy, retrieved a colossal statue of Isis. More recently, in 1994, a survey team led by the French underwater archaeologist Jean-Yves Empereur located statue parts, columns, obelisks, shipwrecks and hundreds of masonry blocks, which, Empereur has suggested, might be the remains of the Pharos lighthouse, one of the Seven Wonders of the Ancient World (the Great Pyramid of Giza being the only surviving 'Wonder'). A second team, lead by another French underwater expert, Franck Goddio, has discovered the remains of a palace.

So, field archaeology in Egypt is flourishing. But away from the sand or the water, as the case may be, a vast amount of work is being undertaken in museums and laboratories, where the finds of the past are being reinvestigated using modern techniques. Perhaps the most dramatic example of this new approach to ancient Egypt is seen in the field of mummy studies. Two hundred years ago mummies were valued only for the jewellery hidden beneath their bandages. The bodies themselves were worthless; they could tell the archaeologist nothing. Unrollings were a legitimate form of entertainment, and we have already seen Belzoni, a man with his finger on the pulse of public taste, open his Piccadilly Hall exhibition in 1821 with the unrolling of a human mummy, 'perfect in every part', and a monkey mummy. The businessman-turned-poet Horace Smith, a man of dubious lyrical talent but high entertainment value, felt the stirrings of the muse. One verse will be enough to satisfy the modern reader:

AN ADDRESS TO THE MUMMY IN
BELZONI'S EXHIBITION
If the tomb's secrets may not be confess'd,
The nature of thy private life unfold:-
A heart has throbbed beneath that leathern breast,
And tears adown that dusty cheek have roll'd:-
Have children climbed those knees and kissed that face?
What was thy name and station, age and race?[4]

The London surgeon Thomas Pettigrew was inspired by Belzoni's unrolling. He started to buy and unwrap his own mummies; soon he too was making a tidy income selling tickets to the public.

Pettigrew kept detailed notes of his work, and his book *History of Egyptian Mummies* (1834) became a popular success. Gradually, however, public sensibilities changed, until it was no longer considered acceptable to unwrap a dead body in public. So it is interesting that in 1976, when the mummy of the 21st Dynasty priest Horemkenesi started to decompose in Bristol Museum, the decision was taken to unroll him in the public eye. The autopsy would be held in private, and Horemkenesi would be accorded the utmost respect at all times, but members of the public would be able to watch events via closed-circuit television. The unrolling of Horemkenesi's relatively insignificant mummy took a full two weeks, and was followed by many more weeks of intensive study. It offered a marked contrast to Gaston Maspero's quarter of an hour stripping of Ramesses II in 1886.

Ramesses, however, was destined to lie on the autopsy table again. The king, stored first in the Bulaq Museum, then in the Giza Museum, then finally in a glass case in the mummy room of the Cairo Museum, had started to decay. Unregulated changes in temperature, humidity and light had caused his skin to crack, and he had been invaded by bacteria, insects and over 80 different species of fungi. A mercury bath, administered in 1907, did little to stem the infestation. Then, in 1975, the French government invited the king on a state visit. In 1976 he flew to Paris where, in a ceremony appropriate to a deceased head of state, he was greeted by a military guard of honour. At the Musée de l'Homme he was examined by a team of over 100 specialists dedicated to his study and preservation. No samples were taken from his body, but a series of samples was taken from his wrappings and his body cavities. Next the cracks in his skin were filled with a compound of natural products, including beeswax, petroleum jelly and turpentine. Finally, Ramesses was rewrapped in his original, now much cleaner, bandages, and the king and his coffin were sterilized with gamma radiation. After eight months in Paris, Ramesses returned to Cairo Museum, where his mummy is displayed today.

Due almost entirely to the generosity of Jesse Haworth, Manchester Museum has a large collection of Egyptian antiquities, including a surprisingly large number of human mummies (24), animal mummies and mummy parts. In 1908 the curator of the Egyptian collection, Margaret Murray, a former pupil of Flinders Petrie and one of Britain's first female Egyptologists, performed a double autopsy, unwrapping a pair of 12th Dynasty mummies known as the 'Two Brothers'. A contemporary photograph shows the diminutive Murray, sensibly dressed in a white apron, as she stands before the operating table, one of the unwrapped bodies stretched before her. Today Manchester, home of the Manchester Mummy Project, is the acknowledged world centre of excellence for mummy studies. The Manchester scientists, led by Professor Rosalie David, are engaged in the study of tissue types, parasites and diseases, and it is hoped that their work will play a part in the eradication of some of Egypt's most persistent parasites. Just one example of their work serves to give a flavour of their methods and results.

In October 1999 Professor David started a multi-disciplinary project to study the mummy of the Third Intermediate Period chantress (temple singer) Asru. Asru became the first mummy in the collections of Manchester Museum when, in 1825, she, her two coffins and her neatly packaged entrails were donated to the museum by the private collectors E. and W. Garratt. Unfortunately, curiosity had got the better of the Garratts, and they had already unwrapped Asru – and presumably stripped her of any jewellery – before giving her to the museum.

The experts felt that although Asru looked extremely thin (non-experts could with some justification argue that all unwrapped mummies look thin), she had no obvious signs of illness and it seemed that she had died a natural death in old age.

Her fingers showed unmistakable signs of degenerative arthritis, and this, combined with signs of calcification in the aorta, the bronchi and in the lower legs and feet, and arthritis in the knee, indicated that Asru was probably somewhere between 50 and 70 years old when she died. The police, having finger- and toe-printed the body, felt that she was probably in her late forties when she died.

X-rays showed that Asru had bad teeth – a common affliction of the elderly in ancient Egypt, where the sand and stone fragments present in the ground flour had a wearing effect on the teeth. Many of her back teeth were missing, and there was evidence of a painful infection in the jaw. Her front teeth were in better condition, but showed evidence of a substantial overbite. A CAT (Computed Axial Tomography) scan allowed the scientist to make a solid polymer replica of Asru's skull, and the skull was subsequently used as the core for a facial reconstruction. We can never expect a reconstruction to provide an exact likeliness of a deceased person, but modern police usage has proved that a reasonable degree of accuracy is more often than not obtained. Asru's reconstruction suggests that she was an elderly lady with high cheekbones, a small pointed chin, a protruding upper lip and deep-set eyes.

So what caused Asru's death? She had suffered from a number of illnesses and parasitic infestations, any one of which might or might not have killed her. Her lung tissue showed the scars of sand pneumoconiosis, an illness caused by the inhalation of windborne sand particles, which would have caused her to wheeze and cough. Her intestines – rehydrated by the scientists – yielded the larval form of the *Nematode strongyloides* worm. Her bladder tissue showed evidence of schistosomiasis or bilharzia infestation. Her chest X-ray revealed an immature form of the dog tapeworm. This medical evidence of sickness and debility offers a marked contrast to the official and highly unrealistic view of elite life preserved on Egypt's tomb walls. Here we see the upper classes, Asru's friends, enjoying themselves in the green fields. They are always fit, always healthy, and seemingly do not have a care in the world.

Our visit to Manchester brings the history of the discovery of ancient Egypt to an end. The subject itself, however, cannot be halted, and continues to develop at an astonishing pace. Who knows what techniques will be used over the next two centuries to bring the long-dead Egyptians back to life? It is perhaps appropriate to give the last word to James Baikie, our Scottish commentator on all matters Egyptological, and the author of the first history of Egyptology:

> ... the true romance of modern excavation lies in this, not that it can reveal the dead monarchs of thirty centuries back in all their splendour, but that by its patient piecing together of innumerable small details it can give back to us the actual life of the period in which the dead monarch lived, and let us see the order of his court, and what is far more important to our knowledge of the past, the traffic of the market place in his cities, and the intercourse of his land with the nations around it ... A science which can accomplish such a miracle of resurrection can never lack the element of true romance in the eyes of anyone who has a real sense of the wonders of life.[5]

ENDNOTES

$\succ\!\!-\!\!\prec$

INTRODUCTION

1 Baikie, J., *A Century of Excavation in the Land of the Pharaohs* (London, 1923), pp. 8–9.

CHAPTER ONE

1 Hednakht was visiting the Step Pyramid of Djoser at Sakkara. The full graffito is quoted in Kitchen, K.A., *Pharaoh Triumphant* (Warminster, 1982), p. 148.
2 Gardiner, A., 'The Great Speos Artemidos Inscription', *Journal of Egyptian Archaeology*, Vol 32 (1946), pp. 47–8.
3 Inscription on the wooden coffin recovered from the Third Giza Pyramid, now displayed in the British Museum, London.
4 Herodotus, *Histories*, Book II. This and all subsequent quotations from Herodotus are based on the translation by George Rawlinson (London, 1858), who obviously felt that the information about urinating and defecating was just too coarse for his sensitive readers, and omitted them from his translation.
5 Ibid.
6 Ibid.
7 Diodorus Siculus, *Bibliotheca Historica*. For a full translation of this work consult Oldfather, C.H. and Sherman, C.L., *Library of History* (London & New York, 1933–67).
8 Strabo, *Geographica*. For a full translation of this work consult *The Geography of Strabo VII*, translated by Jones, H.L. (London & New York, 1932).
9 Pliny, *Natural History*, Book 36, p. 72. For a full translation of this work consult Eichholz, D.E., *Natural History*, Books XXXVI–XXXVII, Vol 10 (New York, 1989).
10 Christian graffito from the Valley of the Kings, quoted in Romer, J., *Valley of the Kings* (London, 1981), p. 31.

CHAPTER TWO

1 Quoted in Rodenbeck, M., *Cairo: The City Victorious* (London, 1988), p.40.
2 Genesis 1: 1–31
3 Quoted in Romer, J., *The Valley of the Kings* (London, 1981), p. 32.
4 Bruce, J., *Travels to Discover the Source of the Nile* (Edinburgh, 1790).
5 Ibid.
6 Denon, V., *Travels in Lower and Upper Egypt* (London, 1803).
7 *Travels in Upper and Lower Egypt III* (London), pp. 217–18: this scroll has since

gone missing, and is now preserved only in Denon's writings.

7 *Description*, Books V and IX. Hieroglyphs had already been decoded by the time the *Description* (1809–29) was complete.

8 A full translation of the text on the stone is given in Simpson, R.S., *Demotic Grammar in the Ptolemaic Sacerdotal Decrees* (Oxford, 1996), pp. 258–71.

CHAPTER THREE

1 Diodorus Siculus, *Bibliotheca Historica*, Vol 1. For a full translation of this work consult Oldfather, C.H. and Sherman, C.L., *Library of History* (London & New York, 1933–67).

2 Ammianus, *Rerum Gestarum Libri*, quoted in Sole, R. and Valbelle, D., *The Rosetta Stone: The Story of the Decoding of Hieroglyphics* (London, 2001), p. 15.

3 Horapollo Niliacus, *Hieroglyphica*, quoted in Snape, S.R., *Decoding the Stones* (London, 1997), p. 7.

4 Vallant, P. (ed.), *Jean-François Champollion: Lettres à son Frère* (Paris, 1984), p. 75.

5 Young, T., 'An Account of Some Recent Discoveries in Hieroglyphical Literature and Egyptian Antiquities Including the Author's Alphabet, as Extended by Mr Champollion with a Translation of Five Unpublished Greek and Egyptian Manuscripts' (1823), in *Miscellaneous Works of the Late Thomas Young*, Vol 3, p. 14; quoted in Sole, R. and Valbelle, D., op.cit., p. 70.

6 Quoted in translation by Adkins, L. and R., *The Keys of Egypt: the Race to Read Hieroglyphics* (London, 2000), p. 259.

CHAPTER FOUR

1 Carter, H. and Mace, A.C., *The Tomb of Tut.ankh.Amen*, Vol. I (London, 1923), pp. 67–8.

2 Depping, G.B., writing for *Le Globe*, 24 July 1827, Paris.

3 Belzoni, G.B., *Narrative of the Operations and Recent Discoveries in Egypt and Nubia* (1820), edited by Alberto Siliotti (Verona & London, 2001), p. 85. This edition of Belzoni's text combines a selective autobiography with tales of daring archaeological exploits.

4 Ibid., p. 91.

5 Ibid., p. 92.

6 Diodorus Siculus, *Histories*, I, p. 47.

7 Hamilton, W.R., *Remarks on Several Parts of Turkey: Part I, Aegyptiaca* (London, 1809).

8 Belzoni, op.cit., p. 104.

9 Ibid., p. 103.

10 Ibid., pp. 112–3.

11 Ibid., pp. 115–6.

12 'Mrs Belzoni's Trifling Account of the Women', in Belzoni, op.cit., pp. 295–318 (quoting pp. 295–6).

13 Belzoni, op p. 142.

CHAPTER FIVE

1 Belzoni, G.B., *Narrative of the Operations and Recent Discoveries in Egypt and Nubia* (1820), edited by Alberto Siliotti (Verona & London, 2001), p. 168.
2 Ibid., pp. 168–9.
3 Ibid., p. 200.
4 Ibid., p. 203.
5 Correspondence quoted in Mayes, S., *The Great Belzoni: The Circus Strongman Who Discovered Egypt's Ancient Treasures* (London, 1959), p. 293.
6 Belzoni, op.cit., p. 253.
7 Herodotus, *Histories*, Book II, trans. Rawlinson, G. (1858), p. 148.
8 Belzoni, op.cit., p. 268.
9 Bonomi, J., *Transactions of the Royal Society of Literature* (2nd Series), Vol. I (1843), p. 108.
10 D'Athanasi, G., *A Brief Account of the Researches and Discoveries in Upper Egypt, Made under the Direction of Henry Salt, Esq* (London, 1836), pp. xi–xii.

CHAPTER SIX

1 Herodotus, *Histories*, Book II, trans. Rawlinson, G. (1858), p. 125.
2 Greaves, J., *Pyramidographia, or a Description of the Pyramids in Egypt* (London, 1646).
3 Ibid.
4 Ibid.
5 Howard Vyse, R. and Perring, J.S., *Operations Carried on at the Pyramids of Gizeh* (London 1840–2).
6 Flaubert, G., Travel notes, 8 December 1849, quoted in Clayton, P.A., *The Rediscovery of Ancient Egypt* (London, 1982), p. 65.
7 Belzoni, G.B., *Narrative of the Operations and Recent Discoveries in Egypt and Nubia* (1820), edited by Alberto Siliotti (Verona & London, 2001), p. 217.
8 Abd el-Latif of Bagdhad, quoted in Cottrell, L., *The Mountains of Pharaoh* (London, 1956), p. 73.
9 Belzoni, op.cit., pp. 221–2.
10 Smyth, C.P., *Our Inheritance in the Great Pyramid* (London, 1866; 4th edn, 1880), p. 5.

CHAPTER SEVEN

1 Kitchen, K.A., *Ramesside Inscriptions Translated and Annotated 2: Ramesses II, Royal Inscriptions* (Oxford, 1996), pp. 569–70.
2 Mariette, A., *Le Sérapeum de Memphis* (Paris, 1882), pp. 5–6.
3 Letter of appointment from Said Pasha, quoted in Reeves, N., *Ancient Egypt: the Great Discoveries* (London, 2000), p. 49.
4 de Morgan, J., *Fouilles à Dachour* (1894); translation after Cottrell, L., *The Mountains of Pharaoh* (London, 1956), p. 159.
5 Brugsch, E., quoted in Wilson, E.L., *Magazine*, 34/1 (May 1887), p. 66.

6 Maspero, G., *Les Momies Royales de Deir el-Bahari* (Cairo, 1889), pp. 547–8.
7 Maspero, G., *Bulletin de l'Institut Égyptien* (Cairo, 1886), pp. 253–5.
8 Smith, G.E., *The Royal Mummies* (Cairo, 1912), p. 57.
9 Edwards, A.B., *A Thousand Miles up the Nile* (London, 1877, rev. 1888), p. 1.
10 Ibid., pp. 284–5.
11 Ibid., pp. 450–1.
12 Letter from Samuel Birch to Amelia Edwards, quoted in Drower, M.S., 'Gaston Maspero and the Egypt Exploration Fund', *Journal of Egyptian Archaeology*, Vol. 68 (1982), pp. 299–317, p. 301.
13 From a letter written by Gaston Maspero to an unknown gentleman (R.S. Poole?), copied by Miss Edwards and reproduced in Dawson, W.R., 'Letters from Maspero to Amelia Edwards', *Journal of Egyptian Archaeology*, Vol. 33 (1947), pp. 66–89, p. 73.
14 Ibid.

CHAPTER EIGHT

1 Petrie, W.M.F., *Seventy Years in Archaeology* (London, 1931), pp. 12–13.
2 Ibid., p. 21.
3 Ibid., pp. 34–5.
4 Ibid., p. 25.
5 Ibid., p. 74.
6 Budge, E.A.W., *By Nile and Tigris*, Vol. 1 (London, 1920), p.133.
7 Petrie, op.cit., pp. 83–4.
8 Ibid., p.87.
9 Ibid., pp. 94–5.
10 Ibid., p. 107.
11 Ibid., p. 234.
12 Quoted in David, A.R., *The Pyramid Builders of Ancient Egypt* (London, 1986), p. 2.
13 Petrie, op.cit., p. 121.
14 Reeves, N., *Ancient Egypt: the Great Discoveries* (London, 2000), p.72.
15 Budge, E.A., quoted in Reeves, N., op.cit., p. 73.
16 Petrie, op.cit., p. 138.
17 Ibid., p. 155–6.
18 Egypt Exploration Fund Annual Report for 1899, p. 26.
19 Quoted in Reeves, N., op.cit., p. 115.
20 Petrie, op.cit., p. 175.

CHAPTER NINE

1 Sayce, A.H., *Reminiscences* (London, 1923), p. 306.
2 Loret, V., 'Les Tombeaux de Thoutmés III et d'Amenophis II', *Bulletin de l'Institut Égyptien* (Cairo, 1988). Translation after Romer, J., *Valley of the Kings* (London, 1988), pp. 161–2.
3 Ibid.

4 Davis, T.M. (ed.), *The Tomb of Hatshopsitu* (London, 1906), p. xiii.

5 Davis, T.M., *The Tomb of Iouiya and Touiyou* (London, 1907), p. xxviii.

6 Quoted in Gardiner, A., 'The so-called tomb of Queen Tiy', *Journal of Egyptian Archaeology*, Vol. 43 (1957), p. 25.

7 Davis, T.M. et al., *The Tomb of Queen Tiyi* (London, 1910), p. 2.

8 Burton, H., quoted in an article published in the *Manchester Guardian*, 27 January 1923.

9 Davis, T. M., *The Tombs of Harmhabi and Touatankhamanou* (London, 1912), p. 3.

10 Edwards, A.B., *A Thousand Miles up the Nile* (London, 1877; rev. 1888), pp. 296–7.

CHAPTER TEN

1 Petrie's diary for 1891–2 is now held in the Petrie Museum, University College London.

2 Private correspondence of Naville, quoted in Drower, M.S., *Flinders Petrie: A Life in Archaeology* (London, 1985), p. 283.

3 Petrie, W.M.F., *Seventy Years in Archaeology* (London, 1931), p. 192.

4 Winifred Burghclere's idiosyncratic introduction to Carter, H. and Mace, A.C., *The Tomb of Tut.ankh.Amen*, I (London, 1923), republished in 2003 with a foreword by N. Reeves, p. 24–5.

5 Carter, H., 'A Tomb Prepared for Queen Hatshepsuit and Other Recent Discoveries at Thebes', *Journal of Egyptian Archaeology*, Vol. 4 (1917), p. 118.

6 Carter, H. and Mace, A.C., op.cit., p. 95.

7 Ibid., p. 105.

8 Ibid., pp. 123–4.

9 Ibid., pp 179–80.

10 Ibid., pp. 143–4.

11 Winifred Burghclere in Carter and Mace, op.cit., p. 39.

12 Ibid., p.1.

13 Carter, H., *The Tomb of Tut.ankh.Amen*, II (London, 1927), republished in 2001 with a foreword by N. Reeves, p. 45.

14 Ibid., pp. 82–3.

15 Ibid., p. 108.

16 Mace, A.C., 'The Egyptian Expedition 1922–23', *Bulletin of the Metropolitan Museum of Art* 18:2 (1923), pp. 5–11.

CHAPTER ELEVEN

1 Davies, N. de G., *The Rock Tombs of el Amarna*, Vol. 6 (London, 1908), p. 10.

2 Letter written by James Henry Breasted from Cairo, dated 24 January 1895, quoted in Larson, J.A., 'Other Amarna Letters', *Amarna Letters*, Vol. 2 (1992), pp. 116–25.

3 Smith, R.W. and Redford, D.B., *The Akhenaten Temple Project* (Warminster, 1976).

4 Reeves, N., *Ancient Egypt: the Great Discoveries* (London, 2000), p. 132.

5 Reisner, G.A., *Mycerinus. The Temples of the Third Pyramid at Giza* (Cambridge, Mass, 1931), p. 108.
6 Dunham, D., *Recollections of an Egyptologist* (Boston, 1972), p. 33.
7 Edwards, A.B., *A Thousand Miles up the Nile* (London, 1877, rev. 1888), pp. 52–3.
8 Edwards, I.E.S., *From the Pyramids to Tutankhamen: Memoirs of an Egyptologist* (Oxford, 2000), p. 125.
9 Pierre Montet writing in a letter to his wife, quoted in Coutts, H. (ed.), *Gold of the Pharaohs* (Edinburgh, 1988), p. 19.
10 Herodotus, *Histories*, Book II, trans. Rawlinson, G. (1858), p. 169.

CHAPTER TWELVE

1 Smith, R.W., *National Geographic Magazine*, 138:5 (1970), pp. 634–5.
2 James Burton, unpublished diaries, MSS 25613-75: British Library.
3 Edgerton, W.F., 'The Strike in Ramesses III's Twenty-ninth Year', *Journal of Near Eastern Studies*, Vol. 10 (1951), pp. 137–45.
4 Poetry lovers the world over will be horrified to learn that Smith was also inspired by Belzoni's acquisition of the Younger Memnon; his poem *On A Stupendous Leg of Granite, Discovered standing by itself in the deserts of Egypt* was inferior to Shelley's identically themed sonnet in every way.
5 Baikie, J., *A Century of Excavation in the Land of the Pharaohs* (London, 1923), pp. 44–5.

FURTHER READING

>—<

The books listed below deal with the history of Egyptology, rather than with the archaeology of the many sites mentioned in this book. Readers interested in archaeology rather than history should consult the *Atlas of Ancient Egypt* by Baines and Malek, which will provide an introduction to the sites themselves. More detailed references will be found in the endnotes that accompany each chapter.

INTRODUCTION

Baikie, J., *A Century of Excavation in the Land of the Pharaohs* (London, 1923)

Baines, J. and Malek, J., *Atlas of Ancient Egypt* (Oxford, 1980)

Baird, K.A. (ed.), *Encyclopedia of the Archaeology of Ancient Egypt* (London, 1999)

Dawson, W.R. and Uphill, E., *Who Was Who in Egyptology* (London, 2nd rev. edn. 1972)

Reeves, N., *Ancient Egypt: The Great Discoveries* (London, 2000)

Shaw, I. and Nicholson, P., *British Museum Dictionary of Ancient Egypt* (London, 1995)

THE EXPLORERS

Adkins, L. and R., *The Keys of Egypt: The Race to Read Hieroglyphics* (London, 2000)

Andrews, C., *The Rosetta Stone* (London, 1982)

Champollion, J.-F., *Monuments de l'Égypte et de la Nubie*, (Paris, 1835–47)

Clayton, P.A., *The Rediscovery of Ancient Egypt* (London, 1982)

Curl, J.S., *Egyptomania: the Egyptian Revival: a Recurring Theme in the History of Taste* (Manchester and New York, 1994)

Denon, V., *Travels in Upper and Lower Egypt During the Campaigns of General Bonaparte* (translated by A. Aiken, London, 1803, reprinted 1986)

Parkinson, R., *Cracking Codes: The Rosetta Stone and Decipherment* (London, 1999)

Roullet, A., *The Egyptian and Egyptianising Monuments of Imperial Rome* (Leiden, 1972)

Snape, S.R., *Decoding the Stones* (London, 1997)

Sole, R. and Valbelle, D., *The Rosetta Stone: The Story of the Decoding of Hieroglyphics* (London, 2001)

THE COLLECTORS

Belzoni, G.B., *Narrative of the Operations and Recent Discoveries in Egypt and Nubia* (1820) (ed. Alberto Siliotti, Verona and London, 2001)

Further Reading

Clair, C., *Strong Man Egyptologist* (London, 1957)
Cottrell, L, *The Mountains of Pharaoh* (London, 1956)
Disher, M.W., *Pharaoh's Fool* (London, 1957)
Halls, J.J., *The Life and Correspondence of Henry Salt Esq* (London, 1834)
Mayes, S., *The Great Belzoni: The Circus Strongman Who Discovered Egypt's Ancient Treasures* (London, 1959)

THE ARCHAEOLOGISTS

Budge, E.A., *By Nile and Tigris* (London, 1920)
Carter, H. and Mace, A.C., *The Tomb of Tut.ankh.Amen*, 3 vols (London 1923–33)
Drower, M.S., *Flinders Petrie: A Life in Archaeology* (London, 1985)
Edwards, A.B., *A Thousand Miles up the Nile* (London, 1877)
James, T.G.H., *Howard Carter: the Path to Tutankhamun* (London and New York, 1992)
James, T.G.H., *Excavating in Egypt: the Egypt Exploration Society 1882–1982* (London, 1982)
Janssen, R.M., *The First Hundred Years: Egyptology at University College London 1892–1992* (London, 1992)
Keay, J., *With Passport and Parasol* (London, 1989)
Maspero, G., *Egypt: Ancient Sites and Modern Scenes* (London, 1910)
Petrie, W.M.F., *Seventy Years in Archaeology* (London, 1931)
Rees, J., *Amelia Edwards: Traveller, Novelist and Egyptologist* (London, 1998)
Reeves, N., *The Complete Tutankhamen: the King, the Tomb, the Royal Treasure* (London, 1990)
Ridley, R.T., *Napoleon's Proconsul in Egypt: The Life and Times of Bernardino Drovetti* (London, 1998)
Romer, J., *Valley of the Kings* (London, 1981)
Smith, G.E., *The Royal Mummies* (Cairo, 1912)
Thomas, N. (ed.), *The American Discovery of Ancient Egypt, Catalogue and Essays* (Los Angeles, 1995)

THE SCIENTISTS

Brier, B., *The Murder of Tutankhamen: a 3000-year-old Murder Mystery* (London, 1998)
David, R. and Archbold, R., *Conversations with Mummies* (London, 2000)
Edwards, I.E.S., *From the Pyramids to Tutankhamen: Memoirs of an Egyptologist* (Oxford, 2000)
Foreman, L., *Cleopatra's Palace: In Search of a Legend* (London, 1999)
Hawass, Z., *Secrets from the Sand: My search for Egypt's Past* (London, 2003)
Tyldesley, J.A., *Private Lives of the Pharaohs* (London, 2000)
Weeks, K., *The Lost Tomb: the Greatest Discovery at the Valley of the Kings Since Tutankhamun* (London, 1998)

INDEX

≻—≺

Index